ecpr PRESS

I0094618

A Political Style of Thinking
Essays on Max Weber

Kari Palonen

ecpr PRESS

© Kari Palonen 2017

First published by the ECPR Press in 2017

The ECPR Press is the publishing imprint of the European Consortium for Political Research (ECPR), a scholarly association, which supports and encourages the training, research and cross-national co-operation of political scientists in institutions throughout Europe and beyond.

ECPR Press
Harbour House
Hythe Quay
Colchester
CO2 8JF
United Kingdom

All rights reserved. No part of this book may be reprinted or reproduced or utilised in any form or by any electronic, mechanical, or other means, now known or hereafter invented, including photocopying and recording, or in any information storage or retrieval system, without permission in writing from the publishers.

Typeset by Lapiz Digital Services

Printed and bound by Lightning Source

British Library Cataloguing in Publication Data

A catalogue record for this book is available from the British Library

HARDBACK ISBN: 978-1-785522-65-9
PAPERBACK ISBN: 978-1-785522-70-3
PDF ISBN: 978-1-785522-71-0
EPUB ISBN: 978-1-785522-72-7
KINDLE ISBN: 978-1-785522-73-4

www.ecpr.eu/ecprpress

ECPR Press Series Editors
Peter Kennealy (European University Institute)
Ian O'Flynn (Newcastle University)
Alexandra Segerberg (Stockholm University)
Laura Sudulich (University of Kent)

Other books available in the Essays series
Citizens in Europe: Essays on Democracy, Constitutionalism and European Integration (ISBN: 9781785522383) Claus Offe, Ulrich K. Preuß
Choice, Rules and Collective Action: The Ostroms on the Study of Institutions and Governance (ISBN: 9781910259139) Elinor Ostrom (Author), Vincent Ostrom (Author), Paul Dragos Aligica (Editor) and Filippo Sabetti (Editor)
Concepts and Reason in Political Theory (ISBN: 978190730170) Iain Hampsher-Monk
Croce, Gramsci, Bobbio and the Italian Political Tradition (ISBN: 9781907301995) Richard Bellamy
From Deliberation to Demonstration: Political Rallies in France, 1868–1939 (ISBN: 9781907301469) Paula Cossart
Globalisation of Nationalism: The Motive-Force Behind 21st Century Politics (ISBN: 9781785522147) Liah Greenfeld
Hans Kelsen and the Case for Democracy (ISBN: 9781907301247) Sandrine Baume
Immigration, Integration and Mobility: New Agendas in Migration Studies. Essays 1998–2014 (ISBN: 9781907301728) Adrian Favell
Is Democracy a Lost Cause? Paradoxes of an Imperfect Invention (ISBN: 9781907301247) Alfio Mastropaolo
Just Democracy: The Rawls-Machiavelli Programme (ISBN: 9781907301148) Philippe Van Parijs
Learning about Politics in Time and Space (ISBN: 9781907301476) Richard Rose
Maestri of Political Science (ISBN: 9781907301193) Donatella Campus, Gianfranco Pasquino, and Martin Bull
Masters of Political Science (ISBN: 9780955820335) Donatella Campus and Gianfranco Pasquino
On Parties, Party Systems and Democracy: Selected Writings of Peter Mair (ISBN: 9781907301780) Peter Mair (Author) Ingrid Van Biezen (Editor)
The Modern State Subverted (ISBN: 9781907301636) Giuseppe Di Palma
Varieties of Political Experience (ISBN: 9781907301759) Gianfranco Poggi

ECPR Classics:

Beyond the Nation-State: Functionalism and International Organization (ISBN: 9780955248870) Ernst Haas

Citizens, Elections, Parties: Approaches to the Comparative Study of the Processes of Development (ISBN: 9780955248887) Stein Rokkan

Comparative Politics: The Problem of Equivalence (ISBN: 9781907301414) Jan Van Deth

Democracy (ISBN: 9780955248801) Jack Lively

Electoral Change: Responses to Evolving Social and Attitudinal Structures in Western Countries (ISBN: 9780955820311) Mark Franklin, Thomas Mackie and Henry Valen

Elite and Specialized Interviewing (ISBN: 9780954796679) Lewis Anthony Dexter

Identity, Competition and Electoral Availability: The Stabilisation of European Electorates 1885–1985 (ISBN: 9780955248832) Peter Mair and Stefano Bartolini

Individualism (ISBN: 9780954796662) Steven Lukes

Modern Social Policies in Britain and Sweden: From Relief to Income Maintenance (ISBN: 9781907301001) Hugh Heclo

Parties and Party Systems: A Framework for Analysis (ISBN: 9780954796617) Giovanni Sartori

Party Identification and Beyond: Representations of Voting and Party Competition (ISBN: 9780955820342) Ian Budge, Ivor Crewe and Dennis Farlie

People, States and Fear: An Agenda for International Security Studies in the Post-Cold War Era (ISBN: 9780955248818) Barry Buzan

Please visit www.ecpr.eu/ecprpress for information about new publications.

Table of Contents

Acknowledgements

For decades Max Weber has been regularly present in my writings, either as a topic of its own or as a source of inspiration for thinking politically. In this respect I consider myself both a Weberologist and a Weberian scholar.

To write on Weber requires cooperation with colleagues. Wolf-Dieter Narr and Sven Eliæson have been my interlocutors in Weberian matters for more than thirty years. *Max Weber Studies* (and its editor Sam Whimster) and the 'Weber Archiv' at the Bayerische Akademie der Wissenschaften (Karl-Ludwig Ay, Edith Hanke) have been my main institutional supports. Ilkka Heiskanen and Quentin Skinner have been two of my 'mentors': Weber is strongly present in the work of both.

With a number of other Weber scholars, such as Rita Aldenhoff-Hübinger, Andreas Anter, Peter Baehr, Jens Borchert, Hans-Henrik Bruun, Catherine Colliot-Thélène, Joshua Derman, Peter Ghosh, Gangolf Hübinger, Duncan Kelly, Marcus Llanque, Peter Lassman, Kyösti Pekonen, Helmut F. Spinner and Keith Tribe, I have had more or less intensive encounters throughout the years.

The articles published from 1999 to 2014 are indebted to research funding from the Academy of Finland, with the University of Jyväskylä as the site of the research. I have cooperated with colleagues and former students, most closely with Taru Haapala, Matti Hyvärinen, Anitta Kananen, Niilo Kauppi, Hanna-Mari Kivistö, Kia Lindroos, Tuija Parvikko, Tuija Pulkkinen, Suvi Soininen, Tapani Turkka and Claudia Wiesner.

For the book I have unified the format of the articles, constructed a single bibliography, used UK English spelling and largely included the translations in the main text and the German originals in the footnotes, except where the translation is my own. I have removed repeated quotations and made minor reformulations of the argument. I have slightly shortened Chapters Five and Eleven as well as some quotations elsewhere, and I have corrected misspellings. I have used the up-to-date English language translations by Lassman and Speirs, and Tribe and Bruun. For the German, I am indebted to Klaus Sondermann; for the English, to Elizabeth Moulton and Bill Hellberg.

The original publications are the following:

Chapter Two: *Alternatives* 28, 2003: 171–86, Copyright SAGE

Chapter Three: *European Political Science* 6, 2007: 69–78, Copyright Palgrave Macmillan

Chapter Four: *Max Weber Studies* 6, 2006: 33–50, Copyright MWS

Chapter Five: Published in French in Catherine Colliot-Thélène et Philippe Portier dir. *Métamorphoses du Prince. Politique et culture dans l'espace occidental*, 2014: 121–44. Copyright Presses de l'Université de Rennes

Chapter Six: *Political Theory* 27, 1999: 523–44, Copyright SAGE

Chapter Seven: *Max Weber Studies* 1, 2001: 196–214, Copyright MWS

Chapter Eight: *Constellations* 15, 2008: 56–71, Copyright Wiley

Chapter Nine: *Max Weber Studies* 11, 2011: 99–117, Copyright MWS
Chapter Ten: *Max Weber Studies* 4, 2004: 273–92, Copyright MWS
Chapter Eleven: *Redescriptions* 12, 2008: 133–56, Copyright *Redescriptions*
Chapter Twelve: *Max Weber Studies* 10, 2010: 71–93, Copyright MWS
Chapter Thirteen: *History of Political Thought* 35, 2014: 519–35, Copyright Imprint Academic

I would like to thank the publishers and journals for the opportunity to republish these pieces in this volume.

Kari Palonen
Helsinki, July 2016

Chapter One

Introduction: Max Weber as a Political Thinker

Max Weber was a life-long *homo politicus*. At age twelve, he read Machiavelli and two years later he criticised Cicero's fluctuating and unsure policy towards Catilina ('schwankende und unsicher Politik', Weber 1936: 3, 13). His letters show that throughout his life Weber continued to analyse the political significance of contemporary phenomena, using his own conceptual apparatus to interpret them. Weber presents original views on the state, parliament or government, types of power and rulership (*Herrschaft*) and on the professional politician. 'Politics' was for him not merely a 'practice', but also a perspective on thinking.

A political mode of thinking

In the first lines of 'Politik als Beruf', Weber says that he will not take a stand on policy issues (1919c: 35). He speaks instead of politics as a concept and of the politician as an ideal type. He thought politically in the sense of analysing, interpreting and judging phenomena from the viewpoint of their political significance. Weber's vision of the research process as a human activity is also shaped by his political mode of thinking.

Chance is the key concept in Weber's political language[1]. *Chance* indicates a type of contingency that is not a residual concept, but a medium of intelligibility that characterises human action in general and politics in particular. As *fortuna* indicates the contingency of the 'Machiavellian moment' (Pocock 1975), *Chance* introduces the Weberian moment in the twentieth-century conceptual history of politics (see Palonen 1998).

Weber introduces *Chance* in his 'Objektivität' essay in order to transcend the conventional distinction between ends and means (*Zwecke und Mittel*). For him, ends and means depend on a judgement of the horizon of chances in a given situation. A discussion of chances and their realisability requires a consideration of ends and means, including the *Nebenfolgen*, or the unintended effects of an action, which refers to the converse side of *Chancen* (Weber 1904b: 149–50).

---

1. In this volume the concept of Chance is used in Weber's sense, which deviates from the standard English meaning of chance.

    The Weberian concept of Chance refers to the distinct and omnipresent contingency of human action. It cannot be translated with a single word but its conceptual horizon includes aspects of possibility, realisability, occasion, opportunity or risk.

    See also p. 18.

Chance allows Weber to 'think outside the box', for he regards judgements about the possible, the situation and unintended effects to be constituent aspects of politics. Weber's view on human action (*Handeln*) and the relationships (*Beziehungen*) between types of action is the basis for reinterpreting key political concepts, such as power (*Macht*), rule (*Herrschaft*), and struggle (*Kampf*) as well as their complex constellations, such as the state (*Staat*), which have distinct profiles based on the presence or absence of chances (see the structure of the 'orders and powers' in *Wirtschaft und Gesellschaft*, 1922).

Chance is for Weber a purely formal concept, which also allows us to discuss destructive or catastrophic chances. There are always *some* other courses of action, and, even if the results do not differ very much in the end or if none of the results seems acceptable, the very moment of choice is what matters politically. In historical interpretation, 'objective possibility' is the correlate of *Chancen*: to understand a 'realised' possibility presupposes speculation about the unrealised and a discussion about its possibility of becoming realised, as Weber writes (1906a: 269–76).

As early as the 1930s, Carl Schmitt (1932b) mentioned in a footnote Weber's frequent use of *Chance*, but regards it as a characteristic expression of an old-fashioned uncommitted liberalism (*see* Chapter Nine in this volume). Insights into the methodological and implicitly political role of *Chancen* in Weber's thinking can be found in the works of several scholars (Hufnagel 1971; Spinner 1989; Freund 1990; Weiß 1992), although many other scholars give no attention to it.

My thesis is that for Weber the contingency of politics, history and research has a political model in the parliamentary principle that any question on the agenda can be fully understood only when it is judged from opposite perspectives. Only then do we have real chances to analyse a question from multiple angles and assess its strengths and weaknesses, as parliament does with a motion on the agenda. The ideal type is Weber's main medium for speculating about unrealised possibilities, while parliamentary practice connects motions to resolutions to be voted on.

Max Weber is free from the widespread academic and populist contempt for practical politics and professional politicians. He would have shared Quentin Skinner's insight that 'political life itself sets the problems for the political theorist' (Skinner 1978: xi; see Palonen 2005b). The point is to render intelligible the professional and the occasional politicians' actions, situations and horizons of the possible and to understand them better than they may do themselves, without offering any direct advice.

My reading is, of course, a truly Weberian 'one-sided accentuation' (1904h: 191) of an ideal–typical perspective: I am looking for the chances to think politically and do not know of anyone who would do this better than Max Weber. Even Weberologists, such as Peter Ghosh in his recent book *Max Weber and the Protestant Ethic* (2014), are opposed to reading Weber from a political perspective. However, Ghosh speaks of politics, as do many others, as a separate sphere, whereas I am interested in politics as a contingent and controversial activity par excellence.

Weber and political science

Jürgen Kocka edited in 1987 a congress volume, *Max Weber, der Historiker*. Together with Wilhelm Hennis's *Max Webers Fragestellung* from the same year, it was among the first to challenge the canonised and US-mediated view on Weber as a sociologist by offering a more historical reading. If we follow Weber's academic career more closely, the multidisciplinarity of his work is very obvious, but this aspect has been more or less completely neglected in recent biographies, one written by a psychohistorian (Radkau 2005) and two by sociologists (Kaube 2014; Käsler 2014).

Weber's dissertation 'Die Geschichte der Handelsgesellschaften im Mittelalter' (1889) and his habilitation thesis 'Die römische Agrargeschichte in ihrer Bedeutung für das Staats- und Privatrecht' (1891) belong to legal history. Under the prompting of his 'supervisor' August Meitzen, Weber became involved in studies on East Elbian Agriculture, on which basis he was appointed to professor of political economy and economic policy in Freiburg. After his studies on the German stock market (Börsenwesen), he was awarded the prestigious economics chair in Heidelberg. Even after his health-related retirement in 1903, he continued to speak of (political) economy as 'our' discipline and served as an expert for appointments in the field. As editor of the renamed journal *Archiv für Sozialwissenschaft und Sozialpolitik* after 1904, he spoke of Sozialwissenschaften (social science) and Kulturwissenschaften (human sciences) as rough synonyms (with economics included in the latter).

Indeed, Weber can be considered a true decathlete of the human sciences. *Die Protestantische Ethik* (1904–5/20) can be read as a contribution to cultural, intellectual and conceptual history as well as to religious studies, British and American politics and so on. With his methodological essays, such as those on 'Objektivität' and 'Wertfreiheit' (value freedom), Weber also contributed to the philosophy of the human sciences, or Wissenschaftstheorie in the German term. With studies on the working conditions in German industry he later gained the reputation of being a pioneer of empirical sociology, social policy or industrial psychology. With the press enquête he initiated, Weber has also been regarded as a pioneer in the study of journalism (Weischenberger 2012). His wartime writings contain important discussions regarding constitutional and international law. When one takes into account his own experience as a speaker and debater as well as his perspectivist theory of knowledge and careful personal revisions of the use of concepts, Weber can also be considered to have made a contribution to rhetorical scholarship. Nearly all of the fields represented in present-day human and social sciences and law can find in Max Weber a classic of their own. Paradoxically, he is probably most forgotten in the field of economics.

What, then, about political science? In the contemporary sense, the discipline did not yet exist in Weber's time. The US chairs in 'political science' since *c.* 1880 were inspired by the German teaching of history and constitutional law, while the French Ècole libre de sciences politiques also had its origins in the German university model, but adapted to the French paradigm of grandes écoles.

In Germany, remnants of the older traditions of Staatswissenchaften (political science), including Weber's Freiburg chair, were at the margins of history, economics and constitutional law.

Weber took for granted that 'political' questions are a central aspect of the research and teaching of Kulturwissenschaften. At one point, he also supported the institutionalisation of something close to 'political science', namely, as an inherent part of a 'Hochschule für Politik oder einer Akademie für Internationales Recht und vergleichende Politik' planned for Heidelberg with the support of the Carnegie foundation, as Lepsius and Mommsen, editors of Weber letters, report (Weber 1994a: 179). With his *Allgemeine Staatslehre* (1900), Weber's Heidelberg colleague the constitutional law professor Georg Jellinek formulated a research programme for a non-judicial study of the state and politics. This was never fully institutionalised in Germany, but it played a founding role in, for example, the establishment of Finnish political science after World War I (see Palonen 1981).

From July to September 1909, Weber wrote several letters to Jellinek in which he discussed several possible disciplinary titles, always including the analysis of politics as an inherent part of the programme. In his letter of 12 September 1909, he accepted Jellinek's proposal for an institute of 'international law and comparative politics' which with his description of the field would today be considered political science (Weber 1994a: 258–59). However, nothing came from this proposal.

Still, the discussion in the letters illustrates well how broadly Weber conceived the study of politics when he returned to teaching in 1918, first in Vienna and then in Munich. Weber's last lecture series, from spring 1929, was cut short by his illness and death. *Allgemeine Staatslehre und Politik* is probably Weber's best example of what today would be called political science (see Chapter Nine in this volume). The same is the case with the Herrschaftsoziologie in *Wirtschaft und Gesellschaft* as well as with his war-time and post-war pamphlets and essays on suffrage, parliament, world politics and the ideal type of the politician, even if some of them also contain standpoints on the politics of the day and therefore do not strictly follow the Weberian principle of Wertfreiheit (value freedom).

Histories of German political science usually trace back to the Deutsche Hochschule für Politik, founded in 1920. Initially it was not a proper academic institution, but moved in that direction during the course of the Weimar Republic. Weber never belonged to the intellectual authorities of that school. The case was different with the re-founding of the Hochschule and new political science chairs after World War II. All the major figures of Berlin political science in the 1950s – Otto Suhr, Franz Neumann, Ernst Fraenkel, Ossip K. Flechtheim, Arkadi Gurland and Otto Stammer – were indebted to Weber, although each interpreted him differently (see Buchstein 1992). However, as discussed in Chapter Thirteen regarding his two types of parliament, Weber's points were often anachronistically misinterpreted by post-war political scientists. At least in Germany, Weber is today included in the range of major political theorists taught at the universities.

At the end of his 'Objektivität' essay, Weber extensively warned against the grave and dangerous consequences of using 'collective concepts of everyday life' in scholarly writings (Weber 1904b: 210–12). Weber teaches us to ask what or who may be hiding behind claims that 'society' or 'the people' demand something (see a letter to Michels of 4 August 1908, in Weber 1990: 615) and reinterprets others, such as 'state' (Chapter Nine) or 'nation' (Chapter Seven) in action-theoretical terms. The dissolution of such thing-like essences is a major achievement of Weber's thinking (see also Palonen 2012c: 168–9).

Contingency, action, freedom and individuality are still viewed with suspicion by many academics today. Even Jean-Paul Sartre with his post-Hegelian dialectics and Hannah Arendt with the consensual aspects of her thinking on politics shrink from radical contingency. As phenomenologists, both Sartre and Arendt locate the possible in the future, whereas for Weber the possible is real in the present situation of an acting (professional or occasional) politician.

The changing profile of Weber scholarship

A remarkable re-vision of Weber studies has taken place since the 1980s. Prompted by the publication of the *Max-Weber-Gesamtausgabe* in the early 1980s, a number of scholars began to acquaint themselves with Weber's lesser-known publications and aspects of his works that post-war studies had neglected. The main target of criticism was the way Weber had been received in post-war US sociology. The journal *Max Weber Studies* has been published since 2001, marking another step in the professionalisation of Weber scholarship. There is today a huge difference in the interpretation and evaluation of Weber's work between professional Weberologists and others who still tend to stick to the textbook Weber.

Wolfgang J. Mommsen with his dissertation *Max Weber und die deutsche Politik (1890–1920)* from 1959 initiated a more historical reading of Weber's work. He found a number of unknown articles and newspaper reports and focused especially on Weber's early writings. This led him to play down Weber's defence of parliamentary government and emphasise his 'nationalism' and late support for the plebiscitary presidency of the Weimar Republic. For Mommsen, Weber appears as a precursor of Carl Schmitt's notorious views, and this reputation is today still part of the textbook view of Weber's politics.

In the 1980s, a number of scholars, most prominently Wilhelm Hennis (1987, 1996) but also others such as Detlef Peukert (1989), Lawrence Scaff (1989) and Catherine Colliot-Thélène (1990, 1992), began to revise the canonised, anachronistic interpretation of Weber. They read his writings as contributions to the debates of his own historical context. Hennis in his *Max Webers Fragestellung* rejected the canonised view of Weber and situated him in the (broadly speaking) 'republican' tradition of political judgment. Scaff recently commented that '[t]he political Weber has never been the same following Hennis's compelling reading of his work' (2014: 129). These more historical approaches to Weber are in strong contrast to the 'evolutionary' interpretations, used by Habermas and others, which discard or ignore how deeply politics was built into Weber's entire mode of thinking.

Wilhelm Hennis was a legal scholar turned political scientist. Besides the earlier important works of Hans Henrik Bruun (1972) and David Beetham (1974), several political scientists have also played a notable role in the new reinterpretations of

Weber, including Scaff (1989), Peter Lassman (the editor of *Political Writings* from 1994 and a major collection of essays on Weber, 2006), Andreas Anter (1995), Peter Breiner (1996), Jens Borchert (2003), Sven Eliæson (2002), Duncan Kelly (2003), Marcus Llanque (2000) and Wolf-Dieter Narr (e.g. 2014), to name a few. Nonetheless, the textbook image of Weber is still powerful enough to marginalise him from the wider contemporary debates on political theory, parliamentarism and research methodology.

Three books on Weber in German

My own work on Weber is connected to the reinterpretation of Weber by emphasising his contributions as a political thinker par excellence. Inspired by Hennis, I started to reread Weber's work from the perspective of contingency. In the 1980s, this concept had arisen to the forefront of scholarly debate, thanks to Richard Rorty (1979, 1989) and the francophone post-modernists, while from another direction it had also became a topic in the new studies of Weber. For my discussion of contingency, however, three historians, namely Reinhart Koselleck (1979), Quentin Skinner (1978, 1988, 1996) and John Pocock (1975, 1985) played a special role. I began to study their work in more detail at roughly the same time as I was writing on Weber.

In the introduction to *Das 'Webersche Moment'* (1998), I hint at common concerns between Weber and post-modernist thinkers. Weber's central theses on contingency, the lack of foundations and so on look from a certain point of view fairly similar to those put forward by Foucault, Derrida, Butler, Ranciere, Laclau, Mouffe and so on. Weber should be credited as a thinker who preceded them by several decades, although they do have different historical, philosophical and political backgrounds.

The leading idea of my *Das 'Webersche Moment': Zur Kontingenz des Politischen* (1998) is to contrast the contingency of the *fortuna* of Machiavelli, as interpreted by John Pocock (1975), with the *Chance* of Weber. I connect Weber's political and methodological views by opposing the residual contingency of *fortuna* with the operative contingency of *Chance*. Weber's concept of *Chance* marks a conceptual innovation formed against the background of the demise of *fortuna* due to an overwhelming tendency towards bureaucratisation. Weber, with his thematisation of the *Chance*-contingency, marked a turn in the political thought of the twentieth century, a break with a politics based on programmes and plans in favour of thinking in terms of situations and possibilities. I illustrated this with a number of thinkers from the 1920s to the 1990s, from Schmitt, Helmuth Plessner and Walter Benjamin via Arendt, Sartre and Michael Oakeshott to Ulrich Beck and William Connolly. This view, more generally, opens up a new perspective on who became the major political theorists of the twentieth century and how and why they became so.

The 'small Weber' (*Eine Lobrede für Politiker: Ein Kommentar zu Max Webers 'Politik als Beruf'*, 2002) offers a line-by-line commentary on Weber's booklet. With the rhetorical title I direct attention to Weber's insight that any defence of politics is futile without a defence of the professional politician. I further connect the quasi-definitions included in 'Politik als Beruf' with aspects of *Chance* contingency. Later, in *Rhetorik des Unbeliebten* (2012b), I set Weber's work in the context of other eulogies for politicians over a 100-year period and discuss the rhetorical topoi used in their defence.

Around 2003, I turned to parliamentary studies and began to regard the parliament as the paradigmatic site for the rhetorical and temporal aspects of politics. I discovered a conceptual link between Weber's 1904 essay on 'Objectivity' and his parliament pamphlet from 1918, especially its section on how parliament can, through various rhetorical means, exert control over officials with their arcane bureaucratic knowledge. This new focus between two hitherto unconnected texts (although Wolf-Dieter Narr told me that he also had noticed this link) led me to write a third book on Weber, *"Objektivität" als faires Spiel: Wissenschaft als Politik bei Max Weber* (2010b). This book was the impetus for using Weber's concept of 'objectivity' as the historical model for my studies on the procedure (*The Politics of Parliamentary Procedure*, 2014b) and the rhetoric (*From Oratory to Debate*, 2016) of the Westminster parliament.

Three foci of the book: politics, concepts and parliament

Weber has a personal idiomatic style in German (see Tribe 2012), and it is a challenge to write about him in English. Weberologists know that the older English translations are hopelessly inadequate. The newer ones, such as Lassman and Speirs' *Political Writings* (Weber 1994b) and Bruun and Whimster's *Collected Methodological Writings* (Weber 2012), are of much better quality, but still controversial in certain details (see e.g. Borchert 2007). For someone like me, for whom both German and English are foreign languages, the main reason to write about Weber in English is that he has become part of the lingua franca of today's academia.

The chapters in this volume are by-products of my work on Weber over a twenty-year period. They illustrate my long-term interest in the history of the concept of politics (e.g. Weber is the most cited thinker in my *The Struggle with Time* 2006; see also *Re-thinking Politics*, 2007). An inherent link exists between the writings on Weber and my studies of Quentin Skinner and Reinhart Koselleck, particularly their principles and practices of 'conceptual history', for Weber is regularly quoted in the essays collected in *Politics and Conceptual Histories* (Palonen 2014a). We could regard Max Weber both as a conceptual historian *avant la lettre* and as a conceptual politician in his own right who reconsidered important concepts in terms of *Chance* (see Palonen 2000).

The first part of the volume is built around Weber's conception of politics and the ideal type of the politician, continuing the themes of the *Lobrede*. They connect to my long-term project of studying the conceptual history of politics as an activity (Palonen 2006 and the articles in Palonen 2007) and include both Weber-inspired theorising and contextualising and strictly textual interpretations of his writings.

Chapter Two, 'The Four Times of Politics: Policy, Polity, Politicking and Politicisation', is a Weber-inspired programmatic essay on the dimensions of the activity of politics. It replaces the triad of policy, polity and politics by splitting the last into two distinct activities, politicking and politicisation. It is opposed to the spatial concept according to which politicking and politicisation are only extensions of the margins of policy and polity. In my interpretation, in contrast, polity and policy are also reconsidered in temporal terms, as special cases of politicisation and politicking. Politicisation marks something as political and opens the horizon for politicking, while polity for its part is a result of distinct politicisations which also set obstacles to competing politicisations. Policy appears as a specific type of politicking, coordinating actions in normative and teleological terms. The Weberian figures of *Chance, Streben, Macht* and *Kampf* are the conceptual instruments by which politics is analysed in strictly temporal and nominalistic terms. This scheme has also been applied by my colleagues and students (see the account of Björk 2015) as well as by myself (see the essays in Palonen 2007) to many different types of studies.

Chapter Three, 'Politics or the Political? A Historical Perspective on a Contemporary Non-debate', opposes the Weberian temporal activity-concept to a spatial order-concept, indebted to Carl Schmitt's *Der Begriff des Politischen* (1932a). Besides summarising the history of the activity-concept, discussed in detail in *The Struggle with Time* (2006), the article also takes up the history of structuralist or system-theoretical attempts to re-think 'the political sphere' using more abstract terms than David Easton did in the 1950s. Such views of the political are fashionable among francophone thinkers, who tend to disparage 'mere politics' and professional politicians (see Marchart 2007, 2010).

In Chapter Four, 'Sombart and Weber on Professional Politicians', I contrast Weber's defence of politicians with the laments of his economist colleague Werner Sombart in 1907. These in a sense exemplify the wider contempt for politics, politicians, democracy and parliamentarism among German academics of that time. Certain formulations in 'Politik als Beruf' allude to Sombart's writings a decade before, although Weber never quotes him there explicitly. The study is connected to an international history of politician-bashing around 1900 and to the counter-literature of apologetics for politicians, discussed in my *Rhetorik des Unbeliebten* (2012b).

In Chapter Five, 'Max Weber's Three Types of Professional Politicians: A Rhetorical Approach', I deviate from Weber's own narrative on the professionalisation of politics. In 'Politik als Beruf', Weber is unduly pessimistic about an eventual victory of functionaries, having supported since early 1919 direct presidential elections as a counterweight to the bureaucratisation of the Weimar Republic. He underestimated the resources of parliamentary politics, and did not discuss full-time parliamentarians as an alternative to rule by the party bosses, for example. In the Westminster tradition so admired by Weber, we can also find resources for supporting a parliamentary professionalisation of politics. I connect the party functionary, the president and the parliamentarian as ideal types to the rhetorical genres of negotiation, acclamation and deliberation.

The second part of the volume consists of sample analyses of Weber's use of concepts. Sharing with Weber an emphasis on the eternal youth of the historical sciences and the corollary that conceptual revisions will never end, I see Weber as a precursor of conceptual history in a broad sense and I apply a 'Weberian conceptual history' perspective to his own work. Weber deals with concepts like a politician, modifying them as needed for a current project, even while maintaining some continuity in vocabulary, as Quentin Skinner's 'innovating ideologist'. With this kind of conceptual historical perspective, the four concepts studied spectacularly illustrate not only the break with the textbook Weber, but also the more detailed rhetorical means that Weber himself employs in his conceptual revisions.

Chapter Six, 'Max Weber's Reconceptualisation of Freedom', summarises some of the main theses in *Das 'Webersche Moment'* (1998) on Weber's rethinking of contingency. With Benjamin Constant, Weber supports 'the modern concept of liberty'. He opposes Aristotle's *zoon politikon* (man as political animal) and Hobbes's reduction of freedom to non-interference, which is inherently opposed to politics. The chapter puts forward the view that the origins of politics in medieval cities was, in line with Weber's interpretation, 'voluntary', as opposed to being a result of imperial power, and that this provides the background for Weber's reconceptualisation of freedom. I also compare Weber's and Sartre's versions of methodological individualism and of the existential dimensions of their defences of freedom.

Chapter Seven, 'Was Max Weber a Nationalist? A Study in the Rhetoric of Conceptual Change', rejects the received view of Mommsen and others of a marked nationalism ascribed to Weber. As a conventional historian, Mommsen is not directing attention to the formulations and rhetorical points in Weber's use of concepts. I oppose his thesis using a strictly rhetorical and conceptual historical reading of Weber's texts. From this perspective, the nationalism thesis holds for the 1890s (with certain qualifications), but Weber changed his views prior to World War I and explicitly rejected a nationalistic policy after the end of the war, in December 1918.

In Chapter Eight, 'Imagining Max Weber's Reply to Hannah Arendt: Remarks on the Arendtian Critique of Representative Democracy', debates on parliaments and representation are at stake. I subscribe to many aspects of Arendt's action concept of politics, but not her apologetics for spontaneity and her suspicions of parliaments and professional politicians in *On Revolution* (1963). Unlike Weber, Arendt never understood the parliament as a dissensual and deliberative assembly that controls government and administration. I trace back their differences to their conceptions of 'power' (*Macht*) and 'rule' (*Herrschaft*): for Arendt, the two are polar opposites, whereas for Weber *Herrschaft* is a special case of *Macht*, having a different range as *Chance* concepts. Elsewhere I discuss Arendt's and Karl Jaspers's critiques of West German parliamentarism from a Weberian point of view (Palonen 2012c).

Chapter Nine, 'The State as a *Chance* Concept: Max Weber's Desubstantialisation and Neutralisation of a Concept', is based on Weber's last lectures, in the spring of 1920, as published in Gangolf Hübinger's edition of

Max-Weber-Gesamtausgabe in 2009. What remains of the lectures are only the notes of two students who were present. They show – more clearly than Weber's published works – how unconventional Weber's concept of the state is. Although his 'definition' is frequently quoted, many commentators tend to ignore the main point of Weber's formulation in *Wirtschaft und Gesellschaft* (1922), which the lecture emphasises. Der Staat is for Weber not an 'acting subject' but another complex of *Chancen*, to which the criteria of area and monopoly on the legitimate use of violence give a distinct profile.

The chapters in the final part deal with the formation of my thesis on Weber's rhetorical and parliamentary revision of the concept of 'objectivity'. They show my initial puzzlement with Weber's use of 'objectivity' (which Weber regularly used in quotation marks), which has nothing to do with the way the concept is used in textbook courses on 'scientific method' and so on. Against my intentions, this puzzlement led me to write a third book on Weber, namely *'Objektivität' als faires Spiel* (2010b). The link between Weber's procedural concept of 'objectivity' with the Westminster parliament as its historical approximation had an effect also in the opposite direction: my reinterpretation of Weber's concept served as a source of inspiration for my more recent works on the Westminster parliamentary procedure (*The Politics of Parliamentary Procedure*, 2014b) and rhetoric (*From Oratory to Debate*, 2016).

Chapter Ten, 'Max Weber, Parliamentarism and the Rhetorical Culture of Politics', is one of the first results of my turn to the study of parliamentary rhetoric and procedure. Weber's essay on 'objectivity' is here linked to his minor but important defence of parliamentarism in the first decade of the twentieth century and to his 1918 'Parlament' pamphlet on the parliamentary control of the allegedly superior knowledge of officials in relation to parliamentarians. As early as this point, I began to speak of Weber's 'parliamentary theory of knowledge', although not yet of his revision of the concept of 'objectivity'.

Chapter Eleven, ' "Objectivity" as Fair Play: Max Weber's Parliamentary Redescription of a Normative Concept', takes up the rhetorical strategies Weber used to justify 'objectivity' as a procedural concept. For Weber the concept relates to how political struggles may be taken as models for dealing with academic disputes. Weber's point in his 'Parlament' pamphlet, that knowledge (*Erkenntnis*) requires a discussion of items from opposed points of view, holds also for everyday knowledge (*Wissen*). In a few pages Weber presents the rhetorical means by which parliamentarians can exercise control of officials and the illegitimate power their knowledge gives them.

Chapter Twelve, 'Max Weber's Rhetoric of "Objectivity" ', summarises the historical role played by dissensus and debate, as seen in the nineteenth-century publications on Westminster parliamentary procedure, rhetoric and political theory. In my interpretation these writings serve as the historical and conceptual background to Weber's procedural rethinking of 'objectivity', which he considered involving a fair debate between opposing theories and approaches. Weber's remarks illustrate the depth of his defence of Westminster parliamentarism; it was part of his rhetorical vision of a knowledge achieved through the process of debating items pro et contra.

In the final chapter, 'Was Max Weber Wrong about Westminster?', I argue on behalf of Weber's procedural and rhetorical view of Westminster parliamentarism against later interpretations of his work in German political science. Critics have misunderstood Weber's defence of the Westminster committee system and how members are obliged to debate items in committee. When Weber speaks of Westminster as an *Arbeitsparlament* (working parliament), he by no means denies its value as also a *Redeparlament* (talking parliament), knowing the critical importance of debate in plenary as well as committee sessions. He does situate Westminster in opposition to a parliament of powerless speeches, such as the Reichstag of the German Empire. At the conclusion of the chapter, a refined typology of parliaments is suggested.

Why politics instead of the political?

In 'Wissenschaft als Beruf' (1919e), Weber emphasises that, in science, what one 'has accomplished will be obsolete' sooner or later, and that 'indeed, that is the very *meaning* of scientific work' (see Weber 2012: 341, the German original in Weber 1919e: 8). A striking fact is that with Weber's own work this has not been the case. Interest in his work as among the few real 'classics' of twentieth-century political thought has grown in the recent decades and new dimensions in his work have been discovered. Even though Max Weber is not currently as fashionable a thinker as Hannah Arendt, Michel Foucault or even Carl Schmitt, I would argue that the very experience of radical contingency in the human world has given an enduring value to Weber's work even beyond his own expectations.

The textbook view of 'Weber, the sociologist' is still powerful. Of course, in Weber's time sociology was not an established discipline and he attempted to conquer the term for an action-theoretical view against the legal theorists (*see* Chapter Nine in this volume) as well as the naturalistic and idealistic theorists of different varieties. But, as Hartmann Tyrell (1994) writes, Weber's is a 'sociology without society' – *eine Soziologie ohne Gesellschaft* (see also Palonen 1998: 109–11). More generally, one of Weber's main merits is his rejection of the 'collective concepts of everyday life' and his corresponding defence of what Schumpeter called 'methodological individualism' (see esp. Weber 1913: 413–14).

Weber's project is one of disenchantment (*Entzauberung*) of allegedly stable or timeless concepts, and this has in turn inspired conceptual histories (see the Weberian title of Palonen 2004a). In contrast, from the Weberian point of view the entire set of concepts that characterises the sociology of the post-war decades – society, structure, function, process, system and so on – and that today dominates administrative language (as if the terms were real entities) should be submitted to Occam's razor. Conventional sociology excludes, and thereby depoliticises, Weber's conceptual horizon of action, chance, objective possibility, life-conduct and so on. The whos, hows and whens of human action hardly ever appear in that view. Against that, it is important to rehabilitate the value of thinking politically with a Weberian imagination.

A more recent trend, initiated in France in the late 1970s and early 1980s, is opposing 'mere' politics to 'the political' (Marchard 2007, 2010). The philosophical contempt for politics and politicking (see Lacoue-Labarthe and Nancy 1981, 1983) is not shared by, for example, Pierre Rosanvallon (2003) or Chantal Mouffe (2005), but they are nonetheless looking for something 'deeper' than politics, a structure or an 'ontology'. I discuss these views in relation to Weber and the activity-concept of politics in Chapter Three and in an article on Rosanvallon (Palonen 2009b).

Discourses on 'the political' as opposed to 'politics' now also exist in German and anglophone scholarship. The studies in the Bielefeld *Sonderforschungbereich*, 'The political as a communicative space' (Steinmetz 2013; Abschlussbericht 2013) have done valuable work on the history of the concept (Steinmetz 2005; Meier *et al.* 2012; Weidner 2012a and b; Steinmetz *et al.* 2013). They apply a spatial concept for interpreting layers of politics beyond the activities of politicians, without, however, seriously considering Weber's work and the activity-concept. In the more philosophically oriented volume of Bedorf and Röttgers (2010), only Michael Greven (2010) introduces Weber into the discussion.

Most authors who focus on the political seem already to 'know' what 'politics' means. For me as a long-term historian of the concept, this is a dilettantism that betrays an unfamiliarity with the rich and complex uses of politics, in particular, since the last third of the nineteenth century (see Palonen 2006). Characteristic of the 'discourse' on the political is that, if Weber is mentioned at all, some of his slogan-like quasi-definitions from 'Politik als Beruf' are repeated, without analysing their nuances or relating them either to the history of the concept or to the text of the book as a whole (see Palonen 2002).

An intriguing anglophone example, which shows a good awareness of both the history and the contemporary debates, are some aspects of Michael Freeden's *Political Theory and Political Thinking* (2013b) (on British twentieth-century uses, see Freeden 2013a). He gives a historical interpretation for the rise of 'the political':

> As the twentieth century entered its final third, processes began to replace institutions and demarcated political space as the loci of politics, and the phrase 'the political' began its unremitting ascendancy, after having been around most of the century in a minor key. The adjectival noun was doubly useful, in intimating vagueness that defied previous attempts at precision – lumping together activities, behaviour, institutions, processes as well as signifying a domain – and suggesting flux rather than stasis.
>
> (Freeden 2013b: 26)

Freeden is critical of the normative uses of the political à la Mouffe and others (Freeden 2013b: 6–7, 57–64) and presents his own interpretation of the concept. His starting point is that ' "the political" generated a shift ... that now signified an entire domain of human interaction as well as the diverse practices that occur in that domain' (Freeden 2013b: 26). He is focused on 'the main recurrent features' of the political (Freeden 2013b: 27). Similarly to the Bielefeld project, Freeden sees the political as a spatial concept, although no longer in the sense of a separate sphere (Freeden 2013b: 28). Freeden condenses his own use of 'the political' in this formula: 'The political is always a cluster of practices and thought-practices that may be malleable, intertwined overlapping, and mutually interacting, but each of which identifies one of the multiple elements peculiar to that field' (Freeden 2013b: 66). In a book review, Freeden accentuates the contrast of his formula to the activity-concept, rejecting 'the over-awareness of contingency and ceaseless contestation' in favour of '[d]econtestation as indispensable for mapping the worlds we traverse and for making the decisions without which the political flounders' (Freeden 2016: 130).

With these uses of 'the political', some less obvious aspects of politics can be identified (see the subtitle of Palonen 1998). Nonetheless, I regard the theorists of the political as trying to save something of the value of politics by giving it a respectable form, beyond the reach of active politicians. It is no accident that this sought-after 'respect' is bound up with maintaining the political as a spatial concept.

In contrast, for Weber as an action-theorist, politics is inseparable from the ideal type of the politician, both the professional and the occasional. Weber helps us to get rid of the populist-cum-academic grand coalition with its shared contempt for politicians. With him we can understand the situation in which they are acting, the debates in which they are engaged and the choices they have to make without ever having sufficient grounds to choose a definite course of action. In *Rhetorik des Unbeliebten* (Palonen 2012b), I have constructed a genre of writings on politicians, which for the most part contain no academic treatises.

A contemporary study that has taken a step in this direction is Peter Riddell's book *In Defence of Politicians (In Spite of Themselves)* (2010), although Weber would never have added the subtitle. The anthropologist Emma Crewe (2015) after closely following Westminster politicians has learnt to appreciate their activity, while Labour backbencher Paul Flynn (2012) has reactivated the genre of the advice-book for the parliamentarian. Parliamentary procedures and politicians' rhetorical competences in applying them are richer, more complex, imaginative and interesting than any 'ontology of the political'.

When Weber claims that 'we all' are occasional politicians (1919c: 41), this can also be understood as a recommendation for studying the activity of politics. We should think of ourselves in situations in which we are acting politically and then apply, *mutatis mutandis*, the case of professional politicians as a model for how to deal with such situations. In present-day academia, in which even the once-protected position of tenured professors has became precarious, it is more important than ever for scholars to play against the 'rule of officialdom', the game of politicians, and to learn from the activities of professional politicians.

PART I

POLITICS AND POLITICIANS –
WEBERIAN THEMES

Chapter Two

Four Times of Politics: Policy, Polity, Politicking and Politicisation

There is just one noun corresponding to the adjective *political* in French, German, Swedish, Finnish and so on, while the English language has three: *policy, polity and politics*. Here, I shall take the tripartite division of the English polit-vocabulary as a point of departure for rethinking politics in a 'de-centring' mode. The English vocabulary provides us with a glimpse into the linguistic chances for the formation of different perspectives from which to conceptualise politics.

I have modified the tripartite division by taking into account two linguistic novelties, *politicking* and *politicisation*. According to the *Oxford English Dictionary* (1989, vol. 16: 34), both politicking and politicisation seem to have been coined no earlier than the inter-war period. My intention is to take each of these nouns as an allusion to four aspects of conceptualising politics (for a previous version of this typology, see Palonen 1993). In addition, two different concepts of politics – namely, politics-as-sphere and politics-as-activity – have been commonly used since the nineteenth century, the first indicating a spatial and the second a temporal mode of conceptualising. Here, I am exclusively interested in the concept of politics-as-activity and, consequently, I will search for the temporal chances present in the four polit-nouns.

In this conceptual horizon, *policy* refers to the regulating aspect of politics, *politicking* alludes to a performative aspect, *polity* implies a metaphorical space with specific possibilities and limits, while *politicisation* marks an opening of something as political, as 'playable'. Policy–politicking and polity–politicisation form two conceptual pairs. In the sphere-concept, the core of politics is occupied by the borders and regulations of the polity–policy space, whereas in the activity-concept politics is constituted by the 'verbal' figures of politicisation and politicking.

I will speculate here on the conceptual chances of this vocabulary. To consider the times of politics is to conceptualise the contingent, fluid and disorderly, and to do so in a manner that does not a priori reduce the contingency of politics through the very act of conceptualising. Here, time constitutes the very activity of politics: it is a medium through which to render a fluid activity intelligible as politics.

Politics as activity: a Weberian perspective

Politics is both a time-consuming and a time-playing activity. We can thus distinguish two modes of playing with time in politics, namely the background time (time in politics) and the operative time (time of politics), or playground-time and playmedium-time.

I will attempt to read the temporal presuppositions and implications of politics as activity, departing from the nominalistic perspective, as expressed in Max Weber's famous formulas on politics, power and struggle. In other words, I want to continue Weber's conceptualisation of politics by programmatically explicating the temporal dimension of the concept.

Let me begin with Weber's main proposal for the understanding of politics in 'Politik als Beruf', in a longer and shorter version: '"Politik" würde für uns also heißen: Streben nach Machtanteil oder nach Beeinflussung der Machtverteilung … Wer Politik treibt, erstrebt Macht' (Weber 1919c: 36). In the translation of Lassman and Speirs: '"Politics" would mean striving for a share of power or for influence on the distribution of power … Anyone engaged in politics is striving for power' (Weber 1994b: 311).

The verbal expressions *streben, erstreben* and *treiben* refer to a temporal activity. Politics is oriented towards changing the existing state of affairs. The temporality of politics is a negative finality, an activity of getting rid of that which is. As an activity, politics has no substantive or purpose 'above' itself. This is the proper temporality of doing, oriented toward change but not in an already determined direction.

With his brief formula, Weber insists that striving for power (*Macht*) is a necessary condition for acting politically. Power is a *medium* of politics, through, and only through, which one can act politically. He who does not strive for power is doomed to powerlessness (*Ohnmacht*) and inactivity. Power expresses the openness of politics as striving, and striving for new power shares leads to the next decision one must take: what to do with these shares. In order to understand this better, let us examine Weber's famous power-formula in *Wirtschaft und Gesellschaft*: '*Macht* bedeutet jede Chance, innerhalb einer sozialen Beziehung, den eigenen Willen auch gegen Widerstreben durchzusetzen, gleichviel worauf die Chance beruht' (Weber 1922: 28). Keith Tribe translates this as follows: 'Power (*Macht*) can be defined as the chance, within a social relationship of enforcing one's own will against resistance, whatever this chance might be based on' (Weber 2004a: 355).

As with all the concepts in the Weberian vocabulary of human actions and relationships, power is a *Chance*-concept. As such, it expresses the contingent character of politics-as-activity; it is 'only' a possibility, an occasion or an opportunity to do something. It opens a horizon of action, but does not specify how to act within this horizon. In a temporal perspective, *Chancen* refer to opportunities that are present and 'real' in the experience of the persons acting politically, while the 'realised reality' is for political agents a contingent result of past political struggles.

Power, in Weber's nominalistic view of politics, consists only of the 'shares' (*Machtanteile*) and their distribution (*Machtverteilung*). The German concept of *Anteil* – as opposed to *Aktie* – refers to an egalitarian enterprise, in which every agent has some *Anteile*. With his conception, Weber gives every political agent some shares of power, without which he or she could not act politically. Nobody who 'strives for power' is entirely powerless, nor are those who resist this striving omnipotent, but rather 'power' is a relative matter of the distribution of shares.

Although there can be some paradigmatic sources of power, there is no obstacle to turning anything into a power share. The lack of conventional resources of power, and even the recourse to the sheer existence of agents, can in principle be turned into a power share. When politics concerns power, it concerns the relationships between different types of power shares, different manners of distribution between them, as well as the relationship between the same types of power share.

Weber's power-formula also indicates a limit-situation. 'To realise one's own will' refers to a situation in which neither the agent nor the 'patient' has any chances left. The latter has been excluded from agency, played out of politics, but the agent's will is also turned into an existing 'fact' and as such can no longer be an object of her strivings. Weber's view of power as *Chance* thus excludes a complete realisation of the 'will'. In this sense, the figure of intentional resistance (*Widerstreben*) to the attempted realisation of a will also marks the difference between human agents' resistance and mechanical obstacles to the realisation of the 'will'.

In the Weberian perspective, any chances is temporary, arising only on specific occasions and having only a limited duration. Time is also something that can be turned into a chances, into a share of power in a relationship with other agents. Time as source of power means the disposable time of the political agent, which allows her a certain temporal sovereignty as a 'player'. In addition to these 'absolute' power chances, which are available through disposable time, we can speak of 'relative' power chances, which are related to the comparative ability of the players, using time as a resource. Even when time is scarce and the margins for its use as a background factor of action are small, the differences in the competence of using time may gain significance, and playing with the margins of temporality can be turned into a decisive instance in a political struggle.

The political dimension of the contingency of *Chancen* not only refers to the formal possibility of having acted otherwise but also to the presence of plural agents conflicting in their strivings for power. Politics as *Streben* is something unpredictable in terms of its results, both because of the sheer facticity of the existing situation and the presence of *Widerstreben*, of an intentional activity against the attempt to gain new power shares. We can distinguish here between the contingency of facticity and the contingency of struggle. This concept is explicated in *Wirtschaft und Gesellschaft*, which explicitly uses the same vocabulary as the power-formula some pages later: '*Kampf* soll eine soziale Beziehung insoweit heißen, als das Handeln an der Absicht der Durchsetzung des eigenen Willens gegen Widerstand des oder der Partner orientiert ist' (Weber 1922: 20). Tribe translates this as follows: 'A social relation will be called a *struggle* where the actor is oriented to the imposition of his own will upon an unwilling partner or partners' (Weber 2004a: 341).

Weber's *Politik als Kampf* topos does not indicate a zero-sum game, but the plurality and mutability of the types of power shares render the struggle an open contest, in which the agents are also obliged to revise their views and redirect their striving for power shares. The struggle against the opposing political agents is, in the Weberian view, a 'moving' instance of politics. In particular, he writes in 'Politik als Beruf' how in politics the results are in a paradoxical relation to the intentions of any of the participants: 'Es ist durchaus wahr und eine – jetzt hier nicht näher zu begründende – Grundtatsache aller Geschichte, daß das schließliche Resultat politischen Handelns oft, nein: regelmäßig, in völlig unadequatem, oft in geradezu paradoxem Verhältnis zu seinem ursprünglichen Sinn steht' (Weber 1919c: 75–6). It is translated by Lassman and Speirs as:

> It is certainly true, and it is a fundamental fact of history (for which no more detailed explanation can be offered here), that the eventual outcome of political action frequently, indeed regularly, stands in a quite inadequate, even paradoxical relation to its original, intended meaning and purpose (*Sinn*).
>
> (Weber 1994b: 355)

The situational drama of the unanticipated consequences of actions (*Nebenfolgen*) is constitutive of politics. Time modifies both the projects of agents and the relations between struggling agents, while the relative competence in time-playing consists of the ability to use *Nebenfolgen* as a special kind of *Chancen* (see esp. Weber 1904: 149–50, translated in Weber 2012: 102). The political point is to turn the scarce margins of time-playing into chances in the changing constellations.

It is now possible to reformulate the four aspects of politics in Weberian terms. *Politicisation* means a share of power and opens a specified horizon of chances in terms of this share, while *politicking* means performative operations in the struggle for power over already existing shares and their redistribution. *Polity* refers to those power shares that have already been politicised but have also created a kind of vested interest that tacitly excludes other kinds of shares, while *policy* means a regulation and co-ordination of performative operations by specific ends and means. The next steps consist of outlining a temporal interpretation of each of them.

Times of policy

So-called policy analysis never poses the question of what constitutes a 'policy' and its political significance. Despite this, we should ask: what kind of politics is to be understood by means of 'policy' and what are its temporal implications?

A policy refers to a direction of activities, to a line, project, plan, programme or doctrine. Policy has, thus, a teleological connotation, an orientation toward the future, which is considered to be a priority over the present state of affairs, as well as the activity itself. In addition, policy has a normative character as a criterion in the selection of what should be realised among possible futures. The construction of a policy signifies the inclusion and coordination of different acts, moves or measures, through which they are turned into the relative unity of activities, into a policy. In addition, a policy presupposes a criterion of judgment that regulates the inclusion and exclusion of activities, types and degrees of coordination, and so on. Thus, we can call a policy a complex of inclusion and coordination of measures into a project unified with a name, such as 'the Paasikivi-Kekkonen line' (for the doctrine of Finnish foreign policy for the cold war era).

The normative and the teleological orientations of a policy remain opposed to one other. A limiting case is *Realpolitik*, a term coined by L. A. von Rochau (1853), in which the realisability of a line is turned into a quasi-norm. Conversely, we can speak of fixed 'moral' aims upheld independently of their realisability. These two situations mark the limits of a policy. In the first case, the flexibility of a policy is turned into a doctrine of passive adaptation, while in the opposite case the policy is limited to a declaration of desirability. Still, we may claim that both of them may also contribute to a change in affairs if used consciously as political strategies.

In the Weberian perspective, none of the agents can perfectly realise a policy established prior to action. This is not acknowledged in the discourse of 'policy-making', if a government has monopolised the relevant power shares. The times conducting a policy, as a mode of politics, can, however, be best understood as being shaped by the insight into limited realisability of any policy. How can the revisions and deviations in the policy itself be calculated? What does the limited realisability mean for the formation and acceptance of a policy?

Understanding a policy does not thus rely merely on the continuity of a line or a project, but makes use of the temporal breaking points within it. The more fixed the policy is, the more dramatic the deviations will be and the more improvisation is needed, in order to achieve at least some of the intended aims of a given policy. Such breaking points can be detected 'before' the confrontation with other policies, either by the inclusion of the measures, by coordinating between them or by naming a policy. 'After' the confrontation we can distinguish between ad hoc corrections, modifications and revisions and giving up on the policy. The teleological character of the policy-time means that, up until the last point, the elements of the break are understood to be subordinated to the internal coherence or consistence of a project.

A lack of policy is commonly regarded as chaotic and, correspondingly, any policy is held to be better than no policy. This assumption relies on the superiority of continuity over discontinuity in politics. My thesis is that it is possible to understand policies as heuristic instruments in politics even when rejecting the continuity assumption. Temporalising policies in relation to their breaking points then becomes a condition of their intelligibility.

In Weberian terms, policies are dependent on the power-shares as chances to which all policy aims must be related. However, striving for power always aims at improving the chances of realising certain purposes (*Zwecke*) formulated in policies. Relating policy to the chances of power, including the *ex post* visible *Nebenfolgen*, means that the normative and teleological dimensions of a policy presuppose an assessment of the horizon of chances. An a priori fixation of a policy is not ideal, but a degree of revisability should always be provided for any comprehensive policy.

Due to the normative-teleological character of this type of politics, a policy cannot dispense with a certain continuity in time. Transcending the actual situation by a consistent line or project is legitimate, on the condition that we acknowledge the value of continuity as relative to different breaking points. Dealing with these breaking points and their relations to continuity also alludes to forms of politicking that transcend the policy-type. The alternative to policy does not consist of a reliance on ad hoc measures but of a type of politicking that is not regulated by normative-teleological criteria, or the priority of the future over the present.

Times of politicking

Politicking has received a minimal amount of attention in literature on the concept of politics, although it refers to a key aspect in the understanding of politics-as-activity. The neglect of politicking is historically related to the fact that *Politics* was originally the title of a discipline (see Palonen 1985, 1990), and in most European languages acting politically is expressed by formulas such as *Politik treiben* or *faire de la politique*. In the English neologism *politicking* and the Finnish *politikoida* (see Palonen 2001: 113–14), a single word suffices.

As a point of departure in the understanding of politicking we can take the Aristotelian idea of a *praxis*, which has its aim in itself, as opposed to *poiesis*, which is oriented towards external aims. A modern version of this idea is Hannah Arendt's metaphor of politics as a performing art that is judged by the criterion of the virtuosity of the performance: 'the Greeks always used such metaphors as flute-playing, dancing, healing and seafaring to distinguish political from other activities, that is that they drew their analogies from those arts in which the virtuosity of performance is decisive' (Arendt 1968: 153).

In the language of the speech act theory, politicking consists of performatives. Politics-as-activity is never to be judged by its 'results' alone, even if we count its unanticipated consequences, or, politicking consists of asking not only *what* should be done but also *how* to do it.

Politicking as a performance relies on available power shares in order to increase the relative advantages in their distribution. The Weberian concept of *Chance* contains a gradation of the degrees of realisability of chances, although only as an analogy to the calculus of probabilities (Weber 1913: 430–42, translated in Weber 2012: 280–2). For the agent, the analogy explicates the character of choices: there is no a priori reason for choosing a more cautious alternative over a riskier one, or vice versa. The key operations of politicking consist of choosing between different types and degrees of chances, which then lead to different styles of performance. The simplest variation concerns the opposition between cautious and daring styles of politicking. More generally, we can speak of genres of politicking, for example between theatrical, filmic, musical or dance-related styles of politicking, or comic, tragic genres of politics between the dramatic and epic variants of theatrical politicking.

When a policy consists of coordinated measures that have sources and limits in time, politicking consists of performances that are both time-consuming and time-playing events. In addition to an origin and an end, politicking has a duration and rhythm of its own, as do the performing arts. This can be viewed as an extension of the present time in politicking into a performative unity that cannot be measured by consumed time but, in a sense, interrupts the time lapse for the duration of the performance. The virtuosity of the performance is judged by its capacity to convey the impression of the temporal autonomy of an extended present as an internal time of politicking.

The continuous moments of politicking consist of performances, of oblique activities, which cannot be rehearsed in advance but presuppose improvisation and taking advantage of the details of the ongoing situation. If the core of the policy is understood to consist of dealing with the breaking point of the continuity, it marks a limit-situation politicking in which the continuities appear as regulations of the improvised performance of politicking.

Although a performance can only take place in the present, this present is not instantaneous but, similar to the artistic performance, it contains internal temporal rhythms with chances to break from common sense views. The stylistic alternatives in politicking have different temporal implications, for example in the rhythms of movement characteristic to each genre or style. Through artistic exaggeration, these 'aesthetic' categories also illustrate temporal chances and modes of using them, which could also be utilised in the closer interpretation of more conventional forms of politicking.

The dual temporality of continuous and discontinuous aspects is thus of equal importance for both politicking and policy, although for politicking the present is the tempus of performance and the mark of its virtuosity. This introduces, however, a second dual temporality, namely that between the lapse of time and the extension of the present in the performing event. The temporality of performance must thus be interrelated to the interruption of the time-lapse by the extended present and the reappearance of this time-lapse at the limits of the performance. The specific quality of politicking consists of dealing with both of these aspects of time.

In politicking, the aims to which policies are oriented serve as instruments in the struggle for power. The limited realisability of the policies marks a limit-situation, which can be turned into a source of new chances, or at least into a relative advantage as compared with the encounter of similar limits by one's adversaries and their policies. The judgment of politicking should therefore be extended to the virtuosity in the competence to deal with the beginnings and ends of the performances. In this sense, politicking, too, presupposes the coordination of activities, not in order to regulate them but as an extension of the event-character of the simple performances to the interconnections and disconnections between performances.

Times of polity

Traditionally, *polity* has referred to a metaphorical space that demarcates the 'political sphere' from other spheres. In terms of activity, polity can be considered as a temporalised space that has been politicised and commonly accepted as political, and that demarcates activity from that which is not accepted as political. In other words, polity can be viewed as a *Spielraum* (play space) for activity, resulting from previous politicisations and established to the extent that it at least tacitly serves as an obstacle to new politicisations.

In Weberian terms, polity refers to a complex in which the power shares are divided into legitimate and illegitimate ones. Certain power shares have gained privileged positions; others have faded away and appear as anachronistic, while attempts to create new ones are viewed with suspicion. The 'core' *Spielraum* of the polity serves as a paradigm for politicking. For example, the public–private dichotomy can be interpreted as a result of contingency, although as well-established politicisations as opposed to a demarcation between two spheres. In naming the polity, such epithets as the 'ordinary', 'proper' or 'strict' sense of the political similarly function as historical criteria for legitimating the established polity as opposed to the concurrent horizons of power shares.

However, the historical and temporal character of the polity means that the 'central' *Spielraum* of the legitimate polity is constantly undermined, due to the shifting significance of the sources of power in the situation. Disputes on the limits or demarcations of the historically and contingently formed polity also contribute to the reinterpretation of the 'core' of the polity.

The struggle for power introduces instability to the formation of a polity as a horizon of politicking. The inventions of new topics on the agenda, new dimensions of human agency or new practices of politicking are liable to destabilise the polity, not only within its margins but also in the interpretation of what is essential and decisive in it. Although these novelties are viewed with suspicion, they can be mixed with old ones and in this way undermine their established character. Thus, it is impossible to render the established polity 'immune' to new politicisations, even among those who in principle accept the established polity as a legitimate 'regime'.

Moreover, we can also speak of the polity of time itself; as a metaphorical space, a polity is also a time-regime. The character of the chances (power shares) illustrates a temporally understood *Spielraum*, or, rather, *Spielzeit* (play time). It is not only characterised by the limits of the available time but also by the specification of the specific occasions within this *Spielzeitraum*. The political competence consists both of playing with the extremities of the legitimate time and of gaining an insight into the specific chances of the time-regime.

Parliamentary politics, controlled by the electorate and by the government–opposition game within the parliament, clearly signifies a time-oriented regime. The complex of parliamentary practices is shaped by the presence of chances and controls, both of them being limited not only 'in time' but also 'by time'. The various types of chances the government has to rule are shaped by temporal distinctions, by the periodisation of governmental politics to times of high and low control by the opposition respectively by the electorate (compare Riescher 1994; Rosanvallon 2000).

A specific calendar of parliamentary politics was successively introduced from the eighteenth century onwards. General elections are decisive chances for either getting rid of or re-electing a government. The government formation in the parliament, the interpellations intended to overthrow the government, the annual debates on the budget, the elections of chairpersons and committees, the decisions over the length of the session periods and on the maximum duration of speeches mark the main instances of a temporal polity. The events of the parliamentary calendar contain occasions for the government to manifest its excellence in politicking and for the opposition to question these manifestations.

'Nur in Terminen rechnet der wahre Politiker', wrote Walter Benjamin in his *Einbahnstraße* (Benjamin 1929: 77). Politicians live according to the items on their calendars. He understood better than many others how crucial the ability to play with time, in this case with one's own 'calendar events', is in politics. When considering time as a decisive criterion of parliamentary politicking, we dispense with the mythologies of the 'right' of certain persons, or of 'the people' to rule. On the contrary, all rulers are subject to temporal control by elections and parliamentary procedures. Even the repeatedly confirmed re-election of a government appears as suspicious, despite the correctness of electoral procedures, for the temporal calendar of the polity tacitly presumes an alternation in government as a condition of avoiding the monopolising tendencies over the shares of governmental power.

Regulating the political chances and their control by temporal measures is an advantage of parliamentary democracy over direct democracy. A simple rotation in office, according to the Athenian model and its imitations (Jacksonian democracy in the United States and the German Greens in the 1980s), also tends to devalue the political competition that is so inherent to democracy. Similarly, the old ideal of 'frequent elections' tends to diminish the chances for governments to use their power shares and to facilitate control by the opposition, without the need to construct a policy alternative.

The parliamentary regime illustrates an ideal type of temporal polity. In nominalistic terms, 'polity' should be understood as any specific regime of power shares, and not as a single 'political system'. We can thus speak of street name polity, university polity, travel polity and so on, which together do not constitute a whole, but a complex myriad of interconnected and disconnected polities transcending juridical, geographical and other limits. If a single polity has a calendar of its own, the interconnectedness of the polities can, rather, be understood by the metaphor of a political timetable, showing the trains and their names, stations and connections. As times are politically controversial, no exact timing can be given, and the very mode of constructing political timetables is contestable and constantly changing. As such, politicking within a complex of polities would largely consist of the competence to read and apply timetables.

Times of politicisation

The word politicisation was first used in German in 1907, when the historian Karl Lamprecht spoke of *die Politisierung der Gesellschaft*, although in the harmless sense of increasing the interest in politics. The neologism, however, was soon turned into a more offensive view of politicisation as a perspectivistic reinterpretation of a phenomenon, especially among the expressionist *literati* Kurt Hiller and Ludwig Rubiner. To speak of politicisation in this sense of creating a new *Spielzeitraum* for the activity of politicking, rendered it open to alternatives and controversies and contributed to the rethinking of the concept of politics. Such a rethinking took place in Germany during the first two decades of the twentieth century, while *politicisation* in English and *politisation* in French seem to have been introduced only during the inter-war era (for the details, see Palonen 1985, 1989, 1990).

Here, politicisation thus means neither the juxtaposition of things with politics nor the increased 'interest in politics' among certain persons. Instead, by politicisation we can mark a phenomenon as political, as a *Spielzeitraum* for contingent action. Politicisation thus refers to the act of *naming* something as political, including the controversies surrounding the acceptance of this naming. There is no politics 'before' politicisation, either in a logical or a temporal sense, and politicking is possible only if a *Spielzeitraum* has been opened for action by politicisation, while a polity is a result of previous politicisations. Still, it seems equally unnecessary to identify initial or original politicisations, for the question of what can be considered to be a politicisation is dependent on the perspective of interpretation.

If a polity is a result of specific politicisations, we cannot refer to a proper or ordinary sense of politics; politicisation has no quasi-natural subject matter. While nothing in human life can be excluded from politicisation, it always demands a specific and concentrated effort to politicise something new, to create a *Spielzeitraum* for which no established practices of politicking are available. Politicisation has to be more than a declaration and must provide at least some indications regarding the forms of politicking that are opened by the specific politicising moves.

Politicisation can be an invention, a construction of chances where none were previously seen or admitted to have existed. This sort of invention requires the construction of a new perspective that makes things appear differently: the feminist slogan 'the personal is political', coined in the late 1960s, seems today to be less of a novelty than it did then – German expressionists, for example, proposed similar views in the early twentieth century. Still, it opened a new horizon for both acting politically and thematising politics as a concept, which could then be used in different and even opposing ways.

In another perspective, politicisation means detecting the political potential of some existing changes, shifts or processes. It will be based on analysing the results or effects of long-term changes, which render some alleged 'necessities' or 'impossibilities' obsolete and using these changes in order to declare a new *Spielzeitraum* for action. Claims that without something 'order' cannot be upheld, or that 'laws of nature' cannot be violated, and so on, have been politicised in the sense of being rendered obsolete by creating the 'impossible' without catastrophes. For example, the arguments for extending suffrage always first had to overcome the resistance to such an 'impossibility'.

The distinction between the inventive and disruptive moments of politicisation is relative. Without some disruptive processes against the old order already made visible, it is difficult to imagine the invention of a perspective of politicisation that is not a realisable horizon of chances. The detection of chances, as an unintended result of erosive changes, already alludes to a tacit shift in the perspective.

When an established polity with a calendar exists, politicisation either introduces new items to it, which alter the relationships between the existing ones, or dismisses existing items. The introduction can concern a new topic on the annual agenda, or a new train added to the timetable and thus changing the significance of other connections. A more radical politicisation could consist of the introduction of a new dimension into the calendar, putting the existing items into a new perspective. The slogan 'the personal is political' represented precisely such a politicising shift in the perspective of questioning the primacy of the conventional parliamentary-governmental-partisan politics, although it obviously was unable to radically alter the calendar and timetables, that is, the connections to the 'old' politics. The politicisation of lifestyles has remained disconnected from the traditional modes of politicking as opposed to altering them or making use of the rich experiences in parliamentary politics in order to construct analogies for lifestyle politicking.

In order to better understand the historical sequences of politicisations, we could make a use of Koselleck's (2000) metaphor of temporal layers. Politicisation describes a novelty that works against an established and sedimented practice and creates links between historical layers of politicisation, when the previous ones have been established, naturalised and spatialised to such an extent that their historical significance as politicising moments has been lost or misrepresented. The rhetoric of politicisation perhaps requires the simplification of an established polity as a space of stagnating and discriminating practices by neglecting its specific politicising origins in order to dramatise the break and the novelty. A radicalising effect can, however, be achieved through reinterpreting history by accentuating forms of politicisation which have been forgotten or marginalised in the established polity. Even if politicisation increases the available *Spielzeitraum* in the future, it also presupposes a redescription or an *Umschreibung* of the past. In this respect Quentin Skinner's and Koselleck's views on rhetorical redescription are parallel (see Skinner 1996 and Koselleck's essay 'Erfahrungswandel and Methodenwechsel', published in Koselleck 2000). In this sense, the Benjaminian figure of 'actualisation' of a past in the present (see his 'Theses' from 1940, published in Benjamin 1980) remains an indispensable temporal resource in the conceptualisation of politicisations.

Thus, politicisation has a dual relationship to politicking. It simultaneously creates new *Spielzeiträume* and makes some old ones obsolete in a given situation. Additionally, we can speak of a second order of politicking, which deals with the different layers of politicisations. This politicking operates with discontinuities in time, creating a relation between a radical break in the present and recourse to the older past as something that provides some analogical resources with a sort of renaissance or rehabilitation in order to accentuate the radical break in the present.

Conclusions

Nobody is able to master time, and the adversity and counter-finality constitutive of political actions place further limits on any attempts to do so. The classical alternative, taming the corruptive *fortuna* of time by creating a space for the *virtù*, appears today to be increasingly unrealistic; it cannot understand time other than as an erosive force. To play with contingency means to accept that time not only marks limits of political activities but also serves as their medium (on *fortuna* and *Chance* as two types of contingency, see Palonen 1998). It is for this purpose that the nuances of the polit-vocabulary provide us with some hints at how to deal with such a fluid and concept-escaping instance as time.

Politics, as presented here, is understood as a correlate between two activities, politicisation and politicking, while polity and policy refer to their 'regulating' limit-situations. Politicisation searches for new power shares, while politicking aims at an increase in disposition over the existing ones. Agents making use of either of these performatives refer to the other one as well as to the past and future variants of the same operation. This reference indicates temporal discrepancies, highlighting chances of revision while simultaneously constituting a new relative continuity in time between historical forms of both politicking and politicisation.

Every politicisation disrupts continuity, although the sequence of breaks forms a second order of continuity in a series of novelties, mediated by the practices of politicking. Politicking contains a performative continuity, which is singularised by the shifting horizons of politicisation and by the critical use of analogies to previous forms of politicking. In this sense, politicisation and politicking signify, each in a different manner, a break with the mere lapse of time. These can be assessed both as an erosive force, alluding to the limits of the chances involved in them, and as a temporal play-limit challenge, to be enclosed in politicking and politicisation as an element of play. As an interruption of continuity, both of these performative operations mark an autonomisation of the present. Politicisation marks a moment: not just an instance, but a new horizon of chances, which can be utilised within a range of time; politicking signifies a performance, which is singular yet has a relative duration of its own.

Chapter Three

Politics or the Political? An Historical Perspective on a Contemporary Non-Debate

In 1981, Régis Debray, the former revolutionary and later advisor to President François Mitterrand, published a book with the classical title, *Critique de la raison politique*. He opposes politics (*la politique*) to the political (*le politique*): 'Bref, la politique m'a longtemps masqué "le politique"' [In short, politics has for a long time masked the political] (Debray 1981: 13).

For Debray, the decline of political activism was indeed combined with the reflection of 'the political' as superior to 'mere' politics. A number of other French authors shared this view, (see Marchart 2007) whereas others, as the title of Alan Badiou's *Peut-on penser la politique* (1985) indicates, have continued to reflect on the practical activity of politics. No real debate between the two modes of conceptualisation exists in France or elsewhere.

Should we understand politics by going behind the term itself to examine 'the political' or by rendering the activity itself more intelligible? In this chapter, I shall track the conceptual origins of the two perspectives to the opposition between Carl Schmitt and Max Weber. The presence of the Schmittian and Weberian problematic already played a role in the inter-war literature and is even more distinct in the post-war conceptualisations of the political and politics. Finally, I shall conclude with the thesis that the Schmittian search for the political devalues the practical activity of politics, whereas the Weberian style of conceptualising politics as contingent activity re-values the politicians.

Schmitt and the concept of the political

Both the expressions 'the political' in English and *le politique* in French refer historically to translations of the German *das Politische*. The catalyst for the rise of the political in recent academic literature is, of course, Carl Schmitt's *Der Begriff des Politischen*. It was first published as an article in 1927, and the book version appeared in 1932 and was subsequently revised during the Nazi regime, although Schmitt himself canonised the 1932 version in 1963. Today, the literature on the political tacitly refers to Schmitt, despite the notoriety of the author.

The use of the adjective as a noun in the expression *das Politische* was certainly not Schmitt's innovation. Friedrich Schiller and Friedrich Schlegel had already used the term in the 1790s (see the references in Palonen 2006: 45–6) as referring to a distinct sphere or sector. The demarcation of the political refers to a new level of abstraction that illustrates the increasing thematisation of the phenomenon over the course of the second half of the nineteenth century. In his

Allgemeine Staatslehre, the leading constitutional lawyer Georg Jellinek used a more abstract expression of the concept of the political, namely *der Begriff des Politischen*, although subordinating it to that of the state (Jellinek 1900: 158).

The question of the criterion for politics or the political was a controversial topic in the Wilhelminian and Weimar debates. In addition to Max Weber and Carl Schmitt, a number of other authors from various backgrounds, including, for example, Hans Morgenthau, Karl Mannheim and Walter Benjamin, should be recognised as relevant to the present-day debates on the concept (see Palonen 1985, 2006).

Schmitt's famous opening sentence on the political as a precondition of the state, '[d]er Begriff des Staates setzt den des Politischen voraus' (Schmitt 1932a: 20), is a direct inversion of Jellinek's view. It is no longer the concept of the state but that of the political that is the key problem for constitutional lawyers. Schmitt's call for radical novelty to become the norm in legal discourse is marked by this emphatic turn against Jellinek's authority. For many practical purposes of legislation and jurisprudence, such as the 'political' character of a crime or an association, the political can no longer be determined in terms of the state (Schmitt 1932a: 22–6).

An intense thematisation of politics and the rise of controversial calls for politicisation took place in the German academic and cultural context during the years between the publication of *Allgemeine Staatslehre* and *Der Begriff des Politischen* (see Palonen 1985, 1989). The criteria of the political were broadly discussed particularly among constitutional and international lawyers, both in relation to the disputes surrounding the Weimar republican constitution and the controversy between the legal positivists and their fierce opponents (see esp. *Veröffentlichugen der Vereinigung der Deutschen Staatsrechtslehrer* vol. 5: 1929 and vol. 7: 1931).

Schmitt's construction of a new 'criterion' for the political took place within the range of legal discourse; he no longer regarded the political as a residual concept that can neither be defined in legal terms nor considered amoral, economic, or any other type of phenomenon. He aimed at identifying the political by its categorically distinctive criteria ('in eigenen letzten Unterscheidungen', Schmitt 1932a: 26). It is to this end that he proposes his famous friend–enemy distinction, 'Unterscheidung von Freund und Feind' (Schmitt 1932a: 26).

Schmitt's understanding of the political was opposed to that of his legal colleagues, such as Heinrich Triepel (1927), who still thought in terms of spheres. Although Schmitt offers distinctive criteria for the moral, aesthetic and economic spheres and compares the political with them, his point is that the political does not form a separate sphere of its own, 'kein eigenes Sachgebiet' (Schmitt 1932a: 38). Although this distinction of *Sachgebiete* is not clearly formulated in the first version (see Schmitt 1927: 4, 10–11), it appears to be the result of the introduction of the degree of intensity as a supplementary component of the criterion, which is indebted to Hans Morgenthau's dissertation from 1929 (Schmitt 1932a: 27–8, 38–9).

From the perspective of conceptual history, the distinction of the political alludes to a higher degree of abstraction. The Schmittian concept of the political constructs a metaphorical space of inclusion and exclusion. The distinction between friend and enemy by the decision (distinction) of a quasi-sovereign agent (in terms of Schmitt's 1922 thesis) also eliminates all the ambiguous intermediate *Spielraum* for action. It is, however, the degree of intensity that gives the distinction between friend and enemy its temporal variability.

With the additional criterion of the necessity of political unity among friends and enemies (*politische Einheit*, Schmitt 1932a: esp. 43–5), Schmitt reaffirms the exclusive character of friendship and enmity and delimits the role of the purely formal criterion of intensity. Schmitt later specified that the figure of the partisan is one who attempts to deny the exclusivity of the distinction between friend and enemy and, correspondingly, to dissolve the definite political units (Schmitt 1963: esp. 93).

Schmitt never explicates the relationship between *das Politische* and *Politik*, although he presupposes the 'real possibility of the struggle' as a precondition of speaking of *Politik* (Schmitt 1932a: 32). The point is that the political does not lie in the struggle itself (Schmitt 1932a: 35). Politics, which is the activity of struggling, is conceptually secondary to the criterion of the political, which also marks the priority of structure over passing temporal events. Accordingly, for Schmitt, the political decision regarding the identification of the enemy has already been made and, as such, is not left to the 'struggling soldier' (Schmitt 1932a: 34). However, the very act of distinguishing or deciding between friend and enemy marks an exceptional situation that refers to time and action within his thinking.

Der Begriff des Politischen evoked intense debates among Schmitt's contemporaries, who frequently transcended his limited juridical problematic as well as the terms of his conceptualisation. As an example of this among historians, we can mention the medievalist Otto Brunner, who uses Schmitt in his polemic against the anachronistic projection of the state onto the Middle Ages and refers to the non-territorial concept of *Fehde* [feud] as the mark of enmity between political units (see Brunner 1942).

Helmuth Plessner's 'Macht und menschliche Natur' (1931) offers the most original application of the Schmittian categories. Plessner was a philosophical anthropologist who was indebted to Weber, and he already defended politics against the popular claims of the community in his 'Grenzen der Gemeinschaft' (Plessner 1924). Plessner incorporates the friend–enemy distinction within *Politik* as existing in the situation of taking a stand for and against ('in einer Situation des Für und Wider zu leben', Plessner 1931: 195). The distinction creates a zone of one's own affirmation against that of the stranger (Plessner 1931). Friendship and enmity are thus relativised and temporalised into zones within the range of the situation at hand and the activity oriented toward it. Plessner's book is a strange combination of Weberian- and Schmittian-inspired views, although Weber clearly takes priority.

Schmitt's joining the Nazi Party in May 1933 changed both his own formulations and the reception of his work both in and outside Germany. In some French works, the very expression *le politique* was regarded as belonging to the Nazi vocabulary (see Palonen 1990: 44–5). Most of the British authors who were conceptualising politics in the 1930s made no reference at all either to the abstraction of 'the political' or to Schmitt. One exception to this general rule is Ernest Barker who, in his *Reflections on Government*, discusses the alternatives to democracy after World War I and analyses those writers who idealised the memory of war. 'The consequent conception of politics and of the nature of "the political" may be seen in a pamphlet published in Germany by Dr Carl Schmitt in 1932' (Barker 1942: 270). Schmitt's strictly juridical justifications for re-determining the criterion of the political were clearly lost in such interpretations.

Weber and politics as an activity

In a footnote, Carl Schmitt (as early as in Schmitt 1927: 2) quotes Max Weber's formula from 'Politik als Beruf' of politics as striving for power shares and influencing their distribution: 'Streben nach Machtanteil oder nach Beeinflussung der Machtverteilung' (Weber 1919c: 35). Characteristically, Schmitt only sees the point in relation to Weber's use of power as the decisive criterion (*entscheidendes Merkmal*, Schmitt, 1927: 2). The activity of striving receives no attention.

Similarly, most of the textbook references to the 'Weberian concept of politics' do not refer to striving. Even specialists in the field frequently disregard the point that, for Weber, even 'social orders' (see Weber 1922) are constituted in terms of human activities, the relationships between them and their contingent constellations. The canonisation of Weber as a sociologist and the almost total neglect of his 'merely political' writings also contributed to the dismissal of the action perspective on politics.

The notion of the striving for power as a characterisation of politics is, as such, nothing new. The legal philosopher Fritz Berolzheimer, for example, considered it to be essential to politics, 'der Wesenszug aller Politik' (Berolzheime 1907/8: 243). He did not, however, further explicate either striving or power.

Weber marks the contrast by presenting politics in terms of verbs referring to activities. In addition to *streben* and *erstreben*, he uses the expression *Politik treiben* (all in Weber 1919c: 35–6) as well as the artisan metaphor of drilling or boring planks: 'Politik bedeutet ein starkes langsames Bohren von harten Brettern' (Weber 1919c: 88). In other words, for Weber, the conceptual reflection on politics takes place in the explication of what the actors are doing and who is acting politically.

One major difference between the politician and its counter concept, namely the official, can be described in terms that refer to the differences in performance. Officials do not need to strive for power, but instead use existing power shares. They are not engaged in politicking, but execute or accomplish a given policy. Above all, they have no need slowly and patiently to remove the obstacles in their way in order to open up a new *Spielraum* for action, but instead remain within the existing one.

The broad range of verbs applied by Weber to describe the activity of politics indicates that there can be no guarantee that politicians will be successful. For

Weber, this is not a sign of the powerlessness of politics, but refers instead to the openness of politics as a struggle. The contingency of politics as an activity is constituted by his concept of *Chance*, which links Weber's political and methodological writings to one another (see Palonen 1998).

When interpreting *Macht* and *Herrschaft* in terms of chances, Weber (1922: 28–9) insists that they be expressed and actualised only in and through action. Power is neither property nor a given structure, but a contingent constellation between struggling or competing political agents. In a consistently nominalistic fashion, for Weber, power is not a whole that is 'distributed' into shares, but, rather, is something that exists only in the form of singular shares and their contingent constellations. Nor does there exist any readily available repertoire of power shares, but, rather, anything can be turned into a crucial power share in the situation at hand. As such, the redistribution of power shares contains the use of existing shares as well as the creation of new shares and the dissolution or devaluation of some of the old ones.

Now we are able to understand better how Weber and Schmitt differ in their problematics of conceptualisation. For Schmitt, the political marks an element in politics that extends beyond its obvious contingency, an ontological foundation anchoring politics in something that is more than politics. Weber, by contrast, attempts to conceptualise the passing, fluid, fragile and contingent activity of politics itself, without reducing its contingency. In this sense, for him, contingency is neither merely residual nor the *fortuna*, but the concept of *Chance* offers him a principle of the intelligibility of the contingent activity. In this sense, we can speak of the 'Weberian moment' as having taken place in his twentieth-century political thought (Palonen 1998).

In its contemporary context, Weber's 'Politik als Beruf' was much less controversial than Schmitt's *Begriff des Politischen*, and his radically nominalistic action perspective was seldom recognised. Nonetheless, the Weberian conception inspired a number of Weimar authors, including Helmuth Plessner and Hans Morgenthau. Weber's views soon gained international recognition in France, especially through the work of Raymond Aron (1938a, b). In the British context, a Weberian inspiration can also be detected in the early work of George Catlin, who referred, for example, to politics as 'an Activity, not a Thing' (Catlin 1929: 68). Independently of Weber, there also exist other attempts to reflect upon politics from the perspective of the politician, such as Louis Barthou's portrait of the French politician (1923) or F. S. Oliver's (1930) introduction to his study on Walpole.

The political in post-war literature

The academic study of politics became institutionalised in the western world during the post-war years, which was quite a discouraging development for the conceptual reflection on politics and the political. The leading metaphor of the academic discipline of political science, the political system, as it was canonised by David Easton (1953) and others, signified the return to a division of sectors, one of them being the political. The political thus refers to a metaphorical space within the holistic order of the system. In the functionalist version of systems thinking, political science was reduced more or less to a sub-discipline of sociology, the imperialistic discipline of the post-war decades. The result was the priority of order over action and struggle, a kind of Hegelianism without history.

Two German sociologists have more recently attributed an autonomous role to the political. Niklas Luhmann has related systems to environment (*Umwelt*) and attributed a constitutive role to contingency. In his posthumous *Die Politik der Gesellschaft* (Luhmann 2000), Luhmann polemicises against voluntarism, but allows room for opportunistic politicking as a part of the vitalisation of the relationship between system and environment. Ulrich Beck's 'reinvention of politics' (1993) has its roots in the radicalisation of risks, the individualisation of life-styles and biographies, and activist movements. He opposes the sub-politics of everyday agency to the systemic view of ordinary politics, not to replace or revolutionise it, but to expand politics into a *Doppeltheater* containing both the systemic ordinary polity and the activities of sub-politics. Beck thus attempts to combine action and systems thinking, although, perhaps unwittingly, still attributing a certain priority to the spatial metaphors.

In Germany, the reception of Schmitt's work among historians led to the modification of his ideas. In his study of the Greek origins of the political, the classicist Christian Meier revises the political into a field of action (*Handlungsfeld*) between political units (Meier 1980: 34–9). Meier wants to incorporate action and time; that is, he wants to incorporate politics into a constitutive element of the political 'field'. He retains the priority of the political, but in the sense of its being an 'element' of movement between political units (1980: 36). Meier's historical interpretation accentuates the opening of the horizon of decidability and controversiality as the main political novelty of the dethroning of the Areopagos and its conceptualisation by Aischylos a few years later (Meier 1980: 144–246). He thus plays with the ambiguity of the German concept of *Entscheidung* [decision] and takes from it much of the Schmittian emphasis on the closure of the situation.

In France, for example, Charles de Visscher (1953) relies on the criterion of the political presented in Morgenthau's early work (1929, 1933) on international law. For the phenomenologist Paul Ricoeur, '[l]e politique est organisation raisonnable, la politique est decision' (Ricoeur 1957: 729). For him, as for Schmitt, politics as action is secondary to the deeper level of the political, but the difference between the juridical criterion and philosophical reason is obvious.

Julien Freund, who as a former *résistant* was initially suspicious of Schmitt, mediated Schmitt's concept of the political to the French audience. The title itself, *L'essence du politique* (1965), already indicates a clear distinction between his thought and that of Schmitt. Instead of a criterion, Freund presents the political as an essence, an invariable condition of *la politique* (Freund 1965: 1–2). The political refers to the weight, *pesanteur*, of the political (1965: 15). For Freund, the Schmittian friend–enemy distinction serves as one of the *présupposés* of the political, the other pairs being those of command and obedience and the public and the private. In the conflict between these presuppositions, dialectical relationships prevail, and the dialectic of friendship and enmity lies in the struggle; it is here that we can detect Freund's debt to Weber.

Similarly to Schmitt, Ricoeur and Freund, the former revolutionary Régis Debray also regards the political as the unchanging element beyond the contingency of politics, although his views are more inspired by the structuralist thinkers. He defines the critique of political reason as the study of 'stable' human groups, their conditions of organisation and functioning (Debray 1981: 45). Such a study aims at the understanding of the limits of the entire political project (*entreprise*) (1981: 60). Debray's work is clearly tinged with the tone of a disappointed activist. Since then, the level of reflection on the political has significantly increased among French philosophers. Much of this reflection remains strictly philosophical and far removed from the dirty world of everyday politics (see Marchart 2007).

Chantal Mouffe, a francophone author writing mainly for an anglophone audience, incarnates the leftist reception of Schmitt's work. In her *Return of the Political*, Mouffe wants 'to think with Schmitt against Schmitt' (Mouffe 1993: 2), particularly to replace the concept of the enemy with that of the adversary (Mouffe 1993: 4; 2005: 20–1). She thus accepts, contra Schmitt, the pluralistic character of democracy and defends agonism as opposed to antagonism. Both the use of Schmitt and the softening of his views is a tool used by Mouffe against the tendency to reduce the role of the political in, for example, Rawlsian, Habermasian or even Marxist thinking. Unlike the French philosophers, Mouffe is certainly not uninterested in daily politics. Still, like the other post-Schmittian thinkers, she looks beyond politics to the 'ontological' level of the political (Mouffe 2005: 8). For her, the political refers to the constitutive 'dimension of antagonism', whereas 'by "politics" I mean the set of practices and institutions through which an order is created' (2005: 9). For Mouffe, politics also remains subordinated to order as a moving historical element, whereas she is not interested in the closer explication of the activity of politicians.

To sum up, the post-war literature on the political decontextualises the concept from Schmitt's strictly juridical aims and frees it from its ideological implications. Still, it shares the Schmittian problematic of the priority of the political over politics, including a certain disregard for the daily activities of politicians and the corresponding search for an 'ontology' behind politics.

The thematisation of the activity of politics

Although the student, feminist, environmental and other movements of the 1960s and 1970s accentuated the activity of politics beyond the conventional polity-sphere, active reflection on the question of what this means for the activity of politics itself has remained strikingly scarce. Is all of this merely the extension of the old criteria for the activity of politics, as presented by Max Weber or, for example, by Hannah Arendt (1958, 1968, 1993) or Michael Oakeshott (1962, 1975), to the politics of 'movements'? Or, do the movements require different types of politicians, perhaps less formalistic and less institutional ones? As much as the agents in those or later contexts spoke of the need for a 'new politics', as little they themselves have specified how this new politics is manifested in the expression and interpretation of the activity of politics itself.

This does not, however, mean that no new ideas were presented concerning the activity-concept of politics. Arendt, Oakeshott and Jean-Paul Sartre are three authors who in their post-war work promoted, each of them in their own direction, the instrumentalisation of contingency as a medium of the intelligibility of politics (in the sense of Palonen 1998).

The Arendtian view accentuates the distinction of politics as action from fabrication by the criterion of novelty, and she uses the metaphor of the performing arts to refer to politics (esp. Arendt 1968: 177). Oakeshott's famous metaphor of politics as 'sailing on a boundless and bottomless sea' (1962: 60) is an indication of his strong anti-foundationalism. Sartre was among the first to regard politics as a 'dimension of person' (Sartre 1964), and he defends the oblique and persuasive activity of the situated politician against the paradigm of the social engineer (Sartre 1972: 261–2).

The action perspective is also close to the thought of those authors who have closely followed the acts of politicians, for example J. D. B. Miller (1958, 1962) and Bertrand de Jouvenel (1963). For both, the Weberian inspiration is clearly visible. A new legitimation of the study of politics through the activity of politicians has been presented in the new rhetoric and the speech act theory. For example, John Pocock once published an article entitled 'Verbalizing a political act' (Pocock 1973), and Quentin Skinner recently affirmed that 'perhaps agency after all deserves to be privileged over structure' (Skinner 2002c: 7).

From this perspective, it would be senseless to go 'behind' politics in order to understand it. On the contrary, it is the very activity of contingent politicking that is the main objective of its understanding. Here, we can already detect a link to the rhetorical tradition.

The point of the non-debate

The political in the Schmittian and politics-as-activity in the Weberian sense transcend much of the harmless daily or academic uses of the polit-vocabulary. They indicate different problematics, both of them legitimate, and the attempts such as Plessner's and Freund's to combine them hardly sound convincing. No real debate between the problematics of the political and politics appears in sight, but clarifying the opposition helps us to understand the lack of debate.

The problematic also has different value orientations. The search for the political, whether as a philosophical foundation or an 'ontological' instance of stability, may be understood as an attempt to create a legitimate place for the political in the order of things. From this point of view, the contingent – temporal, passing and rhetorical – aspect of the activity of politics necessarily remains unintelligible. The reverse side of this attitude lies in the lack of interest in the dirty world of 'mere' politics. Here, the highly academic search for the political comes close to joining the chorus of the widespread popular opinions expressed in politician bashing.

The scholars of politics should rather attempt to understand better the activity of politicking; politicians seldom have either the time or the desire to explicate what they are doing at the very moment at which they are acting as politicians. Journalists often do a better job of that than politicians themselves, and scholars should take politicians' own words as the first step in the assessment of their activity, which can then be explicated and interpreted in greater detail. Historians tend to be better at this than political scientists.

Part of the problem may lie in the very self-conception of those who share Weber's high regard for politicians (see Palonen 2002). He recognised that professional politicians are an indispensable component of a parliamentary democracy, particularly as persons with both the will and the competence to question the powers of bureaucracy (see Weber 1918d).

The interest in the political also provides the scholar with an excuse to retain a pro-political attitude while remaining disinterested in the actions of politicians. However, politicians exist within a highly competitive and contested environment, and from time to time they are obliged to revise both their stands and the legitimation of them. How they accomplish this is a fascinating topic.

Chapter Four

Sombart and Weber on Professional Politicians

Die Protestantische Ethik und der Geist des Kapitalismus is most immediately linked to Weber's 'Politik als Beruf' in the sense that in each case *Beruf* refers both to a profession and to a vocation, as Lassman and Speirs indicate in their translation (Weber 1994b). This distinction refers to the heated debates concerning the role and legitimacy of professional politicians. Among the fierce contemporary critics was the famous economist Werner Sombart. In 1907 he edited a short-lived journal entitled *Morgen*, in which he asked in a series of articles why German academics and literati (*die Gebildeten*) turned away from politics and regarded the rise of professional politicians as one of the main reasons for this disgust with politics.

Max Weber did not share his academic contemporaries' contempt for day-to-day politics and professional politicians. He grew up in a political home, read Machiavelli and Cicero as well as taking part in political debates from a young age. In his student days he entered into a political correspondence with his uncle Hermann Baumgarten. Weber never shared the latter's (and his father's) conciliatory views toward Bismarck (see Baumgarten 1866), and he came to adopt the later Baumgarten's ironic distance from *Realpolitik* and the 'art of the possible' supported by Bismarck and his adepts (see Weber 1936).

Weber also broke with the political generation of Baumgarten and his father by accepting the conditions of democratised mass politics. His reading of James Bryce's *The American Commonwealth*, with its distinction between living for and off politics, was probably decisive (see esp. Bryce 1888: 731–42). Weber adopted this distinction in a preface to an article on German Social Democracy (Weber 1905a). He repeatedly refers to Bryce in the letters he began writing to Robert Michels in 1906 (see Weber 1990). Weber was disappointed by the fact that Michels never properly consulted Bryce's book in his famous work *Zur Soziologie des Parteiwesens in der modernen Demokratie*.[1]

New kinds of professional politicians, who were actually living off politics, had been gaining ground in the United States since the Jacksonian presidency and the introduction of *the spoils system*. Weber was convinced that professional politicians were also becoming indispensable in Europe as a by-product of the process of democratisation. He was disappointed with Michels's failure to analyse the rule of officialdom in the German Social Democratic Party in similar terms as Bryce had done with regard to the US party bosses.

---

1. 'Ich vermisse es, daß Sie nicht Bryce Am[erican] Commonwealth (große Ausgabe! nicht die kleine, die Sie zitieren) benutzt haben' (letter to Michels 31 December 1910, Weber 1994a: 761).

Weber occasionally entered into explicit polemics with some of the critics of parliamentarism (Weber 1904a, 1908). Thanks to the work of Bryce and that of Ostrogorski (1903), he was aware of the movements against partisan politics in the United States, but he seems to have underestimated the anti-political trend among the academics and literati in France and Britain in the early years of mass politics. In his later essays, Weber discussed both the actions and opinions of politicians as well as the empirical literature on politicians and parties but did not deal with the widespread anti-political literature. With the exception of the pedagogue F. W. Foerster (Weber 1919c: 81), anti-political intellectuals are not mentioned in 'Politik als Beruf' either.

Upon closer examination, however, we can detect signs of a polemic against several anti-political thinkers of the time in his formulations. I have found no mention of Sombart's *Morgen* essays in the works and letters of Weber that have been published thus far. We can be quite certain that Weber had heard of these essays when Sombart was the co-editor of the *Archiv für Sozialwissenschaft und Sozialpolitik* and Weber's political friend Naumann responded to him in the journal. Nonetheless, we may ask whether Sombart – who with his war pamphlet *Händler und Helden* (1915) had moved far to the right of Weber – was an explicit or implicit target of Weber's criticism. 'Die Politik als Beruf' was, indeed, the title of one of the articles in Sombart's series, and even if the title of Weber's lecture was suggested by the Freistudenten, he might have remembered that both Baumgarten (1866) and Sombart had used a variation of it in the past.

Politicians as scapegoats

The criticism of politicians was a common topos in Western Europe at the time when Sombart wrote his articles. This was also the case with British politico-literary journals in the early twentieth century. For example, an anonymous author writes in the conservative *Quarterly Review*: 'But one fact stands broadly out – the ill-repute into which politicians generally have fallen' ('Recent political theory and practice', 1900: 359). The writer Hilaire Belloc, himself a disappointed former Liberal MP, stated with a tone of resignation: 'it is rapidly bringing into contempt the reputation and the public position of politicians' (Belloc 1911: 34). The arch-conservative journal *Blackwood's Edinburgh Magazine* conducted a regular campaign against politicians. For example, Arthur Page writes: 'Politics and politicians are out of fashion' (Page 1913: 573).

The declining quality of political life since the introduction of mass elections through the 1867 and 1884/5 parliamentary reforms is a frequent topos. W. H. S. Aubrey for instance remarks: 'It is indisputable that the standard of political life in the country has been lowered of late' (Aubrey 1905: 297). In a review of Bryce, Goldwin Smith wrote on the dangers of the future predominance of the US style of politicians: 'Politics will become in England as well as in the United States a regular trade, and of all trades the vilest' (Smith 1888/9: 245).

In France, similar views were widely shared on opposite sides of the political spectrum. The US-style *politiciens*, a neologism of the 1870s, were viewed as dangerous, although for example Joseph Reinach (1894) did not regard the situation as being as acute as it was in France. Both anti-dreyfusards à la Paul Valéry (1974, from 1910) and dreyfusards à la Charles Péguy (1910) turned against politicians, as did many socialists and anarchists (see Angenot 2003). Both the Bonapartist Jules Delafosse, with his *La psychologie du député* (1904), and Henri Leyret, in two books against *les politiciens* (1909, 1910), were exponents of this genre. Georges Sorel (1908) combined elements of the syndicalist and extreme right wing critiques of politicians. Even the republican political journalist Robert de Jouvenel wrote in his *La république des camarades* (1914: 237) that the French had lost their flair for politics.

In the German context, no such emphasis on the decline of political activity was needed. Old slogans, such as 'Politik verdirbt den Charakter', were still being used, and Bismarck spoke out against professional politicians in his resistance toward payment for the members of the Reichstag, which was not accepted until 1906 (for the debates, see, for example, Butzer 1998). During the first decade of the twentieth century, however, a pro-political attitude was beginning to emerge among the francophile literati, such as Heinrich Mann, Kurt Hiller and Ludwig Rubiner. They, too, however, wanted to protect politics from professional politicians (see Palonen 1985 and 1989).

Werner Sombart as a critic of politicians

In comparison to other contemporary critics of politics and politicians, Sombart seems to use a broader repertoire. His point of departure is the seemingly ahistorical opposition between the *vita activa* and the *vita contemplativa* (1907b: 68). In this argument politics becomes entirely depersonalised. Simultaneously, politics appears to Sombart as overly individual and subjective. In this spirit he does not shy away from going as far as to claim that – with reference to nineteenth-century Russia – politically reactionary ('rückständig') times tend to produce the highest form of culture (1907b: 68). As such, it is consequential that he went on in a later article to claim that the significance of politics for human life is widely over-estimated.[2]

At the same time, Sombart also ponders the question of why so few – or, so many – *Gebildete* participate in German politics. The rise of the '*unseligen Spezies*' of professional politicians lay the groundwork for the development of a hostility toward politics (Sombart 1907a: 41). He regards political participation as natural in democratic cities, whereas in the empires absolutism rules and citizens have no part in politics. The democratisation of empires had created the craft of professional politicians who lived off politics, and whose number was increasing.[3]

---

2. 'daß die Politik in ihrer Bedeutung für die Gestaltung des menschlichen Lebens im allgemeinen ganz ungeheuerlich überschätzt wird' (Sombart 1907f: 420).

3. 'Entstehung eines selbständigen politischen Gewerbes, einer Zunft von Berufspolitikern, die... sich als eine immer zahlreicher werdende Gruppe innerhalb der Bürgerschaft selbst ausbreiteten' (Sombart 1907c: 196).

Unlike most of the contemporary critics, who tended to subscribe to various conspiracy theories, Sombart regards the rise of professional politicians as a quasi-natural consequence of both the increasing complexity and democratisation of politics (Sombart 1907c: 196). As an economist he understands why the occasional occupation with politics among *dilettanti* would no longer suffice for a thorough dealing with matters.[4] Correspondingly, he also finds a return to the politics of *Honoratioren* [local dignitaries] impossible. However, like the French syndicalist critics of parliamentary politics, to whom he refers in his *Morgen* articles, he draws the conclusion that the parliamentary form of democracy is inherently illusory, when the great masses are excluded from politics.[5]

Like many syndicalists and socialists (see Angenot 2003), Sombart shared the views of the technocratic critique of the politician's necessary dilettantism in specialised subjects.[6] Similarly to the technocrats, Sombart saw politics as a mere means of problem solving, without acknowledging that political constellations shape the problems themselves or that political judgment is not a specialist skill. Nonetheless, he admits that politics is a difficult, laborious and boring profession.[7] In line with the anti-parliamentarians in Britain and in France, he also turns against rhetoric of both empty phrases and the increasing business-like speeches in the Reichstag.[8] In the name of both cultural purity and technical efficiency, he denounces the role of the political constellations in deliberations and negotiations, which form the key parliamentary activity in the internal life of a professional politician:[9]

> settling the current business of law-making and everything that belongs to it as well as enabling the measures required by the political machine, require a certain routine and self-denial. This also consists of an unbroken weighting and utilisation of political constellations, in a constant trading and bargaining over votes in parliamentary action.

---

4. 'Die bloß gelegentliche Beschäftigung mit diesen Dingen nicht mehr ausreichte, um sie gründlich uns sachgemäß zu betreiben' (Sombart 1907c: 196).

5. 'Daß nun die große Masse der Bürger von der regulären Mitwitwirkung an der Politik ausgeschlossen blieb' (Sombart 1907c: 196).

6. 'in allen Fragen, die nicht in das von ihm beherrschten Handwerk einschlugen' (Sombart 1907c: 196).

7. '[d]as Gewerbe der Politik selbst aber…zu den schwierigsten, mühsamsten und ödesten von allen Gewerben unserer Zeit gehört' (Sombart 1907c: 196).

8. 'Neben der nüchternen Geschäftsrede dominiert im Reichstag nur noch die Phrase, die man anhört, ohne sich weiter um sie zu kümmern' (Sombart 1907d: 226).

9. '…in der Erledigung der laufenden Geschäfte der Gesetzemacherei und was dazu gehört und der für die Instandsetzung der politischen Maschine erforderlichen Maßregeln, wozu eine gewisse Routine und Selbstverleugnung vonnöten sind, und in einem unausgesetzten Abwägen und Ausnutzen der politischen Konstellationen, einem steten Handeln und Feilschen um Stimmen bei den parlamentarischen Aktionen' (Sombart 1907d: 226). Translations by the author unless otherwise stated.

Here we can detect a teleological and single-agent-oriented conception of a great national policy (perhaps inspired by Nietzsche's enigmatic *große Politik*) to be followed according to plan. The increasing political role played by daily parliamentary and electoral struggles in the absence of stable majorities in the post-Bismarckian Germany was seen by Sombart as disgusting. One of the unwelcome consequences of the mass agitation that occurs during elections lies, according to Sombart, in the necessary simplification of political life, for example in the recourse to slogans. For him, this means above all that professional politicians lose contact with the realities of life.[10]

We can detect his debt to another fashionable intellectual style, namely the *Lebensphilosophie*, as an up-to-date version of the objective spirit. For Sombart, 'life itself' requires a 'concrete' style in terms of the formation of concepts: abstract slogans necessarily lose touch with 'concrete reality'. In this sense politics tends to suppress the truth, as it is incarnated in 'life itself', and to renounce the fine manners as well.[11]

In contrast to Naumann, Sombart claims that politics is doomed to decline once it reaches the lower social strata,[12] which leads him to reject democracy 'in its present form'. His syndicalist critique of powerless people does not, however, lead him to idealise popular rule.

Sometimes Sombart sounds like an academic critic who wants to keep his hands clean of the dirty affairs of parliaments, elections, parties and politicians. On other occasions, however, he manifests political lucidity, as in his critiques of the powerless parliamentary and party politicians in Wilhelmine Germany. This concerns especially the lack of a political career for German parliamentarians.[13]

For the elected representatives of the people, even when they belong to the majority in parliament, it is not possible on the basis of parliament to propel oneself into a seat in government … The parliamentarians always remain in the second rank.

Applying Nietzschean jargon, Sombart insists that German parliamentarians lack the lust for power.[14] In his dark vision nothing is likely to change over

---

10. 'daß die Vorstellungen und Empfindungen des aktiv wie positiv politisch Tätigen schließlich von dem Quell des Lebens ganz abgedrängt werden und nur noch in dieser unwirklichen, verzerrten, verwaschenen Begriffswelt des politischen Schlagwortes eingeschlossen bleiben' (Sombart 1907c: 1978).

11. 'Man geht immer laxer mit der Wahrheit, immer laxer mit der Ehre des Gegners um und man nimmt immer mehr die Manieren eines Rüpels und eines Rowdys an' (Sombart 1907c: 199).

12. '…das politische Leben degeneriert von Tag zu Tag mehr, weil es in immer tiefere Schichten hinabsteigt' (Sombart 1907f: 419).

13. 'Es ist bei uns dem gewählten Vertreter des Volks, auch wenn er der Mehrheit im Parlamente angehört, nicht möglich, mit Hilfe des Parlaments sich einen Platz in der Regierung zu erzwingen… Der Parlamentarier bleibt immer zweite Garnitur' (Sombart 1907e: 257).

14. 'Es fehlt unseren Parlamentariern vollständig das Bewußtsein, Machthaber zu sein oder je es werden zu können' (Sombart 1907e: 258).

the next decades.[15] The celebration of objective spirit and Lebensphilosophie is joined with an extreme pessimism regarding politics. He attributes priority to *Selbstverbesserung* [self-improvement] over *Weltverbesserung* [world improvement] (Sombart 1907h: 514). Despite this, he does not completely renounce his interest in politics, but retains that of an interested spectator, who regards the political views and demands as problems, as if he would be an adversary of every type of partisan politician.[16]

Among the contemporary critics of politicians, Sombart has perhaps the broadest register. He is not content with a simple denunciation of politicians, but discusses different trends in contemporary politics and applies a broad arsenal of diverse arguments in his crusade against them. While he has hardly anything good to say about professional politicians, he still has some nostalgia for the great ideas of the past age, such as the period of the founding of the German Empire (Sombart 1907d: 226–7).

Opposed views on politics

There exists one direct parallel in the texts of Sombart and Weber. It struck me that Sombart, when mentioning the metaphorical extensions of *Politik* in contemporary Germany, expressed the idea that it is possible to speak of 'the wise "policy" of a lover'.[17] The parallel passage in Weber's work lies in the first lines of 'Politik als Beruf',[18] translated by Lassman and Speirs: 'We talk about the bank's politics on foreign exchange, the bank-rate policy of the *Reichsbank* ... and finally we even talk about the policies of the astute wife in her efforts to guide her husband' (Weber 1994b: 309–10). This parallel offers us sufficient grounds to assume that Weber was really well acquainted with Sombart's articles and that he tacitly alluded to his formula in the quoted passage, independently of whether he himself recognised where he had picked it up or not.

Both formulae refer to the old politics-as-art discipline that followed the *phronesis*-vocabulary and was commonly used in the *Privatklugheitslehren* of the seventeenth and eighteenth centuries. In that sense, *politisch* was used in German as a quasi-synonym for expressions such as *klug, listig* and *schlau* [crafty, clever] in a more pejorative manner than the corresponding French expressions *fin, adroit* and *prudent* (see, for example, Sternberger 1978). When both Sombart and Weber refer here to *klug*, they are alluding, perhaps unwittingly, to this older usage, which is comparable to the English *politic*, which was sometimes used in Germany during the early twentieth century (see Palonen 1985).

---

15. 'daß der Gang der Politik in Deutschland in den nächsten Menschenaltern aller Voraussicht nach in den Grundzügen derselbe bleiben wird, der er heute ist' (Sombart 1907g: 479).

16. 'Für uns ist jede politische Ansicht, jede politische Forderung ein Problem; wie sie es für den Parteimann immer nur sind—wenn sie vom Gegner vertreten warden' (Sombart 1907h: 514).

17. '...von der klugen "Politik" der Geliebten' (Sombart 1907a: 42).

18. 'Man spricht von der Devisenpolitik der Banken, von der Diskontpolitik der Reichsbank... ja schließlich von der Politik einer klugen Frau, die ihren Mann zu lenken trachtet' (Weber 1919c: 35).

For Sombart, *Politik* refers to the external normative regulation.[19] In 'Politik als Beruf', Weber is also interested in the 'performative' aspect of the question of the operations which a person carries out in order to be considered a politician (Weber 1919c: esp. 80–8). As such, the politics of a 'wise woman' appears to Sombart to be improper, whereas Weber only demarcates this usage outside 'Politik als Beruf'.

Here we can also detect a difference in the relationship between politics and administration. Sombart almost identifies politics with administration in his definition of politics as regulation. He understands political interest to be one that concerns legislation and administration.[20] He represents, in short, a conception of politics as 'policy-making', or 'fabrication' in Arendtian (1960: 198) terms. Politics is a question of the efficient realisation of a pre-given policy.

From such a perspective we can also better understand his devaluation of the activities of politicians, such as regarding elections as a sport or a carnival, the 'Faschingzeit der Berufspolitiker' (Sombart 1907a: 41, *see* note nine above). Similarly, the deliberative speech that takes place in the parliaments and during elections appears rather as a disturbance. The subjective or performative side of politics is subordinated to its 'functions' within the 'objective spirit'.

Weber, of course, draws a sharp distinction between politics and administration, between the politician and the official, and does not distinguish between words and deeds. On the contrary, he emphasises that politics is an eminently verbal activity, and judging the political role of words is one of the politician's primary activities,[21] for 'politics nowadays is predominantly conducted in public and by means of the written or spoken word' (Weber 1994b: 338; see also 1918d: 237, 263–4; 1994b: 181, 217–8). Connected to this is his idealisation of two professions, advocates and journalists, as the backdrop for the formation of high quality professional politicians, based on the mastery of the spoken and written word respectively.

The defence of advocates and journalists is just one of the unpopular moves Weber made in favour of politicians, explicitly opposing, for example, Bismarck's frequent polemic against both these kinds of professional politicians (see the speeches in the Reichstag, *Stenographische Beriechte* from 5 May 1881 and 26 November 1884; for an analysis of Bismarck's anti-rhetorical rhetoric, see Goldberg 1998). For Weber, the verbal character of politics also signifies an emphasis on both historical and conceptual links between the demagogue and the politician, not in order to depreciate the latter but rather to revaluate the former (Weber 1919c: 38, 65).

---

19. 'Regelung unseres Lebens in der Gesellschaft durch äußere Normen' (Sombart 1907a: 43).

20. 'die Gestaltung der gesellschaftlichen Beziehungen durch Gesetzgebung und Verwaltung' (Sombart 1907a: 43).

21. 'Denn die heutige Politik wird nun einmal in hervorragendem Maße in der Öffentlichkeit mit den Mitteln des gesprochenen oder geschriebenen Wortes geführt' (Weber 1919c: 53).

Anti-political intellectuals vs professional politicians

One of the main topics in Weber's late work on suffrage, parliamentarism and politics is the polemic against anti-politicians. My favourite piece among Weber's writings is 'Wahlrecht und Demokratie in Deutschland', written and published in late 1917. Weber applies an unscrupulous style of rhetoric in his devaluation of the opponents of politicians among the contemporary German *Literaten*. One of the main aspects of his rhetorical strategy is refraining from mentioning the names of the persons and writings which are the object of his polemics.

Weber discusses the entire range of antidemocratic suffrage reforms en bloc (Weber 1917f: 157–68). He regards them as expressions of political childishness (*politische Kindlichkeit*). The literati are characterised as inkpot romantics (*Tintenfaßromantikern*) and coffee house intellectuals (*Kaffeehausintellektuellen*), who are using a speechifier (*Phrasendreschmaschine*) (Weber 1917f: 165, 168, 185, 181). The only footnote in the article is directed against one of his favourite targets, the authoritarian and neo-feudal student corporations (Weber 1917f: 180). The antidemocratic and antiparliamentary opponents are not seen as worthy of serious criticism but serve as an indicator of the fear of the German philistine bourgeoisie to face the specific modern problematics that renders it even more unworldly and unpolitical.[22]

Weber did not attempt to convert these *Literaten* but instead addressed a more general audience by using the rhetoric of ridicule (see Skinner 1996, 2002). Here we can only ask whether he would have also included Sombart's views from 1907 among similar expressions of political illiteracy. The target of the following critique of the classicist tendency in the German academic and literary context could well be Sombart's contempt for the everyday parliamentary and electoral politics.[23]

> The ideas of our classic writers originated in an *un*political epoch even when these ideas concern politics and economics. Inspired by the debates surrounding the French Revolution, these ideas were in part constructed in an atmosphere in which political and economic passions were lacking. The only kind of political passion which inspired them, other than the angry rebellion against foreign rule, lay in their ideal enthusiasm for *moral* demands.

---

22. 'die Wasserscheu des deutschen Spießbürgertums ...vor dem Eintauchen in die spezifisch moderne Problemlage noch zu steigern, es noch weltfremder und unpolitischer zu machen' (Weber 1917f: 180).

23. 'Dieser unpolitischen Epoche entstammen ihre Ideen, auch wo sie politisch und ökonomisch sind. Sie waren teils, angeregt durch die Auseinandersetzung mit der Französischen Revolution, Konstruktionen in einem politisch und ökonomisch leidenschaftsleeren Raum. Soweit aber eine andere politische Leidenschaft in ihnen lebte als die zornige Auflehnung gegen die Fremdherrschaft, war es die ideale Begeisterung für sittliche Forderungen. Was darüber hinaus liegt, blieben philosophische Gedanken, die wir als Mittel der Anregung zu eigener Stellungnahme entsprechend unseren politischen Realitäten und der Forderung unseres Tages benutzen können,—nicht aber: als Wegweiser. Die modernen Probleme des Parlamentarismus und der Demokratie und die Wesensart unseres modernen Staates überhaupt lagen ganz außerhalb ihres Gesichtskreises' (Weber 1917f: 185).

Anything beyond that remained at the level of philosophical ideas which could stimulate us to adopt a position appropriate to *our* political realities and the demands of *today*, but they cannot serve as signposts to the future. The modern problems of parliamentary rule and democracy, and indeed the essential nature of the modern state generally, lay wholly outside their field of vision.

(Weber 1994b: 123–4)

According to Weber, *die Gebildeten* [academics and literati] remained unpolitical in their attitude toward the practical politics of parties, parliaments and elections. This is the reason why he goes so far as to welcome a devaluation of academic degrees through democratisation:[24] 'if the process of "democratisation" were to succeed in *doing away with* the social prestige of the university graduates – this would not destroy any politically valuable social forms' (Weber 1994b: 122).

Although Sombart recognised the secondary political role of the Reichstag, he did not differentiate Wilhelmine Germany from traditional authoritarian regimes. In the Weberian view, his longing for the political role of the *Gebildeten* would, in fact, further strengthen the dominant tendency in the contemporary world, namely the tendency toward bureaucratisation (see as early as Weber 1909a: 277–8). Whether the *Gebildeten* themselves played a political role as the *Honoratioren* did or served as bureaucrats, in both cases the political consequences were fatal. This was one of the main points of Weber's critique of the antidemocratic proposals for franchise reform.

Sombart's claim of the privileged role of the *Gebildeten* and his suspicion of professional politicians are based on a traditional view of knowledge, although one that combines its idealist and positivist versions. Consequently, he remains insensitive to the dangers of bureaucratisation as well as to the politician's special competence with regard to judging the struggle between perspectives. Sombart and Weber were Nietzscheans in different respects, Sombart in claiming privileges for the aristocracy of spirit, whereas Weber extended Nietzsche's perspectivism into the defence of politicians.

In his rejection of the daily parliamentary, electoral and partisan politics (esp. Sombart 1907a: 41), Sombart is a true incarnation of the unpolitical German academics, whom Weber parodies. Sombart, nonetheless, recognises that the career of a professional politician is tempting to intellectuals.[25]

---

24. 'sollte die "Demokratisierung" den Erfolg haben, das soziale Prestige des Prüfungsdiplommenschen zu beseitigen ... so wurde sie damit politisch wertvolle gesellschaftliche Formwerte bei uns nicht vernichten' (Weber 1917f: 184).

25. 'entweder er bleibt allem politischen Leben fern, oder er wird Berufspolitiker oder widmet doch wenigstens einen großen Teils seines Lebens der Beschäftigung mit der Politik. Denn die dritte Möglichkeit fällt für ihn aus: die Rolle des politischen Herdentiers zu spielen' (Sombart 1907c: 199).

He either keeps a distance to all political life, becomes a professional politician or dedicates at least a considerable part of his life to dealing with politics. The third possibility does not arise for him: to play the part of a political sheep.

In Weberian terms, however, we may well question whether he describes the alternatives in a realistic and appropriate manner. The Sombartian *Gebildeten*, who wanted to become professional politicians, were *Honoratioren*, whose election into the parliament was rather unproblematic. Sombart's critique of democratisation refers to the understanding that the chances for the survival of this type of politician were declining. According to Weber, they could only be part-time politicians, not those who lived entirely off politics (1919c: 41–2).

We can, in addition, ask whether Sombart's first alternative of keeping oneself entirely outside the sphere of political life was in fact realisable. Weber's critique of the proverbial 'unpolitical Germans' does not render them politically harmless. On the contrary, they played a definite political role in strengthening the rule of the officialdom in Wilhelmine Germany. The declaration of keeping oneself out of politics is a mark of self-deception and tacit support of the status quo. For this reason, those who take a stand against 'politics' and 'politicians' become, in Weberian terms (Weber 1919c: 41–2), passive and involuntary occasional politicians. The pro-war declarations of German professors are, indeed, not so far removed from the Sombartian *Herdentier* [sheep] either.

But can we count Sombart among the programmatic apoliticians? In his reply to Naumann he denies contributing to the formation of unpolitical persons.[26] Does this limited activity fulfil the Weberian criterion for the occasional politician? It does not correspond to Weber's paradigm of taking a stand.[27] 'We all are "occasional" politicians when we post our ballot slips or express our will in some similar way, such as voicing approval or protest in a "political" meeting, making a "political" speech and so on.' (Weber 1994b: 316–7)

The 'educational' role of talking about politics seems not to be political enough for Weber. But we could also think that an active commitment against politics is a more explicit political act than the support of a contemplative understanding of politics.

Experts vs professional parliamentarians

Democracy without parliamentarism, which was popular among the *literati* in wartime Germany (see Llanque 2000) and perhaps indicated in Sombart's rejection of democracy in its current form, was another target of Weber's polemics.

---

26. 'Im Gegenteil: ich möchte gern dazu verhelfen, die erste und wichtigste Bedingung eines politischen Menschen zu erfüllen: Verständnis für Wesen und Bedeutung des politischen Lebens zu wecken. Dazu aber braucht man keine Politik zu 'machen', braucht man vor allem nicht berufsmäßiger Parteipolitiker zu werden' (Sombart 1907f: 421).

27. ' "Gelegenheits" politiker sind wir alle, wenn wir unseren Wahlzettel abgeben oder eine ähnliche Willensäußerung: etwa Beifall oder Protest in einer "politischen" Versammlung, vollziehen, eine "politische" Rede halten usw' (Weber 1919c: 41).

For Weber, such models further affirm the rule of officialdom:[28] 'What would a democracy without any kind of parliamentary system mean within a constitution such as this, where the officials have authoritarian power? Any merely *passive democratisation* would be the purest form of *uncontrolled bureaucratic rule*, with which we are very familiar here, and which could call itself "monarchic regiment"' (Weber 1994b: 222).

In his pamphlet *Parlament und Regierung im neugeordneten Deutschland*, Weber once again focuses on the irresistible force of bureaucratisation in general and the *Beamtenherrschaft* in imperial Germany in particular. He does not see the possibility of a reversal of the universal tendency but calls instead for counterweights to save at least some 'individualistic freedom of movement' (Weber 1918d: 222; *see* the full quote and – translation on p. 54 below.) His main candidates, and main form of support for a minimal degree of individual freedom and democracy, are the parliamentary politicians.

In the following key sentence, he emphasises the different responsibilities of politicians and officials:[29] ' "above parties", which in truth means that he must remain outside the *struggle* for power of his own. The struggle for personal power and the acceptance of full *personal responsibility for one's cause (Sache)* which is the consequence of such power – this is the very element in which the politician and the entrepreneur live and breathe' (1994b: 161).

Sombart, with his idealisation of experts and contempt for the daily practices of politicians, appears as a good example of those academics and literati who never understood the distinctive demands that a politician must face. Against the Bismarckian tradition, Weber takes a stand in favour of the professional parliamentarian, both as a fact and as a desideratum. For him, the denunciation of professional parliamentarians is seen as very convenient for the bureaucrats (Weber 1918d: 244–5; 1994b: 190–1; *see* the quotes and translation in Chapter Five in this volume).

Sombart emphasises that when it comes to substantial questions politicians are doomed to remain dilettantes. Neither Weber nor the MPs themselves dispute this fact. The point, however, lies in the inability of the officials to recognise the inherent limits of their superior factual knowledge when it comes to political judgment and action. Weber sees the most crucial question to be the political limits of the factual knowledge of the officials and the control of bureaucratisation.[30]

---

28. 'Was würde innerhalb dieser Verfassung mit ihrer obrigkeitlichen Beamtenmacht eine Demokratie ohne allen Parlamentarismus darstellen? Eine solche lediglich passive Demokratisierung wäre eine gänzlich reine Form der uns wohlbekannten kontrollfreien Beamtenherrschaft, die sich "monarchisches Regiment" nennen würde' (Weber 1918d: 267).

29. ' "Über den Parteien", das heißt aber in Wahrheit: außerhalb des Kampfes um eigene Macht, soll der Beamte stehen. Kampf um eigene Macht und die aus dieser Macht folgende Eigenverantwortung für seine Sache ist das Lebenselement des Politikers wie des Unternehmers' (Weber 1918d: 223).

30. 'Leicht ist nämlich festzustellen, daß ihre Leistungsfähigkeit auf dem Gebiet des öffentlichen, staatlich-politischen Betriebes ganz ebenso wie innerhalb der Privatwirtschaft feste innere Grenzen hat. Der leitende Geist: der "Unternehmer" hier, der "Politiker" dort, ist etwas anderes als ein "Beamter". Nicht notwendig der Form, wohl aber der Sache nach' (Weber 1918d: 222).

It is clear that effectiveness has strict internal limits, both in the management of public, political affairs and in the private economic sphere. The *leading* spirit, the 'entrepreneur' in the one case and the 'politician' in the other, is something different from an official. Not necessarily in the form but in substance.

(Weber 1994b: 159)

For the apologists of objective spirit and technical efficiency à la Sombart, the idea that there could ever be too much knowledge and expertise in political decisions is seen as incomprehensible. For Weber, all knowledge consists of a special type of power share and is thus part of the political struggle. The rule of officialdom in the German Empire was for him, to a decisive degree, a result of the situation in which the officials' special knowledge was left outside any realm of parliamentary control. The enablement of such control was the main political project in Weber's wartime political essays and pamphlets.

The core of Weber's critique of expert knowledge concerns the connections between *Sachwissen* [factual knowledge], *Dienstwissen* [official knowledge] and *Geheimwissen* [secret knowledge]. For Weber, they are indispensable aspects of the politics of modern states, but they indicate a view of knowledge which, without counterweights, would be politically fatal. In other words, he disputes a 'monocratic' view of knowledge: the simple distinction between the possession and lack of 'knowledge' of a given subject matter and in terms of a personal division into the categories of those who 'know' and those who 'don't know'.

For Weber, bureaucratisation lies in the situation in which the officials monopolise 'knowing' and regard it as a possession. For Weber's Nietzschean or rhetorical perspectivism, 'knowledge' consists of the competition between different points of view (see Weber 1904b in particular). This is incomprehensible to the ethos of an official, but it is to some degree analogous to the competitive situation of the politicians. I refer to Weber's 'parliamentary' theory of knowledge by taking the rhetorical principle of arguing *in utramque partem* as the core of parliamentary procedures and practices (Palonen 2004b, *see* Chapter Ten in this volume).

In defence of the politicians

The secondary role of the Reichstag in the German Empire and the rise of professional politicians as an indispensable by-product of democratisation are commonly emphasised themes in the work of both Werner Sombart and Max Weber. Their political responses to this situation were, however, almost diametrically opposed. Sombart used a broad register of the contemporary denunciation of professional politicians with certain personal nuances, while simultaneously committing himself to an aristocracy of spirit, which was not at all uncommon among the contemporary German professors.

Although Weber views some of the consequences of the rise of politicians living off politics with disgust, he accepts this situation not only as a fact but also as one containing new chances. They include the breakdown of the rule of the

Honoratioren, which in Germany would have led not only to political dilettantism but also to attempts to create a *parvenu* aristocracy with neo-feudal tendencies (see esp. Weber 1917f). In this respect he is already more radical than contemporary liberal politicians, such as Friedrich Naumann.

The distinctive point in Weber's defence of professional politicians' concerns, however, their chances to act as counterweights to bureaucratisation. This includes at least three distinct aspects: the specific German rule of officialdom, the universal tendency of the age toward the extension of bureaucratic rule (*Herrschaft*) to all spheres of life, and the methodological claim of a monopoly on knowledge. As a critic of the rule of officialdom, Weber was probably more competent and, consequently, more uncompromising than his contemporaries (see Kocka 1981 comparing Weber and Otto Hintze as critics of bureaucracy). The fear of universal bureaucratisation was Weber's personal version of the cultural pessimism shared by many Germans, although he saw in politicians chances to act against the tendencies of stagnation (Weber 1909a: 277–8).

The most original aspect is, however, Weber's methodological view of the politician as a person who is accustomed to arguing *in utramque partem* and able to weigh the political significance of moves in his argumentation. In this respect, the parliamentary politician marks an explicit contrast to the official, the learning to 'weigh the power of words', for 'ein Parlamentarier im Kampf der Parteien zu lernen vermag, die Tragweite des Wortes zu wägen' (Weber 1917f: 187; 1994b: 127). In other words, Max Weber's rhetorical view of knowledge, based on the competition between perspectives without pre-given criteria of judgment, is reflected in his apology on behalf of the parliamentary politician as a person who has become accustomed to struggling, thinking in terms of alternatives and judging political consequences. For Weber, the value of the parliamentary politician transcends the struggles between governments and oppositions and between regimes, including 'parliamentarism' in the technical sense. The politician is the hero of the Weberian cultural criticism, of the distinctively rhetorical political culture that he defends.

In the context of 1917–19, the critique of the anti-politicians was not only directed against right wing antiparliamentary writers, such as Sombart. Weber's critique also turned against the pro-political leftist literati, such as Ernst Toller, who admired Weber, but who did not understand the point of his defence of parliamentarism. Toller and other young admirers of Weber understood even less that in order to defend politics in a plausible manner you have to take a stand in favour of professional politicians.

Chapter Five

Max Weber's Three Types of Professional Politicians: A Rhetorical Approach

This chapter deals with the rhetorical paradigms for the professionalisation of politics. I shall discuss three historical ideal types – party functionary, president and parliamentarian – each of them present in the work of Max Weber. A common reference for them lies in Weber's historical interpretation of bureaucratisation as the dominant tendency of the time, to which the three paradigms offer different types of response. The three types of politician are also related to the history of the democratisation and parliamentarisation of politics.

The tendency towards bureaucratisation

Unlike most of his academic contemporaries, Weber regarded the professionalisation of politics as indispensable in mass democracies. He did not regard it from the perspective of the differentiation of activities or as a sign of historical progress. For Weber, professionalisation of politics served as a counterweight to the process of bureaucratisation. It is important to emphasise the well known fact that Weber considered bureaucracy an indispensable element in modern states and organisations, and it is only to the self-fulfilling process of bureaucratisation that he objects.

At the end of his lexicon article *Agrarverhältnisse im Altertum* in 1909, Weber presents for the first time a dark vision of the self-expansive drive of every bureaucracy, both ancient and modern. Bureaucratisation indicates a process for which order has become an end in itself, and which, according to Weber's prophecy, will dominate capitalism, as it did in antiquity (Weber 1909a: 277–8). In a debate contribution to the Vienna meeting of the *Verein für Sozialpolitik*, Weber emphasises the specific German passion for bureaucratisation. It has led to the formation of a type of *Ordnungsmensch*, who becomes nervous about any minor lack of order. Weber then looks for counterweights to this tendency, for the sake of retaining a 'residual of humanity' (*einen Rest des Menschentums*), free from parcelling out the soul and from the complete rule of bureaucratic ideals over life [Alleinherrschaft bureaukratischer Lebensideale] (Weber 1909b: 128).

The most drastic formulation of the overwhelming tendency towards bureaucratisation is contained in the *Parlament* pamphlet of 1918. Weber calls both the lifeless and the living machine a *geronner Geist*, a concealed spirit, that makes bureaucratic rule seem to be an end in itself.[1] Lassman and Speirs translate the passage as follows:

> It is *only* this fact that gives the machine the power to force men to serve it and thus rule and determine their daily working lives, as it happens in factories. This same *concealed spirit* is, also embedded in that *living machine* which is represented by bureaucratic organisation with its specialisation of trained, technical work, its delimitation of areas of responsibility, its regulations and its graduated hierarchy of relations of obedience. Combined with the dead machine, it is in the process of manufacturing the housing of that future serfdom to which, perhaps, men may have to submit powerlessly, just like the slaves in the ancient state of Egypt, *if they consider that the ultimate and only value by which the conduct of their affairs is to be decided is good administration and provision for their needs by officials (that is good in the pure technical sense of rational administration).* Bureaucracy achieves this, after all, incomparably better than any other structure of rule.
>
> (Weber 1994b: 158)

The political consequences of all-encompassing bureaucratisation provide the theme for his discussion of the chances of parliamentarisation. Weber distinguishes three principles that include chances for opposing bureaucratisation: saving any residuals of 'individualistic' freedom of movement, creating counter-powers in order to guarantee a minimum of democracy in the face of the state bureaucracy and doing what is politically impossible for the bureaucracy, because the *Geist* of officialdom is incapable of independent leadership.[2]

---

1. 'Nur daß sie dies ist, gibt ihr die Macht, die Menschen in ihren Dienst zu zwingen und den Alltag ihres Arbeitslebens so beherrschend zu bestimmen, wie es tatsächlich in der Fabrik der Fall ist. Geronnener Geist ist auch jene lebende Maschine, welche die bürokratische Organisation mit ihrer Spezialisierung der geschulten Facharbeit, ihrer Abgrenzung der Kompetenzen, ihren Reglements und hierarchisch abgestuften Gehorsamsverhältnissen darstellt. Im Verein mit der toten Maschine ist sie an der Arbeit, das Gehäuse jener Hörigkeit der Zukunft herzustellen, in welche vielleicht dereinst die Menschen sich, wie die Fellachen im altägyptischen Staat, ohnmächtig zu fügen gezwungen sein werden, wenn ihnen eine rein technisch gute und das heißt: eine rationale Beamtenverwaltung und -versorgung der letzte und einzige Wert ist, der über die Art der Leitung ihrer Angelegenheiten entscheiden soll. Denn das leistet die Bürokratie ganz unvergleichlich viel besser als jegliche andere Struktur der Herrschaft' (Weber 1918d: 221).

2. '1. Wie ist es angesichts dieser Übermacht der Tendenz zur Bureaukratisierung überhaupt noch möglich, irgendwelche Reste einer in irgendeinem Sinn "individualistischen" Bewegungsfreiheit zu retten? 2. Wie kann, angesichts der steigenden Unentbehrlichkeit und der dadurch bedingten steigenden Machtstellung des uns hier interessierenden staatlichen Beamtentums, irgendwelche Gewähr dafür geboten werden, daß Mächte vorhanden sind, welche die ungeheure Übermacht dieser an Bedeutung stets wachsenden Schicht in Schranken halten und sie wirksam kontrollieren? Wie wird Demokratie auch nur in diesem beschränkten Sinn überhaupt möglich sein? 3. eine dritte Frage, und zwar die wichtigste von allen, ergibt sich aus einer Betrachtung dessen, was die Bureaukratie als solche nicht leistet.... Wenn ein leitender Mann dem Geist seiner Leistung nach ein "Beamter" ist, ... dann ist er weder an der Spitze eines Privatwirtschaftsbetriebes noch an der Spitze eines Staates zu brauchen' (Weber 1918d: 222).

1. How it is *at all possible* to salvage any remnants of 'individual' freedom of movement *in any sense...*
2. In view of the growing indispensability and hence increasing power of state officialdom, which is our concern here, how can there be any guarantee that forces exist which can impose limits on the enormous, crushing power of this constantly growing stratum ... and control it effectively? How is democracy even in this restricted sense to be *at all possible?*
3. A third question, the most important of all, which arises from any consideration of what is *not* performed by bureaucracy as such. ... If a man in a *leading* position performs his leadership ... in the *spirit* of an official, ... then he is useless, whether he is at the head of a private firm or of a state.

(Weber 1994b: 159–60)

Weber emphasises the contrast between the politician and the official: politics consists of a struggle for a standpoint, an activity that the official should avoid.[3]

[I]t is not the task of an official to join in a political conflict and ... in this sense 'engage in politics', which always means struggling. On the contrary, he takes his pride in preserving his impartiality ... as to execute ... what is required of him by the general definition of his duties or by some particular instruction, even – and particularly – when they do *not* coincide with his own political views.

(Weber 1994b: 178, translation modified)

This concern for finding counterweights to oppose the expanding power of bureaucratisation and its spirit of Ordnung is also Weber's point of departure for his discussion of the professionalisation of politics. Which type of person can the professional politician be (Weber 1904b: 189; also Hennis 1987)? Which institutions can serve as an ideal–typical basis for the formation of professional politicians?

For Weber, the party functionary, the president and the parliamentarian contain three partly competing, partly complementary ideal types for the professionalisation of politics. Each type had specific chances to build a counterweight to the 'rule of officialdom' (*Beamtenherrschaft*) in Germany and to respond to the trend towards bureaucratisation in other western countries. In the 'Agrarverhältnisse', Weber's main point concerns the power of bureaucratisation over the capitalist economy. Referring to the works of James Bryce (1888/1914), Moisei Ostrogorski (1903/12) and Robert Michels in particular (besides Michels 1910, see his publications in *Archiv für Sozialwissenschaft und Sozialpolitik*

---

3. 'Es ist... nicht Sache des Beamten ... in den politischen Streit einzutreten und, in diesem Sinn, "Politik zu treiben", die immer: Kampf ist. Sein Stolz ist es im Gegenteil, die Unparteilichkeit zu hüten ... und sinnvoll durchzuführen, was allgemeine Vorschrift oder besondere Anweisung von ihm verlangen, auch und gerade dann, wenn sie seinen eigenen politischen Auffassungen nicht entsprechen' (Weber 1918d: 233).

and Weber's letters to him in Weber 1990 and 1994a), Weber emphasises the bureaucratisation of party organisations.

The party functionary

In 'Politik als Beruf', Weber describes extensively the type of functionary in the party and electoral *Maschine*. He regards the 'machine' as a necessary corollary of mass democracies, with their mass suffrage, advertising and organisation, in the face of which the nineteenth-century pre-democratic parliaments, consisting of amateurish part-time *Honoratioren*, lose their powers (Weber 1919c: 60–1; 1994b: 338). Opposition parties do not have any means to resist the rule of officialdom in the state, other than building their own machine-like apparatus (Weber 1918d: 215).

The differences between the state and the party machine (including the electoral apparatus) – are not negligible. For Weber the party machine operates with *voluntary* membership and candidacy in elections and therefore it must recruit supporters.[4] (Weber 1994b: 99; see also 1918d: 215–16) Candidacy, campaigning and voting are voluntary acts. The voluntary character of party politics is crucial for Weber's fierce opposition to corporative elements (*berufsständische Vertretung*) in representative assemblies (Weber 1917f).

In other words, Weber recognises the competition among the state, party and business machines. We can expect *Spielräume* here for quasi-diplomatic manoeuvrings between the interests of the different machines when they demarcate their overlapping interests and reconcile the interest clashes between them. The voluntarism is mediated to inter-party relationships by the rhetoric of negotiation, following the diplomatic paradigm. Similar to states in their diplomatic relationships, the machine officials view internal disputes as threats to the very existence of both the machine and the wider interests of the party.

The party and electoral machines leave for their members a certain degree of 'individualistic freedom of movement'. It is always possible to leave the party, to threaten to join the competitors, to abstain from voting, to vote blank, even to vote for adversaries. The parties have to select leaders, recruit members and adherents and bring them to the polls, campaign events and party meetings. For this reason two- or multi-party competition is in principle stronger than the inter-ministerial competition between offices.

The more machine-like the party organisation is, the less freedom it leaves to its members. Michels's studies of socialist parties highlight the paradox that parties oriented towards a liberating change in the polity tend to develop the greatest dangers for the freedom of movement of their members. Max Weber noticed that the Social Democratic parties showed a tendency to become huge bureaucratic machines, are 'im Begriff, sich in eine gewaltige bureaukratische Maschine zu verwandeln' (Weber 1907b: 110), and even predicted that in the long run the cities

---

4. 'Gerade daß der Parteiführer auf die formal freie Werbung seiner Gefolgschaft angewiesen ist, ist das schlechthin Entscheidende gegenüber dem reglementierten Avancement des Beamten' (Weber 1917f: 167).

and the state would conquer Social Democracy and not vice versa (Weber 1907b: 110). Nonetheless, the intra-party moments of selection and competition along with their *exit*-options suffice to prevent a complete extinction of the margins of freedom, even in the most tightly organised competitive party machines.

The increasing self-sufficiency of the machine and the order for the sake of order indicate for Weber the limits of what is possible for the rule of officialdom and for the machine-style professionalisation of politics. If the increased efficiency of the party machine further marginalises its voluntary character, the difference of parties to other machines tends to be lost and the possibility of party-based counterweights to bureaucratisation also decreases.

Weber's remarks on party bosses in the United States are instructive. He first offers his impression of an omnipotent *boss*, who has replaced the elected leaders on the basis of centralised power in the party: 'Der Boss ist unentbehrlich für die Organisation der Partei. Die liegt zentralisiert in seiner Hand' (Weber 1919c: 67; 1994b: 346). His next point illustrates, however, that a competent boss is conscious of the limits of his (to use the pronoun of the time) power. A boss strives merely for power over the party funding and backroom manoeuvrings, not for power based on public speaking.[5]

> The typical boss is an absolutely sober man. He has no ambition for social honour; the 'professional' is despised in 'polite society'. His sole aim is power, power as a source for money, but also for its own sake. He works behind the scenes, which is where he differs from the English 'leader'. One does not hear him speak in public; he suggests to the speakers what they ought to say to achieve their goals, but he himself remains silent.
>
> (Weber 1994b: 346)

The party boss typically only aspires to the position of a state senator who possesses powers of patronage according to the service done for the party. The bosses seem thus to have understood their own limits as responsible political leaders (see Weber 1918d: 223). The US presidential campaigns were conducted with bureaucratised machines, but it was rather 'independent notabilities' who were elected presidents:[6] 'The structure of this unprincipled party system with its socially despised wielders of power has thus made it possible for able men to attain the office of the president' (Weber 1994b: 347). Similarly, in British parliamentary politics after the parliamentary reform of 1867 extended the electorate to a mass level, parliamentary leaders – such as William Gladstone in particular – have

---

5. 'Der typische Boss ist ein absolut nüchterner Mann. Er strebt nicht nach sozialer Ehre; der "professional" ist verachtet innerhalb der "guten Gesellschaft". Er sucht ausschließlich Macht, Macht als Geldquelle, aber auch: um ihrer selbst willen. Er arbeitet im Dunklen, das ist sein Gegensatz zum englischen leader. Man wird ihn selbst nicht öffentlich reden hören; er suggeriert den Rednern, was sie in zweckmäßiger Weise zu sagen haben, er selbst aber schweigt' (Weber 1919c: 68).

6. 'Gerade die Struktur dieser gesinnungslosen Parteien mit ihren gesellschaftlich verachteten Machthabern hat daher tüchtigen Männern zur Präsidentschaft verholfen' (Weber 1919c: 68).

been able to turn the party and electoral machine into instruments for their own plebiscitary power: 'Ein cäsaristisch-plebiszitäres Element in der Politik' (Weber 1919c: 64; 1994b: 342).

Weber thus situates the professionalisation of politics in the context of the universal tendency towards bureaucratisation. Against this background, he clearly sees both the indispensability and the inherent limits of machine politics. The traditional counterweights tend to be exhausted and the machine itself is liable to produce order for the sake of order. Nonetheless, the presidential and the parliamentary type of professionalisation have to a certain degree managed to transcend the inherent limits of machine politics. From this perspective must also be seen the slogan *Führerdemokratie mit Maschine*, as opposed to a democracy without the leadership of professional politicians that lack a vocation: a 'Herrschaft der "Berufspolitiker" ohne Beruf, ohne die inneren, charismatischen Qualitäten' (Weber 1919c: 72; 1994b: 351). No machine is self-sufficient, but no lasting effects can be achieved without a machine.

Weber's lucid analysis illustrates that the party functionaries as such are no real threat to the competitive mass democracies. The party bosses are able to run the daily affairs and election campaigns as well as recognise their own limits (see the modest aims and anti-monarchism expressed in the interviews of George Washington Plunkitt, the *Tammany Hall* political boss and New York senator, 1904). Weber in a similar manner saw the limits of the political competence of the German state bureaucracy, despite its claims of superior knowledge (see Weber 1918d: 234–48 and the discussion below).

The plebiscitary leadership of the president

Wolfgang J. Mommsen's famous study, *Max Weber und die deutsche Politik* (Mommsen 1959), gave Weber the reputation of a defender of plebiscitary leadership. However, Weber uses the slogan 'plebiszitäre Führerdemokratie' only once, in a chapter involving an antiauthoritarian reinterpretation of charismatic rule, in *Wirtschaft und Gesellschaft* (Weber 1922: 157). He always defends the value of rulership (*Herrschaft*) as an element of movement against stagnation, while demanding at the same time its political control.

Plebiscitary democracy provides us with a modern expression of politics based on the epideictic genre of rhetoric. The ceremonial application of the genre operates in a binary manner by applauding (*acclamatio*) – or withholding applause. The political paradigm of epideictic rhetoric is, of course, the referendum: you can only vote yes or no. For some thinkers, such as Carl Schmitt, elections are in practice reduced to acclamation, because it is the only manner in which 'the assembled people' can act politically: 'nur das wirklich gesammelte Volk kann das tun, was spezifisch zur Tätigkeit dieses Volkes gehört: es kann *akklamieren*' (Schmitt 1928: 243–4). The preference for the acclamatory style of plebiscitary or presidential regimes is, accordingly, characteristic of Schmitt's political thought in general.

Max Weber clearly distinguishes between elections and acclamation. Characteristic of the selection of a king, a pope or other similar authorities is nomination (*Bezeichung*) by the following (*Jünger und Gefolgsleute*) and confirmation by the acclamation of the people (Weber 1922: 665). The plebiscite is not an election, but a one-time or recurrent recognition of a claimant as one who is personally qualified to rule (Weber 1922: 665). However, the borderline between acclamation and election can be crossed in both directions. Weber recognises the slow, but by no means necessary, historical trend toward the replacement of acclamation by regular, procedural elections. 'The acclamation by the ruled can … also develop into a regular "election procedure", including by norms regulated directly or indirectly by suffrage, with local or regional elections, classes of voters and electoral districts" '.[7]

The development of elections into a representative system has taken place only in the western countries (*im Okzident*). The opposition between election and acclamation is discussed in Weber's chapters on the antiauthoritarian reinterpretation of charisma. Charisma is always dependent on recognition by an audience. When this takes place through the medium of elections, the electorate can always alter its past choice:[8] 'The Ruler is now the freely elected leader'. (Weber 1921: 487–8; 1922: 155–7)

Elections based on personality are the most liable to become interpreted in acclamatory terms, although the example of Gladstone indicates the presence of a plebiscitary dimension in British-type parliamentary elections also. The plebiscitary direct election of a president is for Weber connected to the key role of acclamation. Weber contrasts the US and French practices of his time as the closest examples of, respectively, pure presidential and parliamentary regimes:[9]

> Every kind of direct *election by the people* of the bearer of supreme power, and beyond this every kind of position of political power which in fact rests on the trust of the masses rather than on the parliaments … lies in the road towards these 'pure' forms of Caesarist acclamation. In particular of course the position of power of the president of the United States which is legitimated by (formally) 'democratic' nomination and election; the president's superiority in relation to parliament rests on this very fact.
>
> (Weber 1994b: 221)

---

7. 'Die Akklamation der Beherrschten kann sich aber … zu einem regulären 'Wahlverfahren' entwickeln, mit einem durch Regeln normierten 'Wahlrecht', direkten oder indirekten, 'Bezirks'- oder 'Proportionalwahlen', 'Wahlklassen' und 'Wahlkreisen' (Weber 1922: 666).

8. 'Der Herr ist nun der frei gewählte Führer' (Weber 1922: 156).

9. 'Jede Art von direkter Volkswahl des höchsten Gewaltträgers, darüber hinaus aber jede Art von politischer Machtstellung, welche auf der Tatsache des Vertrauens der Massen, nicht der Parlamente, beruht… liegt auf dem Wege zu jenen "reinen" Formen cäsaristischer Akklamation. Insbesondere natürlich die durch (formell) "demokratische" Nomination und Wahl legitimierte Machtstellung des Präsidenten der Vereinigten Staaten, dessen Überlegenheit gegenüber dem Parlament eben hierauf beruht' (Weber 1918d: 266).

In contrast, parliamentary democracies attempt to exclude plebiscitary methods in the election of leaders, as such methods pose a danger to parliamentary powers. For Weber, this was the case with the French Third Republic, in which the supreme powers lack authority with the masses (Weber 1918d: 266–7, 1994b: 221).

For post-revolutionary Germany, Weber first, in January 1919, opposed the direct election of the *Reichspräsident*. The bureaucratic character of the imperial government had prevented the rise of any kind of political leadership. He argued that in a federal system a directly elected president is incompatible with the parliamentary responsibility of the ministers (Weber 1919a: 40–1). One month later, however, Weber took a stand for the popular election of the president of the *Reich*. His main arguments now referred to the need to give the electorate a choice in political leadership and for a change in the pre-republican party system (Weber 1919d: 75–6; 1994b: 306).

Why did Weber change his mind? The key event between the two publications was the election of the Weimar *Nationalversammlung*. The *Deutsche Demokratische Partei* promised Weber a seat in the Reichstag, but the local politicians of Hessen-Nassau put him on an ineligible list (see Weber 1919b and Mommsen's *Nachwort* and commentary in MWS 1/16, 1991: 156–61, 186–7). His *Reichspräsident* essay criticises bureaucratic and corporatist tendencies in German parties and their old clienteles. He sees the party-list version of the proportional system, when applied to the Weimar constituent assembly elections, as leading to a powerless parliament with a quasi-imperative mandate for its members, as opposed to a deliberating parliament.[10]

The need for this is increased by the *effects of proportional representation*. The next elections will bring into fruition something which was only beginning to become apparent during the last elections: occupational associations ... will force parties to put at the top of their lists the paid secretaries of their associations, simply to win votes. In this way parliament will become a body in which those who set the tone will be persons who regard national politicians as 'Hecuba' and whose actions are in fact subject to the 'imperative' mandate of the vested economic interests, *a parliament of closed, philistine minds*, in no sense capable of serving as a place where political leaders are selected.

(Weber 1994b: 306)

---

10. 'Die Wirkung des Verhältniswahlrechts verstärkt dies Bedürfnis. Bei den nächsten Wahlen wird eintreten, was bei diesen sich erst im Keim zeigte: die Berufsverbände ... werden die Parteien zwingen, lediglich zum Zwecke des Stimmenfangs deren (der Berufsverbände) besoldete Sekretäre an die Spitze der Listen zu stellen. Das Parlament wird so eine Körperschaft werden, innerhalb derer solche Persönlichkeiten, denen die nationale Politik "Hekuba" ist, die vielmehr, der Sache nach, unter einem "imperativen" Mandat von ökonomischen Interessenten handeln, den Ton angeben: ein Banausenparlament – unfähig, in irgendeinem Sinne eine Auslesestätte politischer Führer darzustellen' (Weber 1919d: 76).

The obstacles to a working parliamentary system were specifically bound up with the German electoral and party system as well as the federal character of the state, both of which tended to produce antiparliamentary veto powers against the Reichstag. For Weber the directly elected *Reichspräsident* serves as a *Ventil*, an outlet that brings fresh air into a closed system. Weber used the same metaphor also in 'Politik als Beruf', published in July 1919 (Weber 1919c: 72). The president remains a counter-power to the everyday rule of officialdom. He does not absolve the government from its responsibility to parliament, but creates an element of movement against the bureaucratised party clienteles.

Did Weber, however, recognise that an independent type of professionalisation of politics was developing on the basis of the presidential powers? For Weber, the US president is a non-professional figure, in contrast to party functionaries, parliamentarians and state officials. The present-day US presidential elections, based on a routinised form of the charismatic element, were rather far from Weber's imagination. If judged in Weberian terms, the loss of the *Außeralltäglichkeit* [extraordinariness] of the charismatic element indicates the bureaucratisation of the US presidential election and the loss of the counter-power role of the president towards officials. The massive and continuous campaign for the presidency as well as the decline of *the spoils system* has rather created a new type of professional politician based on the distinct acclamatory practices of the presidential regime. Within this type of politics, with its basis in epideictic rhetoric, the president is only the tip of the iceberg in a hierarchy of acclamatory practices.

The professional parliamentarian

Weber's defence of parliamentarism began in the first decade of the twentieth century (Weber 1904a, 1908; see Palonen 2004; *see* Chapter Ten in this volume). It is in his *Parlament* pamphlet that he explicitly looks for counter-powers to the rule of officialdom, while at the same time recognising that in the modern state the everyday *Herrschaft* lies in the hands of the bureaucracy, while parliaments for him above all 'Vertretungen der durch die Mittel der Bureaukratie *Beherrschten*': 'represent the people ruled by the means of bureaucracy' (Weber 1918d: 226; 1994b: 165). The British type of cabinet government is evidence that the parliament does not 'rule' itself:[11] 'For it is not the many-headed assembly of parliament as such that can "govern" and "make" policy. There is no question of this anywhere in the world, not even in England. ... *That is how things should be*' (Weber 1994b: 174).

In his *Wahlrecht* essay Weber militantly defends parliamentary powers as being a more effective means of controlling the government than any form of

---

11. 'Denn nicht die vielköpfige Versammlung des Parlaments als solche kann "regieren" und die Politik "machen". Davon ist nirgends in der Welt die Rede, auch nicht in England. ... Das soll so sein' (Weber 1918d: 233).

direct democracy. Non-parliamentary forms of democracy are liable to increase the powers of bureaucracy and clientelism.[12]

> First, what organ would democracy have with which to control the administration by officials in turn, if one imagines that parliamentary power did not exist? There is no answer to this question. Secondly, what would be put in place of rule by parliamentary 'cliques'? Rule by much more hidden and – usually – smaller 'cliques'. The system of so-called direct democracy is technically possible only in a small state (canton). In all mass states democracy leads to bureaucratic administration and, without parliamentarisation, to pure rule by officials.
>
> (Weber 1994b: 126–7)

If the representatives were bound by an imperative mandate and the threat of revocation by their voters, they would remain hopelessly powerless in the face of the permanent officials, as compared with parliamentarians elected for the entire term. To this we may add the insight of Earl Grey that in Britain the prolongation of the electoral term from three to seven years in 1716 indeed strengthened the competence and the deliberative powers of the parliament.

> From not being too frequently renewed, the Members of that House have become, as a body, more experienced in the transaction of business, and there has been a greater consistency and steadiness in its conduct than when the duration of Parliaments was limited to three years. Above all, the extension of the term for which the House has been elected, has been favourable to its maintaining its proper character, as a deliberative assembly, instead of becoming an assembly of delegates, not exercising their own judgment on the various questions submitted to them, but merely expressing the wishes of the several bodies of constituents by whom they are returned.
>
> (Grey 1865: 77)

It is common to assume with Mommsen that Weber restricted parliamentarism to the selection of the leader of the government. If we look closely at Weber's own formula for parliamentary government, we will, however, find a much broader conception. For him parliamentary government includes the selection of the Prime Minister from the parliament, parliamentary votes of no confidence in the

---

12. 'Denn 1. Welches Organ hat, wenn man sich die Parlamentsmacht fortdenkt, die Demokratie, um die Verwaltung der Beamten ihrerseits zu kontrollieren? Hierauf gibt es überhaupt keine Antwort. Ferner: 2. Was tauscht sie für die Herrschaft der parlamentarischen "Kliquen" ein? Die Herrschaft noch weit verborgenerer und – meist – noch weit kleinerer, vor allem unentrinnbarerer Kliquen. Das System der sogenannten unmittelbaren Demokratie ist technisch nur in einem Kleinstaat (Kanton) möglich. In jedem Massenstaat führt Demokratie zur bürokratischen Verwaltung, und, ohne Parlamentarisierung, zur reinen Beamtenherrschaft (Weber 1917f: 187).

government, the responsibility of the government to the parliament and, finally, parliamentary control of the administration.[13]

The situation is different in countries where parliament has established the principle that the leaders of the administration must either be directly drawn from its own ranks (a *parliamentary system* in the true sense) or that such leaders require the expressly stated confidence of a majority in parliament if they are to remain in office, or that they must at least yield to an expression of no confidence (*parliamentary selection* of the leaders). For this reason they must give an account of themselves, exhaustively and subject to verification by parliament or its committees (*parliamentary accountability* of the leaders), and they must lead the administration in accordance with guidelines approved by parliament (*parliamentary control of administration*). In this case the leaders of the decisive parties in parliament at any moment share the responsibility for the power of the state.

(Weber 1994b: 166)

Weber's demand for the parliamentarisation of elections and the responsibility of government in Germany opposes, above all, the system of ministers as officials in the Empire. If a member of the Reichstag was selected to be a minister, he was obliged to resign from parliament. For Weber this system was seriously flawed, and he proposed the removal of the constitutional paragraph in question even before the full parliamentarisation and democratisation of the regime (see Weber 1917a, b). For him the German experience demonstrated the complete political failure of officials as politicians (Weber 1918d: 235, 1994b: 177).

As early as his *Parlament* pamphlet Weber directs attention to the plebiscitary aspects of British *cabinet government*. To some extent these aspects complement each other as counterweights to bureaucratisation, while the parliamentary powers strongly restrict the plebiscitary element and support the everyday parliamentary control of government, which in Weber's conception extends the control beyond mere votes of no confidence.[14]

---

13. 'Anders, wo das Parlament durchgesetzt hat, daß die Verwaltungsleiter entweder geradezu aus seiner Mitte entnommen werden müssen ("parlamentarisches System" im eigentlichen Sinn) oder doch, um im Amt zu bleiben, des ausdrücklich ausgesprochenen Vertrauens seiner Mehrheit bedürfen oder wenigstens der Bekundung des Mißtrauens weichen müssen (parlamentarische Auslese der Führer) und aus diesem Grunde, erschöpfend und unter Nachprüfung des Parlaments oder seiner Ausschüsse, Rede und Antwort stehen (parlamentarische Verantwortlichkeit der Führer) und die Verwaltung nach den vom Parlament gebilligten Richtlinien führen müssen (parlamentarische Verwaltungskontrolle). In diesem Fall sind die Führer der jeweils ausschlaggebenden Parteien des Parlaments notwendig positive Mitträger der Staatsgewalt' (Weber 1918d: 227).

14. 'Der Gegensatz zwischen plebiszitärer und parlamentarischer Auslese der Führer besteht also. Aber die Existenz des Parlaments ist deshalb nicht etwa wertlos. Denn gegenüber dem (der Sache nach) cäsaristischen Vertrauensmann der Massen gewährleistet sie in England 1. die Stetigkeit und 2. die Kontrolliertheit seiner Machtstellung; 3. die Erhaltung der bürgerlichen Rechtsgarantien gegen ihn; 4. eine geordnete Form der politischen Bewährung der um das Vertrauen der Massen werbenden Politiker innerhalb der Parlamentsarbeit und 5. eine friedliche Form der Ausschaltung des cäsaristischen Diktators, wenn er das Massenvertrauen verloren hat' (Weber 1918d: 267).

Thus there exists an opposition between the plebiscitary and the parliamentary selection of leaders. But this does not mean that the *existence* of parliament is worthless. For in relation to the (de facto) Caesarist representative of the masses, the existence of parliament guarantees the following things: (1) the *stability* and (2) *controlled nature* of his position of power; (3) the preservation of civil *legal safeguards* against him; (4) an ordered form of *proving*, through parliamentary work, the political abilities of politicians who seek the trust of the masses; (5) a peaceful way of *eliminating* the Caesarist dictator when he has *lost* the trust of the masses.

(Weber 1994b: 222)

Weber's concepts of parliamentary responsibility and control of administration displays a rhetorical dimension in the British variety of *Arbeitsparlament*. He sees the intense participation of parliamentarians in committees as crucial for the British system, enabling them to understand and control the work of officials efficiently. This also leaves specific power shares for individual MPs within a *cabinet government* led by the Prime Minister and controlled by the party *whips*.[15]

The highly developed committee system in the English parliament makes it possible for prospective leaders to join the *work* of committees. All ministers of note during the last few decades have undergone a very real and effective training in this form of work, while the practice of reporting and publicly criticising these deliberations means that this school involves a genuine process of selection which excludes anyone who is a mere demagogue.

(Weber 1994b: 343–4, altered)

The parliament, based on the procedure of speaking pro et contra on every item on the agenda, is a modern paradigm of the deliberative genre of rhetoric. A classical example of the parliamentarian's self-identity is Edmund Burke's speech to his Bristol electors, insisting that the parliament is no 'congress of ambassadors', but a 'deliberative assembly' (Burke 1774), while Weber denounces the powerless *Redeparlament* (*see*, however, the interpretation in Chapter Thirteen in this volume).[16]

Only a *working*, as opposed to a merely talking parliament can be the soil in which not the mere demagogic but the genuinely *political* qualities of leadership

---

15. 'Aber das sehr entwickelte System der Komiteearbeit im englischen Parlament ermöglicht es und zwingt auch jeden Politiker, der auf Teilnahme an der Führung reflektiert, dort mitzuarbeiten. Alle erheblichen Minister der letzten Jahrzehnte haben diese sehr reale und wirksame Arbeitsschulung hinter sich, und die Praxis der Berichterstattung und öffentlichen Kritik an diesen Beratungen bedingt es, daß diese Schule eine wirkliche Auslese bedeutet und den bloßen Demagogen ausschaltet' (Weber 1919c: 65).

16. 'Denn nicht ein redendes, sondern nur ein arbeitendes Parlament kann der Boden sein, auf dem nicht bloß demagogische, sondern echt politische Führerqualitäten wachsen und im Wege der Auslese aufsteigen. Ein arbeitendes Parlament aber ist ein solches, welches die Verwaltung fortlaufend mitarbeitend kontrolliert' (Weber 1918d: 234).

can grow and work up their way through a process of selection. A working parliament is one which *continuously shares in the work of government and the control of the administration.*

(Weber 1994b: 176–7)

Similar to the French and British writers on rhetoric from the period (Reinach 1894; Curzon 1913), Weber targets not parliamentary debate, but merely the *grand style* of the eighteenth-century parliamentary orators. They judged parliamentary speeches rather by aesthetic criteria than as political interventions in a debate, or as the parliamentary version of deliberative rhetoric. Debates oriented towards parliamentary control and based on detailed committee work and on an 'effective system of parliamentary supervision and control' (Weber 1918d: 238; 1994b: 182) are equally rhetorical and more political than plenary speeches in powerless parliaments.

The rhetorical achievement of the parliament is manifest in the section where Weber refers to the knowledge-based power of the ministerial bureaucracy over the parliamentarians:[17] 'Apart from the division of labour which belongs inherently to the techniques of administration, the position of power of all officials rests on *knowledge*' (Weber 1994b: 178). Weber claims that an efficient parliamentary control of this knowledge is possible, but the imperial Reichstag did not possess the political rights and instruments to exercise such a control.

Weber discerns three levels of knowledge in officialdom, representing increasing degrees of power over parliamentarians: *Fachwissen, Dienstwissen* and *Geheimwissen*. First, knowledge that neither the officials nor the parliamentarians possess may be of a merely factual character. Second, officials have through their offices access to special knowledge, hidden from parliamentarians. And third, even if the officials could share their special knowledge with parliamentarians, they have no permission to do so, due to the principle of official secrecy (*Dienstgeheimnis*) (Weber 1918d: 236; 1994b: 178; for a detailed discussion with quotes *see* Chapters Ten and Eleven in this volume).

To enable parliamentary control over officials' supremacy in the possession of knowledge, Weber offers three instruments. The basic form of control is known from legal procedures as well as from the *hearings* of the US Congress, namely the cross-examination of officials (Weber 1918d: 236; 1994b: 178). The method shows parliamentarians that officials do not necessary agree among themselves, but different perspectives inherent to the different ministries tend to oppose each other. With cross-examination, parliamentarians learn better to understand that it is for them and not for the officials to deliberate and decide between the different viewpoints.

The specialised knowledge of the ministerial offices forms another obstacle to parliamentary control. MPs' access to files by on-the-spot examinations is necessary in order to enable control of the situated knowledge of officials. The

---

17. 'Die Machtstellung aller Beamten ruht, außer auf der arbeitsteiligen Technik der Verwaltung als solcher, auf Wissen' (Weber 1918d: 236).

cross-examination of officials serves here as a supplementary measure against both the risk of a monopoly on knowledge and the *deformation professionnelle* of officials, who are bound to the perspective of their specific offices (Weber 1918d: 236; 1994b: 179; *see* Chapters Ten and Eleven in this volume).

Official secrets are rooted in bureaucratic practice, a remnant of the old *arcana imperii* of pre-parliamentary regimes. The secrets serve as the last resort of the powers (*Machtanteile*) of officialdom, and for this reason even stronger measures of parliamentary control are required. Taking Westminster as his model again, Weber proposes parliamentary investigation commissions to provide an extraordinary means of strengthening ordinary parliamentary control of the administration, including through reports, committees and other means. Such inquiry commissions allow the leading officials to present a detailed defence of their views, which is then confronted by criticism from the parliamentarians:[18]

> the right to enquiry is an indispensable aid to be used *on occasion*. Apart from this it is to be used as a rod of chastisement, the mere existence of which forces the administrative chiefs to an account of themselves in a way that obviates the need to use it. The finest achievements of the English parliament have come from using the right of enquiry in this way.
>
> (Weber 1994b: 179)

With these measures Weber aims to reduce the dilettantism in the imperial Reichstag (Weber 1918d: 236). Moreover, his moves illuminate general rhetorical instruments for optimising the parliamentary principle of discussing items on the agenda from opposite perspectives. The Canadian rhetoric professor James De Mille sees the genre of 'parliamentary debate' to be explicitly rhetorical in its character: 'The aim of parliamentary debate is to investigate the subject from many points of view which are presented from two contrary sides. In no other way can a subject be so exhaustively considered' (De Mille 1878: 473).

Max Weber's critique of the allegedly superior knowledge of officials and his proposals to control it rely on well-established procedural principles of the British parliament. His discussions are indebted to the idea of *in utramque partem disputare* of classical and Renaissance rhetoric (see Skinner 1996, 2008) as well as to the contemporary literature on parliamentary procedure. Josef Redlich, for example, writes in his *Recht und Technik des Englischen Parlamentarismus* on the role of *Rede und Gegenrede* [speeches for and against] as constituting one of the basic activities of parliament (for example 1905: 586–7, *see* also Chapters Ten to Twelve in this volume).

The link between parliamentary procedure and rhetorical practice relates to Weber's vision of knowledge and 'objectivity'. In his essay of 1904 Weber

---

18. 'das Enqueterecht ist als gelegentliches Hilfsmittel unentbehrlich und bietet im übrigen: eine Rute, deren Vorhandensein die Verwaltungschefs zwingt, in einer Art Rede zu stehen, die seine Anwendung unnötig macht. In dieser Art der Verwertung dieses Rechts liegen die allerbesten Leistungen des englischen Parlaments' (Weber 1918d: 236).

defends a perspectivist view of all knowledge and the value of confrontation between different perspectives as a condition to prevent stagnation. In Weber's view, knowledge can never be 'possessed' by anyone, but is destined to remain contested and controversial. Through a paradiastolic rhetorical redescription (see Skinner 1996: ch. 4), Weber reinterprets 'objectivity' in the human sciences to mean a fair procedure for dealing with the disputes between perspectives and their adherents in a manner that seeks not to end the dispute nor excommunicate the participants in it (Palonen 2010b; *see* also Chapters Ten to Twelve in this volume).

The parliamentary procedure provides Weber with a paradigm for dealing fairly with scholarly controversies. The pamphlet of 1918 illustrates this rhetorical theory of knowledge with an exposition of how parliamentary procedure provides for the MPs a resource against the monopolising claims for knowledge by state officials (Weber 1918d). Although parliamentarians may lack knowledge, they are better equipped than anyone to judge its political significance with the rhetorical procedures of the parliament and detect its misuse when it favours the rule of the officialdom (Palonen 2010b, *see* also the Chapters Ten to Thirteen in this volume).

This broader background also provides a basis for Weber's discussion of the professional parliamentarian. His ideal is a full-time parliamentarian equipped with an office, which at the time was best represented by the US Congress, but was *in nuce* present even in the Reichstag:[19]

> The professional member of parliament is a man who exercises his mandate in the Reichstag, not as an occasional and subsidiary duty, but as the main content of his life work, equipped with his own office and staff and with every means of information.
>
> (Weber 1994b: 190)

Both state officials and party functionaries were extremely suspicious of a parliament-based professionalisation of politics: 'Denn der Berufsparlamentarier an sich ist den Instinkten der bürokratischen Verwaltungschefs ein Dorn im Auge' – [For the professional parliamentarian as such is instinctively felt as a thorn in the flesh by the heads of bureaucratic administration] (Weber 1918d: 245; 1994b: 191). For Weber, an advantage of the parliamentary type of professional politician lies in their chances to learn from their own practices. Professional parliamentarians are no 'mere' demagogues, but persons who have learnt to think and to discuss items from opposite points of view and to weigh the advantages and disadvantages of the proposals:[20]

---

19. 'Der Berufsparlamentarier ist ein Mann, der das Reichstagsmandat ausübt nicht als gelegentliche Nebenpflicht, sondern – ausgerüstet mit eigenem Arbeitsbüro und -personal und mit allen Informationsmitteln – als Hauptinhalt seiner Lebensarbeit' (Weber 1918d: 244).

20. 'Denn nur qualifizierte Berufsparlamentarier, welche durch die Schule intensiver Ausschußarbeit eines Arbeitsparlaments gegangen sind, können verantwortliche Führer, nicht bloße Demagogen und Dilettanten aus sich hervorgehen lassen. Auf solche Führer und ihre Wirksamkeit muß die ganze innere Struktur des Parlaments zugeschnitten werden, wie es in ihrer Art diejenige des englischen Parlaments und seiner Parteien seit langem ist' (Weber 1918d: 245).

Only qualified, professional parliamentarians who have been through the school of the intensive committee work in a *working* parliament can give rise to responsible leaders, as opposed to mere demagogues and dilettantes. The whole internal structure of parliament must be such as to produce such leaders and enhance their effectiveness, as has long been the case with the structure of the English parliament and its parties.

(Weber 1994b: 191)

Parliamentary procedure can also alter the habits of members, encouraging them to look for alternatives where there seem to be none, to question everything, even what appears self-evident, and to devise objections for the sake of argument. In this rhetorical style of acting politically lies the institutional basis of the parliament and its professionalisation of politics.

Max Weber judged the chances of contemporary parliamentarians pessimistically and readily accepted that parliaments needed both a party machine and a plebiscitary element to appeal directly to the electorate. Nonetheless, as compared with the party functionary and the plebiscitary leader, he saw definite advantages for preferring the parliamentarian to address his main political concern: forming counterweights to the rule of officialdom.

Weber's defence of parliament and parliamentarians as professional politicians concerns the ideal type more than the actual practice of the German MPs. Above all, he does not see any alternative to replace the parliament as an institution that can debate items thoroughly from opposite points of view:[21] 'but *there is no other power which can substitute for it, Or, if there is another, which is it?'* (Weber 1994b: 205). Due to parliamentary procedures and practices themselves, every parliament has some chances to further the procedures and rhetorical practices of the parliamentary style of politics.

Concluding remarks

My interpretation of Max Weber as a theorist of 'political life' (in the sense of Skinner 1978 I: xi) and as a defender of the priority of the parliamentary form of professionalisation implies a different narrative for the history of the professionalisation of politics than Weber sketched in 'Politik als Beruf'. My interpretation insists on the presence of a European rhetorical culture in Weber's *oeuvre*, which, despite its well-known features, such as Weber's juvenile reading of Machiavelli and Cicero (see Weber 1936: 3, 12–15), has so far received hardly any scholarly attention.

I connect his three ideal types for the professionalisation of politics – functionary, president and parliamentarian – to three genres of rhetoric: negotiation, acclamation and deliberation. The genres of rhetoric serve here as

21. 'Es ist schlechterdings durch keine andere Macht zu ersetzen. Oder: durch welche?' (Weber 1918d: 255).

styles of political argumentation, aimed at the different audiences to that decide the cases and related to different modes of both conducting and judging disputes (see also Palonen 2010b). The deliberative genre of rhetoric refers to a fair and open debate in which fixed parties are not a given: the parties will be formed only through the course of the debate and vote on each issue. The rhetorical perspective allows me to emphasise the depth of the parliamentary dimension in the Weberian view of politics, also extending to his perspectivistic theory of knowledge and dealing fairly with scholarly controversies.

Weber's parliamentary model for the professionalisation of politics can be contrasted with the widespread thesis of the 'eclipse of the parliaments', to quote a British book title (Lenman 1992). My point is only to insist that the powers of parliaments, besides the relations between government and parliament, also refer to the inherent rhetorical dimensions of parliamentary procedure and the parliamentary culture of 'government by speaking' (Macaulay 1857). The procedure contains a *longue durée* of parliamentary politics, based on the principles of speaking pro et contra and on fair play between members. Weber further insists on the character-forming power of the parliament: in contrast to the teleological style of the party and the election machine, the parliament teaches its members to think of politics in a procedural style.

Since about 1980, parliamentary powers have been revitalised in West European politics. This is partly an unintended consequence of the full-time salaries for parliamentarians and the improved resources of both the parliamentary and the personal staff of MPs. As party membership and apparatus have declined, the parliamentary basis of professionalisation has gained new ground (see for example Borchert 2003). Also practices such as party financing based on the number of MPs instead of on party membership has contributed to a re-parliamentarisation of party politics and laid the ground for reducing the negotiating rhetoric of the *Parteienstaat* in favour of an activation of the free mandate, in accordance with the deliberative procedural practices of the parliament.

Politics is today increasingly concerned with different perspectives on the world, which are projected into opposing views and crucial questions to be debated in the parliament. In this situation the parliamentarisation of the politics of the agenda is itself on the agenda. The professionalisation of politics refers, today more than ever, to debates over initiatives and moves, their presence and their rank on the agenda. The extension of the principle of *in utramque partem disputare* to the agenda debates would render the parliament itself more conscious of what items on the agenda it should spend time deliberating and what issues deserve to be debated thoroughly. The parliamentarisation of agenda-setting can also change the politics of parliamentary times and the way questions are framed into debatable agenda items.

The examples above illustrate what intra-parliamentary resources for the professionalisation of politics are built into the repertoire of parliamentary procedure, although they have not always been activated in the rhetorical practices of parliamentary speaking. Finally, concerning the parliamentary principle on the relationship between voting and debating, the latter should not be viewed as a prelude to the vote, but rather the vote should be seen as the last rhetorical move to be taken when nothing new is said in the debate. Instead of the unity created by the majority vote, we should then emphasise the value of keeping a dissensus of perspectives and standpoints in debate on all the major issues on the parliamentary agenda.

PART II

WEBER AS A CONCEPTUAL POLITICIAN

Chapter Six

Max Weber's Reconceptualisation of Freedom

It is not customary to count Max Weber among the theorists on freedom. On the contrary, he has a reputation for analysing the situation of his contemporary world in terms of the 'iron cage', as the Parsonsian mistranslation of *stahlhartes Gehäuse* (on the translation see Chalcraft 1994) goes. It is also obvious that Weber does not fit easily into the common oppositions of the contemporary Anglo-American debate in terms of positive and negative liberty or the liberal and republican view on liberty. Despite his obvious sympathies for Anglo-American politics and the Protestant ethic (see Roth 1995), the 'conventions of English-speaking "society"' (Weber 1916b: 39) did not correspond to his understanding of freedom, either.

Weber never made a concise exposition of his conception of freedom. In the huge secondary literature on his work, I have found no systematic exposition of his conception of liberty (on some aspects of it, see Draus 1995), as opposed to the discussion of whether he was 'a liberal' (compare Hennis 1987 with Beetham 1994). My intention here is to assess the context-transcending singularity of Weber's understanding of freedom by presenting first its different aspects and then indicating conceptual connections between them.

The significance of the Weberian conception of freedom to political theory can be crystallised into the following main points. In Constantian terms, Weber is definitely a proponent of a 'modern concept of liberty'. The Weberian variant does not, however, oppose individual freedom to political action but maintains a close connection between them. As opposed to the strictly contractualist thinkers, Weber does not defend human rights as limits to politics but understands them as power shares in political action, and the same is the case with the competitive market.

These unorthodox commitments refer, furthermore, to his situational analysis, in which freedom appears as a counter-concept for order, with the universal tendency toward bureaucratisation as a paradigmatic expression of a danger of extinguishing freedom. The critique of conventional legitimations of freedom and the search for alternatives to bureaucratisation can be made intelligible when considering Weber's rethinking of contingency: instead of a residual of non-understanding, the specific operative contingency of *Chancen* plays a key role in both Weber's methodological and political writings. To understand human actions and relations between them in terms of *Chancen* makes freedom omnipresent in his work and also allows one to understand all orders as products of freedom. The concept of *Chance* also shows a connection between Weber and the existential dimension of twentieth-century political thought, which is illustrated here with a short comparison between Sartre and Weber.

The plurality of meanings of *Freiheit*

Max Weber consciously used *freedom (Freiheit)* in different context-bound meanings. In the index of Johannes Winkelmann's edition of *Wirtschaft und Gesellschaft*, the entry *Freiheit* is divided into subcategories, and *Freiheitsbegriff* [concept of freedom] is qualified as a notion the meaning of which varies according to circumstances (Weber 1922: 890). The situation characterises a key aspect of Weber's idiosyncratic nominalistic language. In the case of freedom, it thus becomes necessary to identify the contextual brackets in the Weberian conceptual horizon.

An expression of Weber's nominalistic view on language is that he often uses *Freiheit* in quotation marks. He does not try to determine 'true' or 'false' meanings of freedom but starts from the actual usage. For him, a qualification is always required when one wants to speak of freedom: freedom in which respect and for whom? This should always be specified. This nominalism can be also used as a clue to the analysis of Weber's own views of freedom, which can be read in his actual uses of the word. A close attention to Weber's vocabulary and the textual history of his *oeuvre* can be considered as a precondition of the discussion of 'the Weberian views on liberty'.

To understand the range of freedom in the Weberian vocabulary, I will just mention some of its common meanings. An obvious connotation is the idea of liberty as a *status*, as opposed to slavery in his lexicon article on antiquity (Weber 1909a) and serfdom, including the non-free status of peasants and agrarian labourers in the East Elbian *latifundias* in Prussia, which is taken up in Weber's early Prussian studies (see Weber 1893a, 471–2; 1894, 506). The chances to choose between individual forms of living appear to Weber as a political question concerning the control of these forms. In his early agrarian studies, he discusses the 'magic of freedom' arising in the Prussian countryside when the traditional order shows signs of breaking down (Weber 1895a: 7).

Another meaning refers to the independence of states or to the autonomy of cities, as opposed to empires, which is a central subject especially in *Die Stadt*. In this respect, Weber's view is close to the 'republican' view on liberty (see Skinner 1984 on Machiavelli as a paradigmatic example of republican liberty), but it should be blurred neither with the Kantian philosophy of autonomy nor with the ideal of national self-determination.

Freedom is also discussed in more specific meanings, such as free competition (see Weber 1898) and free agitation as the basis of the parties (for example Weber 1918d: 215) or academic freedom (above all, Weber 1919e). For Weber, *Wertfreiheit* has a double significance: it refers both to freedom of research from given value premises and to freedom as an irrevocable condition of political choices, which should not be patronised in the name of 'science' (the three classical essays on 'Objectivity' (Weber 1904b), 'Value freedom' (1917a), and 'Science as a vocation' (1919e). The first aspect was important in Wilhelmine Germany, not only due to state intervention in appointments ('System Althoff', see Hennis 1994), but also in relation to the central role of the Schmollerian neocameralist view of human sciences as a service to the state. Still, the specificity of the Weberian value of freedom lies in the insistence on the responsible decisions of the politicians, as a recognition that political questions cannot be solved 'by the development of science' but that they must be decided upon by the political agents themselves.

In *Die protestantische Ethik*, Weber opposes the space for individual choice created by the Reformation to the new and severe forms of the regulation of life-conduct by Protestant doctrines (Weber 1904–5/20). He analyses the forms of factory discipline restricting and forming the chances of individual life-conduct (Weber 1907a). For Weber, the chances in individual lives and the control of these do not primarily signify drawing a line between the private and the public sphere. The concept of life-conduct refers, rather, to the political character of the individual choices, their conditions, and their *Spielraum*.

These examples show that Weber's remarks on freedom form a kind of subnarrative, which I regard as relevant both to the interpretation of the singularity of the Weberian political theory and to the discussion of the concept of liberty in present-day political theory. My viewpoint in this chapter is to sketch out a perspective that makes the politically central aspects in the Weberian subnarrative on freedom more intelligible. The points referred to above and treated in the following sections can be called Weberian dimensions of freedom: the modern, the legitimatory, the situational, the contingent and the existential.

Ancient and modern liberties: Constant and Weber

During recent decades, Sir Isaiah Berlin's dichotomy between negative and positive liberty has become the usual starting point of any discussion of liberty and freedom. Berlin sees Benjamin Constant as one of 'the most eloquent defenders of freedom and privacy', as well as a kind of precursor of his own defence of negative liberty (Berlin 1958: 126, 163–4). This annexation of Constant in Berlin's case has been criticised by Stephen Holmes, who insists that Constant himself was a politician who could not, at least in the Restoration period, defend an apolitical privacy implied by Berlin's negative liberty (Holmes 1984).

Regarding a discussion of Weber's conception of liberty, Constant's dichotomy between ancient and modern liberty seems to be a more relevant reference than Berlin's. Weber, indeed, seems to have been well aware of Constant's distinction between the two liberties and their roles in the estimation of the difference between ancient and modern polities. In his programmatic essay on objectivity, Weber uses Constant's theory of the ancient state as an example by which he illustrates the character of the ideal type. As such, it can be used as an auxiliary construction, as a *Nothafen*, until the ocean of facts has been properly treated (Weber 1904b: 206, mentioned also by Holmes 1988: 53). This is the only reference to Constant in Weber's work that I have found.

Constant gives a new turn to the seventeenth-century *querelle* between ancients and moderns in terms of liberty in the postrevolutionary period. In the French context, his work has been recently assessed as a kind of liberalism that is primarily political rather than economic and opposed to the republican traditions of political thought (compare Nicolet 1982: 357, 479–84 with Rosanvallon 1992: 246–7). The term liberalism is, however, criticised as anachronistic: Constant did not use it himself (as noted by Fontana 1991: xiii).

The famous formulation of Constant's dichotomy is presented in his lecture 'De la liberté des anciens comparée à celle des modernes' in 1819. Its idea has been found, however, in his writings as early as 1798 and published for the first time in 'De l'esprit de conquete et de l'usurpation' in 1814 (for the dating, see Holmes 1984 34–6; Gauchet 1980). This idea formed a part of Constant's general project for a representative government, discussed in the books of Holmes and Fontana.

Constant's two distinctions, that between ancient and modern liberties and that between individual and political liberties, served as legitimating devices for this programme. He used the historical interpretation as a polemical measure against the apology of antiquity in the revolutionary rhetoric. Constant's interpretation contained another perspective to 'modernity', in which direct and widespread participation in public affairs appeared as a questionable return to an idealised past.

In 1814, Constant linked the opposition between ancient and modern liberty with two forms of enjoyment (*jouissance*): the ancients did enjoy participation in 'collective power', while the moderns prefer individual independence. According to Constant, under modern conditions, sacrificing individual enjoyment is absurd and impossible (Constant 1814: 182). He contrasts two ideals of human beings: the ancients enjoyed action, while the moderns enjoy reflection (Constant 1814: 184). The political point of modern liberty is to resist arbitrary government (Constant 1814: 196–7).

Constant's lecture in 1819 presents the idea with specified arguments that are partly related to a new political constellation: the Jacobin militancy turned out to be no longer actual, and the monarchist *ultras* had become the main target of critique (Holmes 1984: 36–9). The language of enjoyment was still used at that time, and in its terms the enjoyment of 'participation in power' was opposed to the 'security in private enjoyments' (Constant 1819: 502). However, Constant also uses the language of rights: they are seen as instances in terms of which the contemporary English, French, and Americans understand liberty (Constant 1819: 494–5). As opposed to the active participation of the ancients, 'our liberty' consists of 'peaceful enjoyment of private independence' (Constant 1819: 501).

The main point of his argument consists of demonstrating the unwanted consequences of ancient liberty. It was compatible with the 'complete subordination of the individual to the authority of the whole'. All private actions were severely controlled; nothing was left to individual independence. The movements of individuals were restricted, observed and repressed (Constant 1819: 495–6).

While the ancient individual was sovereign in public, but not in private affairs, the modern situation was the opposite. The independence of individuals in private life corresponded with restricted sovereignty, even in free states, and when it was sometimes exercised, this was done only to abdicate it (Constant 1819: 496). The difference between the ancient and the modern is related to the size of the polities, to the abolishment of slavery and to the replacement of war by commerce, which also strengthens the love for individual independence (Constant 1819: 499).

Constant's point is to stress that individual independence should never be sacrificed to obtain political liberty (Constant 1819: 501). The argument is based on an analysis of a situation, according to which individual existence is less touched by political existence in the contemporary world than in the ancient world (Constant 1819: 511). Political freedom is, however, the guarantee of individual liberty, but this liberty is organised otherwise than in ancient liberty (Constant 1819: 509, 511–12). Constant combines this principle with a defence of the representative system of government (Constant 1819: 512–13).

Remarkable in Constant's reasoning are the close connections between the two concepts of liberty, their division into the political-public and the individual-private spheres, and the conclusions about the governmental system. This argument presupposes a parallelity in the oppositions between ancient and modern polities at these three levels.

None of the meanings of *Freiheit* in the Weberian list of 'freedoms' corresponds to the 'ancient liberty' as presented by Constant. Although Weber criticises the lack of a 'public spirit' among his contemporaries, he does not name it as a lack of 'freedom'. The Weberian horizon of meaning belongs exclusively to the horizon of Constant's modern concept of liberty. Within this horizon, his conception of freedom, however, differs in important respects from that of Constant's.

Weber's note above indicates that he was well aware of Constant's critique of the ancient polis as a realm of unfreedom. There are even some parallels in the formulations, although Weber, having the ancient agrarian and urban history as one of his specialities, had, of course, first-hand sources for his critique. In 'Agrarverhältnisse im Altertum', Weber emphasises above all the primarily military character of the ancient polis as a 'military camp' and of the *ekklesia* as the assembled army (*das versammelte Heer*) (Weber 1909a: 124, compare also 262). The extension of the suffrage in the polis signifies, according to him, a democratisation of militarism (Weber 1909a: 108).

This perspective is combined with a critique à la Constant in the City essay, which continues the problematic of the 'Agrarverhältnisse'. The military character of the polis is now described as a craft of warriors *(Kriegerzunft)* (Weber 1922: 809), and the military duties form, besides the 'Khadi justice' of the people's tribunals, a paradigm for the limitation of individual freedom. If some degree of freedom were obtained, as in 'democratic' Athens, it would be achieved at the cost of military efficiency (Weber 1922: 809–10).

Weber's general thesis is to emphasise that under the conditions of the ancient polis it was not possible to speak of 'freedom of personal life-conduct' (Weber 1922: 809). The concept of life-conduct indicates a conceptual difference from the Constantian view. Freedom is neither a mere question of rights nor a mere absence of dependence: it refers to choices concerning the individual's way of life.[1] Life as such is not a sufficient goal for Weber, as we can see in his remark concerning the medical prolongation of life. The length of the life is not a question of maximation to be followed at all costs, but is a value choice (Weber 1917c: 496) For the nominalist Weber, no 'good life' in the unproblematic classical sense is possible, but, as Weber puts it in 'Wissenschaft als Beruf', each person has to decide on the sense of his or her own life (Weber 1919e: 20).

Unlike in the case of Constant, Weber's replacement of the ancient liberty with the modern one cannot, thus, be interpreted as a reversal of *vita activa* in favour of a reflective *vita contemplativa*. The personal freedom of life-conduct demands an exercise of freedom in a more or less open horizon of action. The attempts to control or regulate this horizon form, for Weber, a central topic in modern politics.

A Weberian distinction between the ancient and modern world is presented, in both his studies on the ancient and medieval politics, in terms of the opposition between *homines politici* and *homines oeconomici* (Weber 1909a: 262; 1922: 805). This vocabulary deserves, however, a specification. It points out the difference in the criteria of the 'citizenship' between the *politai* or the *cives* of antiquity and the *Stadtbürger* of medieval cities. The ancient citizenship was, for the full citizens of the *polis*, political 'by nature', that is, a citizenship based on administrative and military criteria as well as a sort of *ius sanguinis* principle.

The medieval cities were, according to Weber, primarily units of commerce and trade (*Handel und Gewerbe*) (Weber 1922: 804–5). According to Weber's historical interpretation, the origin of the modern citizenship is related to the practices of the medieval autonomous cities. It is in this sense that Weber sees the modern European citizens as *homines oeconomici*. But, yet, this title does not make them apolitical. On the contrary, the *Stadtbürger* always had chances to act politically. The 'the city air renders free' (*Stadtluft macht frei*) principle (Weber 1922: 742–809) did not only mean a chance for liberation from serfdom for the peasants but also formed a basis for the opposition of the cities to the power of the empires to which they formally belonged. The right – or to put it in specific Weberian terms, the *Chance* – to act politically was gained by belonging to the economic unit of the city.

This is the perspective through which Weber discusses the chances and consequences of the struggle of the autonomous cities against imperial, patrimonial and, later, etatist forms of ruling. Weber's discussion both in *Die Stadt* and in the chapter on patriarchal and patrimonial rule (in *Wirtschaft und Gesellschaft*) makes

---

1. Although the concept of Lebensführung has played a dominant role in Weber studies since Hennis's *Max Webers Fragestellung*, there exists no systematic Werkgeschichte concerning this concept and the parallel expressions – Lebenshaltung, Lebensstil, Lebensanschauung, Lebensentscheidung – or the regulative dimension of Lebensordnung. I just want to remark that the concept is used by Weber on various occasions, as early as in the study of developmental tendencies in East Elbian agriculture (Weber 1893a: 472) and then in the *Protestantische Ethik*, as well as in the later studies on the sociology of religion, in the Russian studies of 1906, in the older part of *Wirtschaft und Gesellschaft*, for example, in the comments on the role of the play (Spiel) in the feudal mode of life (Weber 1922: 650–l, and in the 'Stadt' essay (1907b [1999]), but also in the methodological writings, such as Weber 1917c: 508; 1919e: 7, 17, 22; and 1919c: 35, 76).

it clear that he was by no means an admirer of the formation of centralised modern states, which unmade the autonomy of cities.

The *homo oeconomicus* character of modern persons makes Weber worry about the growth of apolitism and ask for the chances for political activity under modern conditions. Since his letters to Herman Baumgarten in the late 1880s (Weber 1936), he criticised the apolitical tendencies in contemporary Germany. Although Weber is, like Constant, an advocate of representative government, he does not want politics to be the monopoly of the professional politicians. Even in his Freiburg inaugural lecture (Weber 1895a). Weber makes clear that the representative system presupposes politically conscious citizens.

In 'Politik als Beruf' Max Weber introduces the concept of the 'occasional politician' *(Gelegenheitspolitiker)* (Weber 1919c: 41; see also 1917f, 1918d). He plays with the double meaning of occasion: a *Gelegenheitspolitiker* is not merely one who occasionally participates in politics but also one who always has an occasion to participate in order to control the professional politicians or to try to become a professional politician himself. In Weber's usage, it aptly describes the political idea of citizenship in a culture based on *homines oeconomici.* Political action is experienced as freedom if it remains a voluntary, self-chosen activity.

Legitimating liberty

For the classical contractualist theorists, liberty was an antonym of power. Even the late-eighteenth-century declarations of human rights were presented as programmes that could put a 'sphere of freedom' beyond the reach of political powers. Weber discusses human rights in the 'Rechtssoziologie' of *Wirtschaft und Gesellschaft* and in the Russian studies (Weber 1906b, d), both times in a manner that manifests his dissent with the classical legitimation of freedom.

In Weber's 'Rechtssoziologie', the theories of natural law and social contract, although he recognised their historical roles, are submitted to Occam's razor (Weber 1922: 498–503). A key point in his argumentation is to insist that it is by no means a priori decided whether the extension of contractual relations means 'an increase of individual liberty in the determination of one's own life-conduct' or whether it leads, rather, to an 'increase of the compulsory schematisation of the life-conduct' (Weber 1922: 439).

Weber had both philosophical and strategic grounds not to legitimate politics in favour of the individual life-conduct by the natural law or its analogies. Weber himself also spoke of freedom in the sense of rights, *Freiheitsrechte.* He refused, however, to understand human rights only as an instrument to limit political power. On the contrary, his legitimation of *Freiheitsrechte* or *Freiheit im Rechtssinn* (Weber 1922: 399) is openly political. For Weber, subjective rights are sources of power *(Machtquellen)* (Weber 1922: 398). They are political means of expression of the chances of the individual life-conduct. Weber sees in juridical formalism a guarantee that gives the individual interested in her or his rights 'the relative maximum of *Spielraum* in freedom of movement', especially related to calculating the juridical consequences and chances of her or his intended action. This insight does not hinder the possibility that these rights are, in some cases, turned into an instrument of reglementation (Weber 1922: 469).

As noted by David Beetham (1974: 44–69), Weber discusses most systematically the relations between individual and political freedom as well as the political significance of human rights in his studies on Russia in 1906. According to his analysis, the anti-centralist liberals, represented by the self-government organs, the *zemstvos*, were, for Weber, the most important movement against Czarist autocracy and bureaucracy (Weber 1906b: 263–79). The programme of Russian liberals, such as Struwe, explicitly defends the political individualism of the 'West European human rights' (Weber 1906b: 164, 188). Weber sympathises with the programme, although he rejects its traditional legitimation. In another passage, Weber explicitly accepts the basic individualistic idea of 'inalienable human rights' with the argument that they have become trivial to 'us West Europeans' (Weber 1906b: 269).

The defence of human rights is thus clearly distinguished from the argument of putting law above politics, and the rights are seen, on the contrary, as a legal instrument of political action. Although Weber's critique of the Czarist regime contains conventional 'liberal' objections against arbitrary rule, he sees the bureaucratic depoliticisation of problems of government as still more dangerous (Weber 1906d: 406–11).

The defence of human rights, understood as a part of the West European political heritage of liberty, is also explicitly mentioned when Weber, in his parliament pamphlet of 1918, asks for the remaining chances of individual freedom (Weber 1918d: 222). The significance of these Weberian analyses lies in the demonstration that individual and subjective rights are, for him, above all, a political matter. The rights are instruments for individuality in life-conduct, and they can be used in politics against an imminent victory of order for the sake of order (Weber 1922: 503).

Another common legitimation of liberty, which was used by Struwe as well as by most other nineteenth- and early twentieth-century liberals, is the appeal to the 'invisible hand'. For Weber, this argument is still less acceptable than the classical natural law doctrine: all the figures appeal to harmonising the interests between individuals (Weber 1906b: 165), implying a depoliticisation of the economy. Weber's economic theory, as indicated by his agrarian writings and sketched later in *Wirtschaft und Gesellschaft*, differs from that of the liberals in its 'conflictual' character of economic actions and relations. Conceived as a struggle (on the 'market struggle', see esp. Weber 1922: 48–53), 'the economy' always has a political dimension, as was understood by Julien Freund (1990: 179). In Weber's argumentation, the advantage of the competitive market is not in its eventual contribution to economic progress but in the freedom to resist the monopolistic and centralist tendencies.

Weber's most vehement critique of Struwe and his friends is, however, directed against their philosophy of history, with its reliance on more or less automatic 'progress'. For him, individualism and human rights are no 'necessary' consequences of 'economic development'. The contemporary 'high capitalism' does not have any 'elective affinity' [*Wahlverwandtschaft*] with 'democracy' or indeed with 'freedom'. On the contrary, the 'housing for new serfdom' [*das Gehäuse für neue Hörigkeit*] is present everywhere (Weber 1906b: 269–70).

To this situational analysis, Weber connects a normative proposal. 'We, the "individualists" and partisans of "democratic institutions", are obliged to struggle against the current – the centralistic and authoritarian tendencies in capitalism and bureaucratisation in the state – instead of being a "weather-vane of a developmental trend"'. 'The connection between capitalism and modern freedom' was a product of unique historical constellations. For an individual of the masses, freedom, the only hope to win an 'inalienable sphere of freedom and personality', is mediated by the 'anarchy of production' and ' "subjectivism" still not extinguished by bureaucratisation' (Weber 1906b: 270–1).

When Weber spoke of Russia, he always had Germany and Western Europe in mind, too (see Weber 1906d: 477–9). In the Weberian analysis of Russia as well as in his remarks on Germany and the Western countries, we can detect fragments of an original but implicit reading of the history of European politics and culture in the era after the American and French revolutions. This analysis gives hints of a different view of legitimating the freedom of human rights and parliamentary politics.

According to my thesis, Weber saw, more clearly than the nineteenth-century philosophers of any political colour, how the democratisation and parliamentarisation of politics had led to a new kind of openness in the polity as an important expression of freedom. This dimension of freedom was manifested for Weber in the competition between parties and in the possibility of alternance in government.

Max Weber stressed the key role of elections as early as in his analysis of the Russian situation in the first Duma elections. In 'Politik als Beruf', when Weber is analysing the late nineteenth-century types of politicians formed in Britain and in the United States, his analysis presupposes a view of elections as a contingent phenomenon of parliamentary politics par excellence, referring both to a possibility of an alternation in government and to the temporariness of any government. This very temporariness makes *Herrschaft* combinable with political freedom in a representative government (compare Weber's two letters to Robert Michels from 1908 and 1910: Weber 1990: 618 and 1994a: 761).

It was from this perspective – and not from any normative ideal of democracy – that Weber appreciated the studies on party politics by Bryce (1888), Ostrogorski (1903) and Michels (1910). He understood the oligarchic and centralistic tendencies as related to an increase of freedom created by the new partisan forms of political life, which were more or less depreciated by all the thinkers longing for national unity and effective government (for the French discussion around 1900, see Rosanvallon 1998).

The studies on party politics by the authors mentioned above and by Weber himself (besides the letters from 1906 to 1910 – see Senigaglia 1995) refer to tendencies and remedies by which the political agents tended to diminish or control openness in the polity (see also Rosanvallon 1992, esp. 299–338). He did not consider the professionalisation of party and electoral politics or even the formation of a party machine as dangerous. This was the case only with the tendency to turn partisan freedom into a party monopoly. He saw in these phenomena a threat that could have closed down the new chances of parliamentary politics from within and, by doing so, extinguished the openness of governance and policies in a far more radical manner than was possible for the *Ancien Régime*.

Bureaucratisation and the chances of politics

Max Weber was, since his youth, a fierce critic of apolitism. This critique was closely related to his global historical perspective. The presence of politics and politicians belongs to the characteristics of Weber's occidental *Sonderweg* (Weber 1919c: 38, 41; compare also Weber 1922: 793), which was, however, threatened by several sorts of apolitism, some of which he presents as analogous to those practised in ancient cultures. In this perspective, the political powerlessness of the Liberal and Social Democratic parties in Germany and the political immaturity of judgement among the German citizens in general, as well as the tendency to seek solutions from 'science' to political questions, are the key critiques as early as in his Freiburg inaugural lecture. His perspective of analysing these expressions of the apolitical spirit concentrates on finding realistic chances to overcome them.

Beginning around 1905, Weber sees the most important form of apolitism in the tendency toward bureaucratisation (see Weber 1906b: 279; 1906d: 442). It appears to him as a danger of the return of apolitism under modern conditions. Bureaucracy is, according to Weber, an indispensable political instrument in the modern state, in capitalist enterprises as well as in parties. Bureaucracy as a means should thus be sharply distinguished from the apparently irresistible tendency toward bureaucratisation, which was still unknown to Constant in the early nineteenth century. The triumph of bureaucratisation actualises, according to Weber, the opposition between order and freedom in a new form.

Thus, when criticising universal bureaucratisation (see esp. Weber 1909a: 277–8; 1918d: 220–3), Weber understands *Freiheit* as a counter-concept not only to tyranny or despotism but also to order in general, even if he sometimes uses the concept of *freiheitliche Ordnung* (Weber 1918d: 275). In this critique, Weber cannot rely on the conventional critique of state intervention, because bureaucratisation also concerns capitalist enterprises, parties and so on. In the final pages of the 'Agrarverhältnisse' Weber presents a kind of prophecy, a historical interpretation according to which bureaucratisation will one day (*irgendwann*) win over capitalism (Weber 1909a: 278). The 'anarchy of production' would then be replaced by an irresistible order, such as in ancient Egypt. In his contributions to the sessions of 'Verein für Sozialpolitik', Weber accentuates the critique of order and asks whether there are chances to find counterweights to the inevitable tendency toward bureaucratisation (Weber 1910b: 407, 414).

The Russian studies manifest Weber's own turn toward a clear advocacy of parliamentary government and even democracy. In his letters to Friedrich

Naumann in subsequent years, we can detect his growing concern for the proposals to limit the powers of the emperor and make the government responsible to the parliament of the German *Reich* (Weber 1990: 202–5, 546–7, 587–8, 711–15). Against a substantialist egalitarianism, still upheld by Michels, Weber insists that only political democratisation is perhaps realisable in the foreseeable future, but that is *gar nicht so wenig* [certainly worth appreciation] (Weber 1990: 423).

During World War I, Weber recurrently presented proposals for reforming the constitution of the Reich in order to improve the parliamentary and public control of state officials (see Weber 1917a, b). The *locus classicus* of Weber's critique of order and bureaucratisation is his book *Parlament und Regierung im neugeordneten Deutschland* from 1918. In it, Weber restates his thesis on the inevitability of bureaucratisation and searches for political counterweights to it. The point of these essays is to assert a parallel with the chances to save some parcels of the ' "individualistic" freedom of movement' or democracy as a medium to control the rule of officials, as well as of politicians against officials, incompetent in specifically political matters (Weber 1918d: 222).

The representative system of government serves for Constant as an instrument of political freedom compatible with both the independence of the private sphere and the control of the rulers. In Weber's conceptual horizon, the representative system, combined with universal suffrage and parliamentary responsibility of government, has the additional advantage of giving the chances for the formation of professional politicians. They can control the officials and, of course, compete with each other for posts in the parties, the parliament, government and administration. Politicians worth the name also exercise a freedom in making politically responsible choices between policy alternatives, something unknown to the officials' style of thinking and acting. The opposition between freedom and order is also visible in the opposition between the ideal types of politicians and officials (see esp. Weber 1918d: 233; 1919c: 53–4). The professional politicians can, however, only get their legitimation through the audience of 'occasional politicians'.

Freedom also meant for Weber, in this respect, a clear opposition to the 'identitarian' assumptions of ancient liberty. Although Weber speaks of the equality of the citizens (Weber 1917f: 167, 172), this does not prevent a differentiation in degree in their political engagement according to choice, political competence or political trust.

Despite his rejection of 'ancient liberty', Weber's apology for the politician's freedom of action has some similarities to the ancient republics' celebration of the virtuosity of politicians. He rejects the suspicion common to liberal, socialist or anarchist views, which tend to understand action as a licence or caprice that should be held in check by laws. Weber considered laws as instruments in the political struggle, which was the most concrete manifestation of freedom. Weber's critique of the nominal *Bürger* of the German empire is directed against their passive *Untertan* [loyal subject] mentality (besides Weber 1917f, see 1909a: 278). We can interpret his notion of the occasional politician as a provocative counter-concept to the *Untertan* and as a form of citizenship that implies a political self-understanding in the fight against the claim of bureaucratic orders.

Freedom as contingency

Against this background, I find it important to discuss Weber's nominalistic rethinking of the concepts of human sciences, his theory of action and his late political writings in terms of the key concept, *Chancen*, connecting them to each other. The theory of action also gives perspective to his discussion of *Freiheit* as a precondition of life-conduct (for a clear expression of this concept, see Weber 1904–5/20: 14).

Considering the contemporary situation to be dominated by a universal tendency toward bureaucratisation, Weber is not content in his apology for freedom with the commonplace arguments on tolerance and pluralism. As the examples analysed above indicate, his view could, rather, be summarised by two more radical principles: 'freedom as openness to change' and 'freedom as conflict'. Both of them stress that freedom does not refer to the results of activities or to the goals to be achieved by human actions but, rather, to the situation of acting. To understand the connection between conflict and openness as dimensions of freedom, we have to discuss in detail Weber's theory of action and reflect on its significance for his political theory.

In the polemical or programmatic essays of his *Wissenschaftslehre*, Weber also discusses the philosophical questions of freedom, although with a tendency to move them from the 'metaphysical' level to that of empirical research and with a political dimension always implied. Weber's polemics are directed not only against naturalism and evolutionism but also against essentialist forms of both determinism and antideterminism (Weber 1903/06). In the 'Objektivität' article of 1904, Weber sketches a programme for the human sciences (*Kulturwissenschaften*) in which human freedom is no limit – either as an obstacle or as a refuge – to the intelligibility of action but is, rather, its point of departure. In short, freedom refers to the contingency of action (for an interpretation, see Palonen 1998: 111–42).

Weber understands action in finalistic terms. But the point of his conception is to overcome the ends–means dualism without rejecting it. In the programmatic discussion, the dualism is relativised, both from its origins in *Chancen* and from hindsight through *Nebenfolgen* (Weber 1904b: 149–50). These 'side effects' consist of a special sort of chances that refers to something that is not expected. Weber's point is that some side effects are always to be expected: the horizon of chances is only partially intelligible before the event.

Chances and side effects refer to the 'action face' of the 'objective possibility', which Weber discussed from the perspective of historiography in a polemic against Eduard Meyer (Weber 1906a); the concepts also hint at a more general presupposition in Weber's thinking. They legitimate the specific Weberian view on freedom as openness, dependent on the plurality of human actions and the conflicts between them. In this view, freedom is a condition of the openness of action, which turns the complete realisation of any predetermined project to be not only impossible but also undesirable: the side effects can make the non-desirability of the earlier chosen ends visible. In this perspective, freedom is thus related to the horizon of chances – the side effects indicate ex post some unexpected forms of them – rather than to the choice of some definite ends which are always related to the horizon of chances.

It is characteristic that, in his polemic against Meyer, Weber presents the politician as a paradigm for a person acting in a situation in which actions are both contingent and intelligible. Historians should also treat past situations according to this paradigm, as ones in which actions other than those which were followed would have also been possible, in order to understand the course of action that was realised (Weber 1906a: 267–8).

In the Weberian conceptual horizon, the possible (*Möglichkeit*) appears more real than the 'reality' (*Wirklichkeit*). In his perspectivist view of knowledge, *Wirklichkeit* is a limiting concept only for something that can never be exhaustively conceptualised (Weber 1903/06: 13–35). The possible is, on the contrary, something 'real' in the experience of the person acting, as a chances open for action and as a side effect to be taken into consideration in action (compare Weber's formula of politics as 'the art of the impossible', 1917c: 514, against the inverse formula of Bismarckian *Realpolitik*). The normative ends and the instrumental means, aiming at altering reality, are always related to this double horizon of the possible in action. The 'weighing' of alternative courses of action thus becomes more complicated and more demanding than in the simple means–ends model in which chances and side effects are treated as secondary or as given.

Weber's *Chancen* should not be understood as extraordinary but as rare chances in the sense of the classical concept of *kairos*. The human situation is, rather, characterised by the insight that there are always some *Chancen* available, some chances to act otherwise, even if their practical significances tend to be the same. The politically important question is not, primarily, whether one can use chances but, rather, whether one can construct different chances in situations, so that one can weigh their degrees of risk and choose between them.

My point is to emphasise that this model of Weberian theories of knowledge and action is also included both in his view of individual life-conduct and in his vocabulary of political theory. I argue that, in both cases, the conception could be expressed in the formula of 'freedom-as-contingency' (of human actions). It is not only a 'recognition of contingency' (Rorty 1989: 26, 46), but it is 'dealing with the contingent event', as Pocock's formula for politics points out (1975: 156). Indeed, freedom and action, life-conduct and politics, are for Weber more or less different aspects of naming the same complex of contingency.

When quoting Pocock's formula, I am, however, not identifying the Weberian conceptions of politics and contingency with the Machiavellian ones. The Weberian contingency is not to be understood as a relation between *fortuna*, *virtù* and corruption. The universal tendency toward bureaucratisation has, according to Weber, made the *fortuna* more or less disappear from the experience of the contemporary world, and it is against bureaucratisation that new elements of contingency are to be found. In Weber's historiography, contingency is reconceptualised in terms of objective possibilities and, in his action theory, in terms of the *Chancen* (for a closer discussion, compare Palonen 1998: 130–42, 209, 216).

In the Weberian conceptual horizon, freedom refers to three sorts of contingency of action and, in particular, of politics. The first is the lack of 'sufficient grounds', the necessity of the agents to choose the course and manner of action. The second is the fragility, if not futility, of all chosen projects, susceptible to be turned down or changed in their sense, due to the side effects of the action in the context, which also obliges – and gives a chances – to revise earlier choices (see Weber 1919c: 75–6). A third is inherent in the action, an operative figure of playing in action, of making the action intelligible in terms of chances and side effects. This view makes use of the constitutive aspects of the situation, such as the strategies of the action of others and the historical constellation of the chances.

In comparison with both teleological and normative-instrumental views on liberty, the Weberian freedom-as-contingency is, of course, elusive and disillusioning, related to the historical process of *Entzauberung* [breaking the spell]. It does not promise anything more than that there are always chances to act in opposed ways, but none of them are '100 percent' chances. The realisability of chances is never sure, their side effects are impossible to count in detail, and the actions of other agents may have to be intentionally resisted in order to prevent the use of some chances or to alter their consequences. This situation contains, however, the condition for learning to play with contingency as the 'exercise' of human and political freedom. Weber himself remained critical toward the 'opportunistic' consequences of freedom-as-contingency and demanded the politician to be a person with a clear hierarchy of value choices in the judgment and use of chances (Weber 1919c: 73–6).

The choices concerning individual life-conduct always contain a political dimension. In the Weberian nominalism, the political choices are always actions of individuals who are in insecure relations with their opponents, allies and adherents. The individuals' choices are related to the contingent constellations and regulations of the horizon of chances, but they are also exemplary in creating new profiles, which per se already alter the available horizons of chances.

Weber and existential freedom

The politician serves for Weber, as I have already indicated, as a kind of paradigm for a person facing the multiple freedom of the contingency in her or his choices of action. Although the choices of the professional politician do not, at least primarily, concern her or his own life-conduct, the insight into the contingency of the individual's life-conduct gives the 'occasional politician' a chance to take the professional politician as a model. Weber's 'existential' model in 'Wissenschaft als Beruf' concerning 'the last sense [Sinn] of one's own activity' (Weber 1919e: 20) is parallel to the situation of the politician. The individual and the political aspect are both intelligible through his conception of freedom-as-contingency as an operative principle of action.

Conversely, the individual life-conduct may also become a paradigm for exemplary political action for others. This becomes important especially in an era in which the nineteenth-century politicising phenomena – parties, votes and elections – were threatened from within by bureaucratisation. Both the inventions of profiled individual forms of life-conduct and the breaks with some norms or conventions regulating life-conduct may become objects of both imitation and invention of different choices of similar type. The Weberian conception of liberty marks both a break with 'liberal' and 'republican' views on liberty and a beginning for a new type of freedom, individual and political at the same time.

This sort of freedom, although its proponents hardly acknowledge the 'debt to Max Weber', has become an important part of twentieth-century continental political thought. In a sense, Weber can be considered as a precursor of the 'existentialist' view of freedom. For this reason, I want to end my analysis of Weber's rethinking of freedom with a short comparison with Sartre's views, which also depart from the assumptions that human beings are always free, that unfreedom is a product of human freedom and that individual freedom is always political.

Human beings are 'condemned to be free', as Sartre's famous formula in *L'être et le neant* (*Being and Nothingness*) goes (Sartre 1943: 537, 541). The political point of this formula is that the limitations of freedom are produced from within as results of free actions. A dimension of the freedom of life-conduct is also present in situations in which the range of choices is extremely narrow, as is clearly manifested by Sartre's plays. Sartre's concept of sovereignty in *Critique de la raison dialectique* (*Critique of Dialectical Reason*) signifies a political extension of the situation of being condemned to be free (Sartre 1960: esp. 666, 672). The specific contingent aspect in the human situation, which makes it impossible to leave freedom, is in *L'être et le neant* a negative fact, the lack *(manque)*, in the *Critique*, a negative condition of human history, the scarcity *(rareté)* that makes history possible. Sartre's story of a self-loss of freedom in the first volume of the *Critique* manifests how it is possible to go from a radical existential premise of freedom to a more or less complete practical unfreedom in which the sovereignty of the *praxis* is made powerless by its alienation. However, the project of the recovery of freedom is also, from its beginning, subject to alienating tendencies (see Palonen 1992: 72–7).

The initial chapter of Weber's *Wirtschaft und Gesellschaft* (Weber 1922: 1–30) can be seen as a parallel to the Sartrean story in the *Critique*. For Weber also, freedom remains omnipresent and inalienable in the formal sense that any agent has some chances, some 'shares of power' at her or his disposal. Departing from human actions and from the relations between individual agents, Weber constructs a net of social orders *(gesellschaftliche Ordnungen und Mächte*, as they are called in his original title for the volume) in which the chances within the specific types of order appear to be by each new step more structured and hierarchised. The point is, more clearly than in the case of Sartre, that Weber's story is a purely formal one: he only tries to make the formation of tight orders intelligible as a product of inter-individual actions and relations. Also, the state, as a *Herrschaftsverband* of a special kind (Weber 1922: 28–30), is nothing more than a complex of chances whose realisation is never secure. The existential implication of Weber's programme consists in the nominalistic insight that even tight and extremely bureaucratised orders have no ontological existence of their own, but their legitimacy is based on specific structures of chances. This moment of chances as an expression of freedom makes any legitimation fragile and subject to sudden erosions or delegitimating policies.

There are, of course, well-known differences between Weber and Sartre. Weber did not want to have anything to do with the Hegelian dialectic, and I do not think that a Sartrean nominalisation would have made him more favourable toward it. Sartre's pathos of revolution, despite his scepticism about the realisability of revolutionary changes, remains entirely alien to Weber. A theoretical ground for this difference might be seen in the fact that, for Sartre, the possibilities refer to projects in the future, while for Weber, *Chancen* are available in the present situation (see Palonen 1998: 272–3).

Despite these differences, the argumentation structure of freedom within a nominalistic perspective is surprisingly similar between Weber and Sartre. Above all, freedom, power and politics are for them no antonymic concepts but, on the contrary, different faces of the same phenomenon. In this sense, it is refreshing both to read Sartre as a 'Weberian' thinker and to consider Weber more generally as a political theorist of existential freedom.

Chapter Seven

Was Max Weber a 'Nationalist'? A Study in the Rhetoric of Conceptual Change

The rhetoric of self-identification

Max Weber is commonly regarded as having been a German 'nationalist'. In this article I will question this thesis by analysing in rhetorical terms the conceptual changes concerning Weber's 'nationalism'. I discuss the inclusions and exclusions, identifications and disidentifications, confessions and rejections that can be reconstructed in Weber's work with regard to the figure of 'nationalism'. My point of departure is a strict nominalist view, according to which concepts 'are' the way in which agents use them. Thus, I refuse to discuss the essentialist question of whether or not Weber 'really' was a nationalist or such related topics as what is meant by 'nationalism' in general. Questions like these tend to assume that 'nationalism' is an 'objectively' existing entity with a well-known 'ordinary meaning', which then could be used as a measure for judgement.

The anglophone political theory still largely operates by constructing and classifying 'isms' or 'ideologies' as if these were independent of the specific perspectives and problematics of political agents or theorists. For theorists such as Max Weber, these types of projections of party lines on the level of intellectual and conceptual history appear especially misleading. Even a more sophisticated attempt, such as Michael Freeden's 'morphological' approach to the political ideologies (Freeden 1996), retains an objectivistic 'core' in each of the 'ideologies', allowing rhetorical and conceptual variation only in their peripheral dimensions. The agent's own rhetoric of self-identification and dis-identification as well as the historical changes due to the nuances in vocabulary, meaning, evaluation and range of the reference of the concepts are regarded as secondary.

Weber's relation to 'nationalism' provides me with an occasion for a study of conceptual change within the *oeuvre* of a single author. For this purpose, I am interested only in Weber's conceptual horizon as expressed in his texts, and I use historical events and so on here purely as a background for the understanding of conceptual change. The 'truth' of Weber's views is bracketed. As Quentin Skinner writes on Machiavelli's beliefs on mercenary armies, asking for the 'truth' of these beliefs 'will be something analogous to asking whether the king of France is bald' (Skinner 1988: 256).

From my conceptual perspective, a classification of Weber's writings as 'academic' and 'polemical' does not make sense. Weber's pamphlets on suffrage, democracy, presidential powers and so on are key sources for our understanding of his theorising about politics. His nominalist striving for conceptual revision also shapes his interventions in daily politics. He does not simply adapt himself to the vocabulary of the audience, but makes new distinctions and introduces revisions in meaning or vocabulary (see Palonen 2000). Weber's explicit remarks on 'nationalism' become intelligible only when connected to his nominalist style of concept formation.

My starting point is a comparison of the rhetoric of identification in two formulas: the first from Weber's inaugural lecture at Freiburg University, published in 1895, and the second from a speech given in December 1918.

In a well-known statement from the Freiburg lecture Weber makes a kind of confession and declares himself as an 'economic nationalist':[1] 'We economic nationalists measure the classes who lead the nation or aspire to do so with the one political criterion that we regard as sovereign' (Weber 1994b: 20). To my knowledge this is the only passage in Weber's published work in which he commits himself to 'nationalism' of any kind. This passage does not justify the use of 'nationalism' as a global label for Weber's *oeuvre*. Changes in Weber's political thinking and in his relationships to political practices in Germany should rather be considered as occasions for a conceptual change in this respect.

I was struck to find in Weber's writings in 1918 a formulation that directly contradicts the nationalism thesis. According to a newspaper report on a speech given in Wiesbaden on 5 December 1918, Weber advocates an 'anti-nationalistic' but 'national' policy for the post-war Germany: 'Our policy will, furthermore, necessarily be anti-nationalistic, not antinational.'[2] 'Unsere Politik wird ferner antinationalistisch, nicht antinational sein müssen' (Weber 1918c: 122).

My first question is: has Weber changed his self-identity from 'nationalist' to 'national anti-nationalist'? I will briefly present the controversy among the Weberologists regarding this topic. Both Weber's formulae are rhetorically ambivalent, and I shall check them by comparing the passages with other formulations in Weber's work. I remain, however, convinced that the second formulation is significant for Weber's changing relation to the concept of nationalism.

The next question is: why did Weber change his mind? Is this change related to a revised view of the meaning of 'nationalism' or, rather, to a revised attitude toward 'nationalism'? Or, in the technical terms of Quentin Skinner (1974), is Weber's changing relation to the concept of nationalism due to a change in the 'range of reference' of the concept of nationalism or to a change in 'attitude' towards it, independently of a change in the concept of 'nationalism'?

In the final section I shall make some critical remarks on the study of 'isms', such as 'nationalism', as objects of study in a historically oriented political theory, and discuss the chances of a historical and rhetorical study of concepts – as an alternative to the more conventional approaches to political thought.

---

1. 'Denn an jenem politischen Wertmassstab, der uns ökonomischen Nationalisten der einzig für uns souveräne ist, messen wir auch die Klassen, welche die Leitung der Nation in der Hand haben oder erstreben' (Weber 1895b: 560).

2. Translations by the author unless otherwise stated.

The controversy over Weber's 'nationalism'

Weber has always appeared as an author difficult to classify according to the common textbook criteria of 'isms' (see Schelting 1934). The initial move in the present Weberologist controversy was undertaken by Wolfgang Mommsen in his book *Max Weber und die deutsche Politik 1890–1920* (1959, expanded edition 1974). His critique was supported by Raymond Aron in his lecture 'Max Weber und die Machtpolitik' (1964). Contrary to Weber's liberal and democratic reputation in post-war Germany, both of them insisted that Weber was a nationalist. In the 1980s Mommsen's interpretation of the Freiburg inaugural lecture was criticised by Wilhelm Hennis (1987), and later also by others, such as Lawrence Scaff (1989) and Catherine Colliot-Thélène (1990), although it did also have its supporters (e.g. Anter 1995).

Mommsen first quotes the view of Weber's former fellow member in the Deutsche Demokratische Partei (DDP), Theodor Heuss, who later was the first Bundespräsident of the Federal Republic. According to Heuss, Max Weber had been 'nationalist in all his instincts'. Mommsen also claims that this judgement was justified at least by the tone (Tenor) of the Freiburg inaugural lecture, in which Weber consciously declared himself to be an 'economic nationalist' (Mommsen 1974: 40).

Although here Mommsen makes use of Weber's own words I think he is too hasty in his judgement, because he does not pay attention to the question of how they are used. To declare himself as an 'economic nationalist' cannot be judged simply as an inclusion into a broader concept of 'nationalist'; rather the qualification already marks a differentiation from unqualified 'nationalist' identification. However, in general Mommsen's tone concerning Weber's nationalism is nuanced insofar as he acknowledges both the specificity of and historical changes in Weber's concept of the nation. Mommsen concludes that Weber did not question the validity of the national idea and, in this respect, says Mommsen, he was a prisoner of his epoch (Mommsen 1974: 68).

However, here Mommsen neither distinguishes between 'national' and 'nationalist', as Weber himself does, nor does he pay attention to passages in which this distinction is explicitly made. In general, among the proponents of the nationalist thesis, Weber's views are judged without problematising either his conception of nationalism or the rhetoric of its advocacy in his texts. In Mommsen's case this is not surprising, as the programmatic history of concepts was not yet sketched in the late 1950s, nor were there any signs of 'the rhetorical turn' in historiography.

In his *Max Webers Fragestellung*, Wilhelm Hennis revised Weber's place in intellectual history, especially his relations to the older historical economics. It is from this perspective that Hennis rereads Weber's early work. By 1893, Weber had declared that the East Elbian agrarian workers' situation should be analysed 'unter dem Gesichtspunkt der Staatsräson' [in terms of reasons of state] (Weber 1893b: 180). Against Mommsen's interpretation of the nation as the supreme value and purpose of the Weberian political theory (Mommsen 1974: 67–8), Hennis saw the role of the nation, rather, as marking for Weber the 'radius' of the *Lebensordnung* without a normative and teleological commitment (Hennis 1987: 87). His specific concern was to reinterpret the famous passage in Weber's lecture on the value criterion of economic policy: 'The economic policy of a German state, and, equally, the criterion of value used by a German economic theorist, can therefore only be a German policy or criterion'[3] (Weber 1994b: 15).

According to Hennis, this sentence had always been misunderstood as 'nationalistic'. He, however, emphasises the word *deshalb*, which refers to the previous sentence, in which the 'Qualität der Menschen' [quality of human beings] is seen as the normative purpose of using the *Staatsräson* (Hennis 1987: 139). Although Hennis does not explicitly refer to Weber's 'economic nationalism', he understands the point of Weber's formula, namely the political control of economic judgements in the name of *Staatsräson*. For Hennis, this control is necessary for the higher 'cultural' purpose of improving the *Lebensführung* in each country (see also Scaff 1989: 31). But his interpretation is still insufficient for the understanding of Weber's conceptual and rhetorical point, and Weber's later distance from 'nationalism' remains unanalysed by Hennis.

Catherine Colliot-Thélène, in her introduction to the French translation of Weber's inaugural lecture, first acknowledges that it seems that the principle of his engagement with the national state did not remain unchanged from 1895 to 1920. As opposed to Aron, she denies that the 'nationalism' of the young Weber was an unreflected adoption of the dominant Wilhelmine ideology. It should, rather, be looked at from a Nietzschean perspective: the national power (*puissance*) is not desirable per se but as a means in the service of human greatness (Colliot-Thélène 1990: 104, 107, 110). However, no explicit reference can be found in her article to 'economic nationalism'.

To sum up, the revisions of Weber's views do not question his 'nationalism', but rather emphasise the peculiarities and the historical changes in his 'nationalism'. They have provided textual and contextual evidence against the received view, but, in order to better understand the Weberian formulas quoted at the beginning and the historical differences between them, a more detailed conceptual and rhetorical analysis remains to be done. In this chapter, I present some illustrative examples based on the best available sources – representative anecdotes in the sense of Kenneth Burke (1945) – for such a study.

From 'economic nationalist' to 'anti-nationalist national policy'

It seems worth asking whether Weber's 'economic nationalism' also marks a self-irony by using the title of 'nationalism' in an unconventional context. Economic nationalism does not, in his case, simply signify a protectionist economic policy, but, more generally, a control of economic development by political means. This has several layers, including the Hennisian 'cultural' dimension of the 'quality of

---

3.   'Die Volkswirtschaftspolitik eines deutschen Staatswesens ebenso wie der Wertmaßstab eines deutschen volkswirtschaftlichen Theoretikers können deshalb nur deutsche sein' (Weber 1895b: 560).

human beings'. However, the primacy of the political in economic judgements as used by Weber also means an overcoming of the narrow private economic interests of the Prussian Junkers in favour of a wider and political criterion of the *Machtinteressen der Nation* or *Staatsräson* (Weber 1895b: 560–1).

In the Junker practice of hiring cheaper Polish agrarian workers (from Russian areas) to do seasonal work, Weber sees a neglect of the *Staatsräson* and a lack of political judgement regarding economic questions (Weber 1895b: 550–3). The private interests of the Junkers neglected the political interests of Germany in its relations both to Russia and to the other European powers. The Weberian concept of *Staatsräson* always refers to his view on European politics as a balance of great powers (*Mächte*). In the 1890s, the era of *Weltpolitik*, Weber saw Germany's position as world power threatened by its domestic policy, especially by its subordination to the private interests of the Junkers. In this context, the 'national' character of the German state was for Weber, strictly speaking, not a value criterion but rather a historical condition for playing the role of great power in the late nineteenth century (Weber 1895b: 560–1; for the role of *Staatsräson* as a criterion of political judgment in Weber's early critique of depoliticising tendencies, see Palonen 1998: 60–1).

Had Weber, thus, given up his 'nationalism' (of this special kind), when a month after the end of the World War I he advocated an anti-nationalist yet national policy? Could someone like Weber have been turned into a 'national anti-nationalist'? Before considering this question, a closer look at Weber's nation-vocabulary in the post-war context is necessary.

In his Afterword to the volume on Weber's contributions to post-war German politics, Wolfgang Mommsen speaks without hesitation of 'nationalistic elements' when he assesses Weber's speeches around the foundation of the DDP and the campaign for the Constituent Assembly in January 1919 (Mommsen 1991: 159). Mommsen thus did not see any reduction of 'nationalism' in Weber's post-war writings. In order to criticise this view, I shall analyse Weber's own vocabulary in detail. Mommsen does not make use of the nuances in Weber's formulations, which, however, would be necessary for understanding the seemingly small yet potentially significant shifts in Weber's conceptual horizon.

One way of analysing Weber's horizon of 'nationalism' is to draw attention to its rhetorical redescriptions (see Skinner 1996: Ch. 4; 1999b), that is, to expressions which are sometimes used synonymously with nationalism, but which have different normative connotations. One such expression was, of course, 'chauvinism'. If we compare Weber's vocabulary from the 1890s with his post-war vocabulary, the role of chauvinism is clearly different. According to the index of volume I/4 of the *Max-Weber-Gesamtausgabe*, Weber refers only once in the 1890s to 'chauvinism', and then in quotation marks, in order to avoid obvious objection to his views on the 'national' policy of Germany in the East Elbian areas: 'anyone, who might think that it is for "chauvinistic" reasons, that we follow a national policy in the eastern areas either cannot or does not want to understand what is the issue'.[4]

---

4. 'Wer glauben sollte, daß wir im Osten nationale Politik aus 'Chauvinismus' treiben – nun, der kann oder will nicht verstehen, um was es sich handelt' (Weber 1893b: 182).

Weber then clearly saw that his defence of a 'national policy' was falsely accused of 'chauvinism'. This was a defensive argument. However, in his post-war writings, he himself on several occasions turned 'chauvinism' into a description of the probable and dangerous consequences which would threaten Germany if it were not treated in an 'honourable' manner in the peace negotiations:[5]

> all this would obviously lead to a situation in which even the politically most radical German worker would turn to chauvinists – not now but after a year and a day, after the present unrest and the following exhaustion have passed away.

A reference to German *Irredenta* is interpreted by Mommsen (1991: 159) as a 'crescendo' of Weber's post-war nationalism. Weber refers to *Irredenta* on two occasions, again in the manner of a prognosis of the consequences of a peace not worthy of a great power, and not as a claim of self-identification (Weber 1918a: 126; 1919a: 31). On the first occasion Weber uses the word 'nationalism' with a certain positive connotation in the imaginary situation of defending the German *Irridenta* in the east against 'foreign' rule. Here 'nationalism' refers to a kind of defence of the German *Staatsräson*, as opposed to the sort of 'nationalism' that was practised by the proto-militarist student corporations:[6]

> The speaker addressed the students … Who, in the face of a danger to German irridenta, is not ready to make use of revolutionary methods and to risk scaffold and prison, should not in the future call himself a nationalist.

Once again, 'nationalism' is given a slightly ironic tone, referring to the Weberian distinction between an ethics of conviction and an ethics of responsibility presented a couple of months later in 'Politik als Beruf' (Weber 1919c). The nationalism of the student corporations was only a *Gesinnung* [mindset], while a consequent 'nationalistic' value orientation in the post-war situation would have required taking responsibility for a definite policy and all of its consequences. However, there is no hint in the quoted passage that Weber would have identified himself with this sort of 'nationalistic' variant of the ethic of responsibility.

On the contrary, there are clear hints that Weber, in the post-war context, consciously dissociated the 'national' from neighbouring concepts (Skinner 1996) with which it was often associated. In early November 1918, a few days before the German capitulation, a newspaper report used the following formula for Weber's

---

5. 'Das alles würde selbstverständlich dazu führen, daß auch der politisch radikalste Arbeiter Deutschlands – nicht jetzt, wohl aber nach Jahr und Tag, wenn der jetzige Taumel und die folgende Ermattung vorüber sind – zum Chauvinisten würde' (Weber 1919f: 61).

6. 'Der Redner wandte sich an die Studentenschaft … Wer in der drohenden deutschen Irridenta nicht bereit ist, revolutionäre Methoden anzuwenden und Schafott und Zuchthaus zu riskieren, der soll sich künftig nicht einen Nationalisten nennen' (Weber 1918a: 126).

speech: 'We are now facing the necessity of a complete re-orientation of foreign policy. This should be a national but not an imperialistic one.'[7]

'National' is here used as a counter-concept to 'imperialistic'. The qualification of the policy *antinationalistisch, nicht antinational* a month later is clearly a variation of this thesis, although a more radical formulation. Not only is 'nationalism' then distinguished from its 'compromised' variants, but Weber takes a step further in the rhetorical redescription and replaces the opposition 'national vs imperialistic' with a distinction between 'national' and 'nationalistic'. In addition, although we must once again be cautious in regarding this as Weber's conviction, it is remarkable that, at least with regard to a situational strategy for German foreign policy after the defeat, he is prepared to support an 'anti-nationalistic' policy.

Weber speaks in a similar sense, but again using 'imperialistic' as a counter-attribute to the 'national', in his brochure *Deutschlands künftige Staatsform*, written at approximately the same time as the Wiesbaden speech. In his thesis, he writes in the first paragraph on new 'tasks' of renouncing the imperialist dreams:[8]

> A clear renunciation of imperialistic dreams and adoption of a purely autonomous ideal of nationality. Self-determination of all German areas aiming at unification into an independent state for the purpose of peaceful care of our own qualities within the sphere of the League of Nations.

Thus, although Weber's use of the 'anti-nationalistic' attribute is only occasional and is quoted from a newspaper report, there are other expressions in Weber's post-war writings which distinguish between 'national' and 'nationalistic'. These expressions make it wholly plausible that Weber really could advocate an 'anti-nationalistic' policy. In other words, close attention to rhetoric and vocabulary indicate that Mommsen's attribution of the title of 'nationalism' to Weber's post-war writings is contrary to Weber's own usage.

In this sense, I argue that the shift in Weber's conceptual horizon from the (qualified) 'nationalism' of the 1890s to a distancing from the use of this concept in 1918–19 represents a real and significant conceptual change.

Weber's changing conception of 'nationalism'

The arguments I have presented so far seem to imply a clear tendency towards narrowing the meaning of 'nationalism' in Weber's vocabulary. Now I shall check this thesis by taking 'snapshots' from Weber's other writings and also through the contextual evidence provided by the secondary literature. Weber's attitude toward this narrower concept of 'nationalism' was clearly much more critical than

---

7.　'Wir stehen nun vor der Notwendigkeit einer vollständigen Neuorientierung der äusseren Politik. Dies soll national, aber nicht imperialistisch sein' (Weber 1918b: 114).

8.　'Klare Verzicht auf imperialistische Träume und also rein autonomistisches Nationalitätsideal. Selbstbestimmung aller deutscher Gebiete zur Einigung in einem unabhängigen Staat zur rückhaltslos friedlicher Pflege unsrer Eigenart im Kreise des Volkerbunds' (Weber 1919a: 30).

that toward his earlier use of the concept. The eventual change in attitude will be discussed in the next section.

Weber's intellectual background was in the National Liberal party, which accepted Bismarck's policy in 1866. His 'uncle', the historian Hermann Baumgarten, was an important ideologist of this political move (see Baumgarten 1866), and his father also sat for some time on the Reichstag. From his early youth onwards, Max Weber was accustomed to talking politics, and in the 1880s Baumgarten, who by then, however, had severed ties with Bismarck, became Weber's political mentor (see Weber 1936). In the early 1890s, Weber moved towards pastor Friedrich Naumann's 'National-social' Association. It is Weber's reformist interest in the social and political consequences of the German–Prussian economic policy that can be seen in the background of his 'economic nationalism' (see Mommsen 1974: 1–36, 132–46; Scaff 1989: 11–72). The older, purely etatist, view on *Staatsräson* was not alone sufficient, and both domestic and socio-economic elements had to be included in the concept and in the political judgement of the relations between the great powers.

The introduction of the socio-economic dimension to the concept of the 'nation', especially the aspects of social integration and political participation, added a 'French' connotation to Weber's views, as opposed to the *Staatsräson* of the Prussian *Obrigkeitsstaat* [authoritarian state]. This does not, however, mean the neglect of the international dimension of the *Staatsräson*; on the contrary, this dimension was explicitly present in Weber's extension of the concept to domestic issues. Weber was committed to the *Weltpolitik*, to the extension of the competition between the 'great powers' outside Europe, which is visible, for example, in his advocacy of an export-oriented view on the German economy (e.g. Weber 1897). In contexts such as this, Weber does not, however, speak of 'nationalism'.

Weber joined the *Alldeutscher Verband* in 1893. According to Mommsen he originally did not reject clearly the 'ethnic' nationalism of the association. But Weber left the association in 1899 on the grounds that it was not radically enough opposed to the agrarian interests on their use of Polish agrarian workers (Mommsen 1974: 58–9). A new *völkisch* type of 'nationalism' with anti-Semitic connotations arose in the 1890s in both Germany and France, and the *Alldeutscher Verband* soon became one of the representatives of this kind of nationalism in Germany, of which Weber wanted no part. The Social Darwinist legitimation of nationalism was another aspect that aroused Weber's opposition (see his critique of 'rein zoologischen Nationalismus' [purely zoological nationalism] from 1911, quoted in Mommsen 1974: 70).

'Cultural' nationalism, however, remained a challenge for him, and he seems to have found a new perspective on this through his studies on the Russian Revolution of 1906. He speaks of 'extreme nationalism' without the slightest sympathies (Weber 1906c: 29, 60). He was impressed above all by the programmes of Russian liberals, especially those based on the views of the Ukrainian federalist Dragomanov from the 1880s on cultural autonomy as a means to deal with the nationality questions (Weber 1906c: esp. 21–31; see Mommsen 1974: 60–4).

During World War I, he used this idea in his proposals to integrate the Poles into the German Empire (Weber 1916a: 75).

Weber's most explicit discussions on the concept of the nation can be found in two discussion statements at a meeting of the German Sociological Association in 1912 as well as in two chapters of the older parts of *Wirtschaft und Gesellschaft*, written around 1913 (Mommsen 1974: 55–6). His remarks on all of these occasions are primarily academic and non-committed. The general tone stresses the complexity of the problematics, but in his reply to Paul Barth, Weber does cautiously formulate a kind of working 'definition' of the nation as a community based on emotions:[9]

> It would be possible to define the concept of the nation roughly as follows: it is a community based on feelings, for which an independent state would be an adequate expression; it is normally the case that the community brings about such a state.

From today's perspective, this view looks anachronistic when universalising the connection between 'nation' and 'state'. The same is even more clearly true for two discussion statements, in which Weber speaks of 'nationalist' reaction against the papal imperialism in the late Middle Ages (Weber 1912: 486).

Instead of this unhistorical use of concepts, Weber proposes a kind of 'deconstruction' of the concept in *Wirtschaft und Gesellschaft*. The general point of the chapter on the *Nation*, as political community in particular, is to illustrate with historical counter-examples the insufficiency of all commonly proposed candidates for 'defining' the nation and the hopelessness of the search for a definite concept. Weber, however, offers a minimalist and paradoxical proposal:[10]

> If the concept of 'nation' can in any way be defined unambiguously, it certainly cannot be stated in terms of empirical qualities common to those who count as members of the nation. In the sense of those using the term at a given time, the concept undoubtedly means, above all, that it is proper to expect from certain groups a specific sentiment of solidarity in the face of other groups. Thus, the concept belongs in the sphere of values.
>
> (Weber 1978: 922)

What, however, remains of such an allegedly common value after Weber's nominalistic destruction of all attempts to 'define' the concept by empirical

---

9. 'Es liesse sich ein Begriff von Nation wohl nur etwa so definieren: sie ist eine gefühlsmässige Gemeinschaft, deren adäquater Ausdruck ein eigener Staat wäre, die also normalerweise die Tendenz hat, einen solchen aus sich hervorzutreiben' (Weber 1912: 484).

10. '"Nation" ist ein Begriff, der, wenn überhaupt eindeutig, dann jedenfalls nicht nach empirischen gemeinsamen Qualitaten der ihr Zugerechneten definiert werden kann. Er besagt, im Sinne derer, die ihn jeweilig brauchen, zunächst unzweifelhaft, dass gewisse Menschengruppen ein spezifisches Solidaritätsempfinden anderen gegenüber zuzumuten sei, gehört also der Wertsphäre an' (Weber 1922: 528).

criteria? The minimalist 'definition' turns the concept into a mere matter of value. As an analytic concept, 'nation' only refers to a vague expectation of a feeling of solidarity. Weber's concept of 'nation' can thus be characterised as a 'descriptive-evaluative concept' (Skinner 1974), in which a tacit normative connotation is used to cover the emptiness of the common content among the users of this concept.

The normative, but, in its reference, empty character of the concept is also alluded to in an ironic passage emphasising the most eager 'nationalists' to be often of foreign origin (Weber 1922: 528). This is the only mention of 'nationalism' in the *Nation* chapter, and, according to Winckelmann's index, this is the only appearance of the concept in *Wirtschaft und Gesellschaft*.

After these moves to dissolve the core of the concept of 'nation', it becomes more intelligible that Weber himself, despite his continuous commitment to the 'value' of the nation, distances himself from 'nationalism'. He obviously viewed nationalism as presupposing the 'givenness' of the nation and hypostatising a policy into an 'ism'.

As is commonly known, Weber did, as many others, initially show some enthusiasm for the war and served a year as a voluntary administrative chief of a military hospital. Then, from autumn 1915 until the end of the war, he wrote several contributions against expansionist war aims – how far his own aims could be judged as 'expansionist' in retrospect does not matter here – and urged for a democratisation of the suffrage in Prussia. A commitment to a 'national viewpoint' remains central in Weber's wartime writings (e.g. Weber 1916a: 63), and he used the distinction between *Machtstaaten*, such as Germany, and *Kleinstaaten*, such as Denmark or Switzerland, as an instrument against the pacifist propaganda (esp. Weber 1916b: 39–41). This distinction was again based on his view of world politics as one in which only the great powers were the real players and the small states were dependent on the balance between the great powers.

The only reference to 'nationalism' in the index of the volume *Zur Politik im Weltkrieg* alludes to a passage from Weber's plea for universal suffrage and parliamentarism in Germany. Weber claims that just democratic parties are everywhere the main agents of nationalism:[11]

Democratic parties which *share in government* are bearers of nationalism everywhere. It is only natural that nationalism should be spreading amongst the masses in particular in an age that is becoming increasingly democratic in the way it provides access to the goods of national culture, the bearer of which is, after all, the *language* of the nation.

(Weber 1994b: 82

11. 'Überall sind mitherrschende [sic] demokratische Parteien Träger des Nationalismus. Der zunehmende Nationalismus der gerade der Massen ist nur natürlich in einem Zeitalter, welches die Teilnahme an den Gütern der nationalen Kultur, deren Träger nun einmal die nationale Sprache ist, zunehmend demokratisiert' (Weber 1917: 156).

This is a cool academic statement on the consequences of democratisation in a brochure in which Weber argues in great detail against all kinds of 'alternatives' to a democratised suffrage. According to Weber, bourgeois parties have no reason to be afraid of democratisation and democratisation by no means favours a Socialist revolution per se. At the same time in the quoted passage he alludes to a situation in which the dangers of nationalism are faced as a by-product of democratisation.

Even before World War I, Weber, then, was careful not to identify himself as a 'nationalist', and his wartime writings did not mean a backsliding into his earlier vocabulary. I can think of at least two different reasons why, while keeping with the 'nation' and 'national policy', he dissociated himself from 'nationalism' – to the point of advocating an 'anti-nationalist' policy in the situation following Germany's defeat in the war. First, the most vociferous 'nationalists' advocated extremist policies to which Weber was strictly opposed, that is, anti-Semitic, racist, chauvinist or expansionist policies. Any advocate of a 'national' policy at this time had explicitly to deny any support of these sorts of policies.

Second and more interesting is Weber's own style of concept formation. He was a strict nominalist who abhorred any essentialist, substantialist or collectivist concepts. If we look closely at his conceptualisation of the nation in *Wirtschaft und Gesellschaft*, it is based on the expectation of a feeling of solidarity. Like other concepts of expectation (see Weber 1913), it should be understood in terms of *Chancen*, which is a key concept for Weber. (For a closer discussion, see Palonen 1998: 133–42, 209–16). The 'nation' is based on an expectation of the availability of certain chances of solidarity. For Weber 'nation', like other *Ordnungen und Mächte* (his original subtitle for *Wirtschaft und Gesellschaft*), is a highly contingent product. For him to advocate 'nationalism' would obscure its contingent character.

Nationalism and nation

A shift in Weber's relation to 'nationalism' can thus be made intelligible. He moved towards using the concept in a narrower sense, and this move also enabled him to sever the link between 'nation' and 'nationalism' which he clearly presupposed in the 1890s. Or, using a football metaphor: Max Weber remained an engaged 'fan of Germany', but over the course of time he made it explicit that this did not imply harming the competitors, in particular, the smaller states. Their 'cultural tasks' in world politics were merely different from those of Germany as a great power (Weber 1916a).

However, my discussion leaves open the question of whether we can speak of a change in his normative orientation toward 'nationalism', independently of the changes in the concept. In order to answer this question, a certain link between 'nation' and 'nationalism' cannot be denied. Did Weber's increasingly critical attitude towards 'nationalism' also mean that the value of the core concept 'nation' was to some extent devalued, especially as compared with the state?

Weber's concept of the nation is not entirely distinguishable from the state, and both in the Freiburg lecture and later he explicitly uses the concept

Nationalstaat, although he also problematises, if not deconstructs, the relation between them in his discussion in *Wirtschaft und Gesellschaft*. His views in the 1890s transcended the conventional view on the *Staatsräson* in the name of the nation, but then, for example, his views on the cultural autonomy within a federal state again meant a step toward the primacy of the state. In his wartime writings, however, the 'nation' – in the 'French' sense of an integrative and participative unit – again gained superiority over the state, but was now dissociated from its *völkisch* connotations.

The advocacy of an 'anti-nationalist' policy for the defeated Germany meant perhaps a renewed emphasis on the state, as the key unit that participates in the competition of great powers. The affirmation of Germany's role as a *Machtstaat* appears in Weber's thinking to have retained its priority over the nation throughout the period. In other words, his ultimate point of reference is the political struggle between the great powers. Weber's post-war commitments, including his rejection of the Versailles Treaty, seem to refer to a danger of replacing the balance between competing powers by the hegemonic situation of one of them (see his remarks on Woodrow Wilson as 'der erste wirkliche Weltbeherrscher' [the first true world leader]: Weber 1918b: 113). It is not the fate of Germany but the presence of a plurality of 'powers' in world politics that is Weber's main anxiety after World War I.

I could invoke other Weberian value concepts, such as freedom and individuality (see Palonen 1999), but he hardly ever opposed them to the 'nation'. They, however, illustrate a perspective towards which his 'deconstruction' of the concept of the 'nation' was never followed at the level of his own political identifications. Unlike *Macht* and *Staat*, explicated as complexes of chances (Weber 1922: 28–9), *Nation* remained for Weber a quasi-mythical label containing a positive value, and he upheld this value by disregarding the specific chances contained in his own nominalist dissolution of the concept. In this sense, it seems to me that the relatively marginal change at the level of attitudes justifies calling Weber, although not a 'nationalist', an apologist of the nation state within the concert of great powers.

Conclusions

The received view of Weber as a 'nationalist' remains strong, not only in the Weber literature, but also through an 'impressionistic' reading of Weber's own texts. A revised interpretation of Weber's standpoint is achieved here through giving more systematic attention to his own vocabulary and rhetoric as well as to the conceptual shifts over time.

It seems to me that the critique of textbooks and anachronisms, present in anglophone political thought at least since Collingwood (1939, 1946), is even today not fully recognised. I regard this as remnant of a 'foundationalism' which assumes that at least some common core must be presupposed when using common concepts. Both rhetoric and history of concepts can, however, be used as heuristic instruments of analysis in order to avoid this sort of foundationalism. A source for this anti-foundationalism can also be found in Max Weber's perspectivist view of knowledge, as presented in his famous 'Objektivität' article (Weber 1904b).

Weber's writing on the concept of the *Nation* in *Wirtschaft und Gesellschaft* could also be used as a fine example of dissolving the foundationalist assumption. The clue, suggested by Weber himself in his 1918 Wiesbaden speech, is problematising the link between 'nation' and 'nationalism'. The *Spielräume* for both historical changes and rhetorical variations in Weber's thought can be analysed in terms of his own rhetorical moves. Interpreting Weber as a nominalist theorist who rethinks politics in terms of the operative contingency of *Chancen* (Palonen 1998) allows me to make the gap between 'nation' and 'nationalism' intelligible. Furthermore, we can ask whether his commitment, after all *(dennoch)*, to the 'nation' or 'Germany' remains a private belief, poorly adapted to his nominalist perspective to action and politics.

In this chapter I have practised a kind of microscopic variant in the study of the history of concepts. I have used a single author, a single concept, and two short quotations of different periods as a point of departure, which is then completed by further textual evidence and contextual background knowledge both of Weber and of politics and history in his time. While the programmatic history of concepts (e.g. Koselleck 1979) is mainly interested in macroscopic studies with extensive materials, my study indicates that a concentration on conceptual changes can gain advantages over conventional history ideas, including when short-term changes in the political usage of concepts are studied.

Chapter Eight

Imagining Max Weber's Reply to Hannah Arendt: Remarks on the Arendtian Critique of Representative Democracy[1]

Max Weber and Hannah Arendt are two major German political thinkers of the twentieth century. Since the 1980s, a remarkable reappraisal of the work of both has taken place: Weber is no longer judged solely as a sociologist and also Arendt has got rid of her reputation as nostalgic for the ancient polis. Currently specialist studies on both Arendt and Weber are booming, but remain, especially when their political thought is concerned, strangely unrelated to each other.

Hannah Arendt's work, especially her *On Revolution* (1963), has its value in the critique of the conventions of representative democracy in post-war Europe and the United States. Max Weber in his late pamphlets and essays presents arguments in favour of parliamentary democracy which have not lost their cogency in the age of praising new forms of direct action. Here, I want to carry out an exercise in political imagination: how would Weber reply to Arendt's arguments on suffrage and political representation? (see Palonen 1998, 2002, 2004a) I will follow the Weberian methodological principle that, in order to better understand realised history, one must construct an unrealised comparative alternative to it (Weber 1906a: 267). My thesis is that the depoliticising aspects in Arendt's thought are indebted to her contractarian assumptions.

I want also to connect the work of Weber and Arendt with contemporary debates on democracy, representation, parliamentarism and political liberty, as actualised in the work of such scholars as Pierre Rosanvallon, Frank Ankersmit and Quentin Skinner. None of them seems to deal in detail with the political writings of Weber or Arendt, but their work offer clues to an improved interpretation of the political significance of both. At the same time, invoking the work of both Arendt and Weber may produce a certain *Verfremdungseffekt* [effect of distanciation] for this contemporary discussion.

Jaspers and Arendt on Weber

Karl Jaspers served as a kind of personal link between Max Weber and Hannah Arendt. Arendt mentions hardly anything about Weber's political thought in

1.   This is a revised English version of my article 'Was hätte Max Weber zu Hannah Arendt gesagt? Reflexionen zu Hannah Arendts Kritik der repräsentativen Demokratie', published in Hubertus Buchstein and Rainer Schmalz-Bruns, eds, *Politik der Integration. Symbole, Repräsentation, Institution. Festschrift für Gerhard Göhler zum 65. Geburtstag* (Baden-Baden: Nomos, 2006): 199–213. I would like to thank Tuija Parvikko for her critical remarks on a previous version of this article.

her published work, although there is, however, one interesting exchange in her correspondence with Jaspers in 1950. Jaspers tells Arendt about a dream he had, in which Weber gave Arendt as a present some of his best political documents and works of art from a trip to East Asia, because her understanding of politics surpassed Jaspers's own ('weil Sie mehr von der Politik verstehen als ich', Arendt–Jaspers 1985: 184). The passage ends with Jaspers's recommendation to Arendt to reread Max Weber. Two months later, Arendt wrote back and told Jaspers that his flattery had worked and that as a result she had reread much of Max Weber's work. She recognised, however, that it was impossible for her to match the Weberian masterful sobriety (*Meisterstück der Nüchternheit*), as she was unable to completely rid her own work of its inherently dogmatic elements, which she attributes to being Jewish (Arendt–Jaspers 1985: 186).

This confession serves as my point of departure. I will not deal here with the conceptual link between Arendt and the 'Weberian moment' of contingency or debates on their intellectual relationships (discussed in Palonen 1998: 256–72; see also Parvikko 2004 and Baehr 2005). My point is rather that the difference in the degree of sobriety alludes to an inherently different attitude toward day-to-day politics in the works of Weber and Arendt. I want to more closely examine the extent to which this is visible in their relationship to parliaments, elections, parties and representative democracy.

Suffrage and politics

The democratisation of suffrage and the parliamentarisation of government are the most decisive political changes of the nineteenth and twentieth centuries, the significance of which has still to be properly estimated. Social scientists still recourse to anachronistic 'explanations' of politics by allegedly deeper factors, and to many philosophers the past struggles over suffrage and parliamentarism hardly appear worth studying. In terms of conceptual history and rhetorical analysis, however, some excellent works by Pierre Rosanvallon (1992, 1998, 2002) and Frank Ankersmit (1996; 2002) in particular are slowly altering the overall picture.

Despite its pamphlet-like character, Weber's late work remains unsurpassed in terms of its understanding of political conflicts as the result of the democratisation and parliamentarisation of politics. This holds true not only for Wilhelmine Germany but also for the conceptual analysis of the political transition in general. One example of his inherent 'sobriety' lies in his characterisation of the parties as voluntary organisations aiming at maximising the number of adherents: the ballot (*Wahl- und Stimmzettel*) is the *ultima ratio* of modern party politics (Weber 1917f: 167).

Admitting that the principles of election [*Wahl*] and number [*Zahl*] serve as the last resort of partisan, electoral and parliamentary politics marks the radical contingency of politics itself. Political choices must always be made, but there is no sufficient ground for following any definite course of action, and therefore certain procedural principles are required. The fierce competition in parliamentary regimes and the increased number of voters under democratic suffrage radicalise the contingency of politics. To accept the principles of representative democracy means accepting elections as a procedural principle of the choice of persons, as opposed to the always controversial appeals to the weight of the arguments. It is the number of adherents which serves as the final criterion for decision making.

This would, of course, be a hard test for many academics, many of whom would surely be quite reluctant to reject the Platonic–Hegelian claim of the best arguments in favour of the prosaic counting of the votes and the adherents to proposals. It is thus not only the principle of numbers but also the contingency of politics as such that has been difficult for academics to accept. It is my guess that we must also count Hannah Arendt among them, despite her intimate acquaintance with rhetorical and Sophist thinking, manifested in her *Denktagebuch* (Arendt 2002). In her *On Revolution* (1963), Arendt aims at reducing the contingency in terms of outlining a constitutional history of a new political order in a broad universal historical perspective.

Weber's studies on democratised politics were supported to a considerable extent by the empirical analysis of the party and electoral politics of three contemporary scholars – James Bryce (1888), Moisei Ostrogorski (1903) and Robert Michels (1910) – although judged in Weber's own terms. One of the main points of their studies lies in the question of how to judge the rise of new types of professional politicians, which neither the proponents nor opponents of the democratisation of suffrage could ever have imagined. This is another example of a case in which Weber does not denounce the vulgarity of the party bosses and election agents but, rather, accepts their presence as part of the implicit conditions for democratised mass politics (see Weber 1918d, 1919c).

For Arendt, on the other hand, the democratisation of suffrage does not mark any major break in constitutional history. For her, universal suffrage is merely a 'negative' right and not an example of an individual's participation in the use of the powers of the state:

> However, the liberties which the laws of constitutional government guarantees are all of a negative character, and this includes the right of representation for the purposes of taxation which later became the right to vote … they claim not a share in government but a safeguard against government.
>
> (Arendt 1963: 143)

In other words, by defining freedom in terms of participation in the polity, Arendt, in accordance with Jefferson and Tocqueville, explicitly defends democracy on the local level as a medium of connecting individuals into the community. The chance for individual intervention in political deliberations and decisions is not on her agenda:

> If the ultimate end of revolution was freedom and the constitution of a public space in which freedom could appear, the *constitutio libertatis*, then the elementary republics of the wards, the only tangible place where everyone

could be free, actually were the end of the great republic whose chief purpose in domestic affairs should have been to protect and provide the people with such places of freedom (in the German edition she uses explicitly the formula 'in einem positivem Sinne frei' [free in a positive sense].

(Arendt 1964b: 326)

As Quentin Skinner's studies on Machiavelli and English 'neo-Roman' authors illustrate, it was historically possible to combine the republic and the right to political intervention with a negative concept of liberty, one opposed to the dependent status of the individual (see esp. Skinner 2002b and the essays in 2002c). The argument also plays a role in the British suffrage debates from the 1860s. Whereas, for example, Robert Lowe (1867: 9) regards freedom solely as the absence of coercion, John Bright compares the status of 84 per cent of the male population in Britain (he does not mention women) to the dependent status of Russians without any parliament:

Out of every 100 grown men in the United Kingdom 84 have no votes. Those 84 might just as well, for all purposes of constitutional government, so far as they are directly concerned – those 84 might as well live in Russia, where there is no electoral system of parliament, or in those other countries, now very few indeed, in which Parliaments and representations are unknown.

(Bright 1866: 29)

Max Weber's defence of negative liberty is most clearly visible in his redescription of the citizen as an 'occasional politician' (Gelegenheitspolitiker) (Weber 1919c: 41). For Weber, the paradigmatic role of voting as an act of the occasional politician refers to the role of elections as the occasion par excellence upon which the citizens in democratic polities are expected to take a personal stand and, thus, act politically. As compared to this, the Arendtian integrative view on political participation tends to underestimate the political significance of the individual's electoral choice as a paradigmatic manifestation of contingency in democratic polities.

From the Weberian view, we can consider elections as a deliberative situation for the voter as an occasional politician; we can also ask whether it makes sense to judge political interventions in the purely quantitative terms of the amount of time spent participating in the polity. With the concept of *Interessentenbetrieb* [organisation run by the interested parties] (Weber 1919c: 57; see also the comments of Lassman and Speirs in Weber 1994b: 334, 372), Max Weber takes a strong stand in favour of the voluntary character of political activity. In addition to being related to the voluntary basis of the parties, *Interessentenbetrieb* also refers to regarding the occasional politician not only as a person who has occasional chances to intervene in politics by voting – for example by making a political speech – but also as someone with opportunities to attempt to become a professional politician.

Universal suffrage has undoubtedly played a crucial role for Weber in dethroning the monopoly of the politics of the old privileged stands and the part-time politics of the notables (Honoratioren). As the procedure of election by universal suffrage became increasingly politically significant, the elected representatives in the parliament and the lower level assemblies became much more heterogeneous in terms of the socio-cultural background of the representatives. This breakdown of the social homogeneity of the parliamentary assemblies also opened new types of chances for political activity, and Weber characterised the assemblies elected on the basis of universal suffrage as a free stage (*freie Bühne*) (Weber 1917b: 99–100).

Parliament and representation

Similarly to many other twentieth-century intellectuals, Arendt tends to view representative democracy and professional politicians as its key agents with suspicion. In the context of her interpretation of the US Constitution, she presents reflections regarding the principle of representation, concisely describing the main dilemma of political representation as follows:

> The traditional alternative between representation as a mere substitute for direct action of the people and representation as a popularly controlled rule of the people's representatives over the people constitutes one of those dilemmas which permit of no solution. If the elected representatives are so bound by instructions that they gather together only to discharge the will of their masters, they may still have a choice of regarding themselves as either glorified messenger boys or hired experts who, like lawyers, are specialists in representing the interests of their clients. But in both instances the assumption is, of course, that the electorate's business is more urgent and more important than theirs; they are paid agents of people, who, for whatever reasons, are not able, or do not wish, to attend the public business. If, on the contrary, the representatives are understood to become for a limited time the appointed rulers of those who elected them – with rotation in office, there is of course no representative government, strictly speaking – representation means that the voters surrender their own power, albeit voluntarily, and the old adage 'All power resides in the people,' is true only for the day of the election.
>
> (Arendt 1963: 237)

In the first part of her argument, she presents a precise critique of the imperative mandate and its substitutes, all of which render the parliamentarian dependent on any and all directives decided by others. This critique marks a difference between Arendt and most of the protagonists of direct democracy (see for example Rühle 1924). For the latter, the high profile political activity of the MP is viewed as suspicious, because there is no danger of deviation from the will of the mandators among the passive representatives. However, the political implication of the free mandate, the distinct deliberative (in the rhetorical sense, of course) role of the parliament, is also never explicitly defended by Arendt, despite the key role given to the deliberative dimension of speech in her conception of politics (esp. in Arendt 1960 and 2002).

The second critique put forth by Arendt in the quoted passage is, however, off target and misleading. Referring to the vote as a surrender might allude to the *Wahlkapitulation* in the old Holy Roman Empire or to the literal sense of the contemporary German expression *Stimmabgabe* [giving up one's voice]. Both concepts see the act of voting as relinquishing one's vote. Her view resembles the slogan of the German antiparliamentary *Spontis* from the 1970s: 'Wer seine Stimme abgibt, hat sie nicht mehr' ['A person who gives away his or her vote, has none left']. But for what purpose might the vote be saved if not for using it as a ballot in the elections? The idea behind this is probably that a vote is too weak as a personal voice and that a more powerful means of expressing one's voice should thus be found. But can the act of voting be completely abandoned? Arendt does not advocate abstention from voting either.

It appears as though Arendt sees the contingency of elections as simultaneously too overwhelming – one vote never decides the outcome – and too marginal in the sense of assuming that the results are politically insignificant anyway. In either case, she tends to underestimate the chances of the political decision involved in the electoral choice leading to the changing of majorities, governments and policies. Nor does she consider citizens in the Weberian sense as MPs of election day, deciding their own political identities at regular intervals, independently of whether or not their vote plays any decisive role in the results (see Palonen 2004c). From the voter's political standpoint, the paradigmatic significance of the elections and the chances of changing that standpoint in the next elections appear to Arendt to be so self-evident that perhaps she does not think they deserve any special emphasis.

In Arendtian terms, voting for a candidate is like refraining from criticising or controlling the elected candidate until the next elections. But even if a voter publicly declares support for a candidate, why should this require her to hide her opinion during the incumbent's electoral term? We might rather imagine that, through the act of voting, the voter acquires a greater power share by criticising her 'own' MP and ultimately declaring that she will not support her in the next elections.

Arendt justifies her Rousseauvian position on the limits of the power of the people to the election day with a reference to Benjamin Rush's interpretation of the US Constitution. According to him, the people are the source of all power, but after the election power becomes the property of the government (Arendt 1963: 319). The idea of power as a form of property and elections as a means of transferring power is of contractarian origin. The procedures of the secret ballot and the free mandate of the parliamentarian allow no such bind between voters and their representatives, and the very idea of treating elections as a contract fails to see the political point of elections in a representative democracy.

Let us consider the promises candidates make to do something if elected. This idea also appears as quite illusionary. It gives the impression of the individual MP as having the power to 'realise' her own hobbyhorses in the parliament, which is a rare occurrence. More crucially, the time-lag between the date of the promise and that of acting in parliament can always be used as a justified excuse for not acting according to the electoral promise, based on the fact that the situation has changed. In other words, the electoral promises contain a *ceteris paribus* clause that an MP may justifiably invoke at any time. It is too easy to forgive a broken promise due to the never-ending chances to have recourse to the changing situation, including a better insight into the realisability of the promise. In the case of electoral promises, the forgiving thus turns into an excuse that can be invoked at any time. It is only in a static world that the exceptional character of forgiving as a counterpart of keeping promises is imaginable.

For Arendt, the real danger lies in the mutation of the relationship between the represented and their representatives into that of rulership (*Herrschaft*):

> In the second instance, somewhat closer to the realities, the age-old distinction between ruler and ruled which the Revolution had set out to abolish through the establishment of a republic has asserted itself again; once more, the people are not admitted to the public realm, once more the business of government has become the privilege of the few, who alone may 'exercise [their] virtuous dispositions' (as Jefferson still called men's political talents).
>
> (Arendt 1963: 237)

The strong Arendtian dualism between power and rule, *Macht* and *Herrschaft*, is, of course, indebted to her interpretation of the ancient polis (Arendt 1960: 193–202). Arendt's distinction is based on a form of spatial phenomenology in which all concepts have a distinct and stable *locus* of their own. From this perspective the elimination of such asymmetric relations of rulership is an obvious demand.

In Weber's formal analysis, on the contrary, both concepts refer to certain types of chances, and the difference between them lies in the fact that *Herrschaft* contains a structural asymmetry of power chances, whereas *Macht* does not; it is amorphous (Weber 1922: 28–9; see Palonen 1998: 168–76). Understanding both power and rulership in terms of chances also means that Weber, despite speaking of the 'will' in his definitions, is no theorist of sovereignty, because the chances of 'realisation' of the will are dependent on the judgment of the situation.

The difference between the Weberian and the Arendtian views on *Herrschaft* is also related to German conceptual history (see Koselleck *et al.* 1982). It is the Arendtian view that corresponds to the older tradition of linking *Herrschaft* to the old feudal or patrimonial tradition of local and personalised rulership, to the *Herr* and *Knecht*. The Weberian view, on the other hand, is more in tune with the changes that took place during the nineteenth century, which rendered the old Prussian paradigm of *Herrschaft* obsolete. With this conceptual change, all claims of *Herrschaft* began to require a specific legitimacy, and this is, of course, the key to the Weberian view of the concept.

In the words of Reinhart Koselleck, Weber has 'sociologically neutralised' the concept of *Herrschaft* (Koselleck 1979: 128). Or, to put it differently, Weber constructed a new and more formal concept of *Herrschaft*, in the sense of the

German *auf den Begriff bringen* [conceptualising] (see Koselleck 1983). The
crucial aim of the construction of this new concept was to free the concept of its
ties to the historical paradigmatic forms of personal rule, which simultaneously
meant also neutralising the normative tone of the concept.

In other words, Weber turns *Herrschaft* into an historical concept that can be
filled with a wide range of forms of asymmetric relationships between variable
positions of 'rulers' and 'ruled'. An excellent example of this neutralisation,
expressed in the nominalistic language of Max Weber, lies in his letter to Robert
Michels on 31 December 1910, in which he comments on the latter's famous book
Zur Soziologie des Parteiwesens in der modernen Demokratie, which had been
published a few weeks earlier. If Weber had met Arendt somewhere other than in
Jaspers's dream, it is my guess that he would have repeated this example to her.
The key passage is as follows:

> Alles in Allem: der Begriff 'Herrschaft' ist nicht eindeutig. Er ist fabelhaft
> dehnbar. Jede menschliche, auch: gänzlich individuelle Beziehung enthält
> Herrschafts-Elemente, vielleicht gegenseitige (dies ist sogar die Regel. so z.B.
> in der Ehe). Im gewissen Sinn herrscht der Schuster über mich, in gewissen
> anderen ich über ihn – trotz seiner Unentbehrlichkeit u. alleinigen Competenz.
> Ihr Schema ist zu einfach.
>
> (Weber 1994a: 761)

> [All in all, the concept of 'Herrschaft' is not a univocal one. It may be
> tremendously amplified. Every human relationship, no matter how individual
> such a relationship might appear to be, bears elements of Herrschaft, leading
> eventually to mutual ones (this is, indeed, the rule for example in a marriage).
> In a certain respect, it is the shoemaker who rules over me; in another respect it
> is me that rules over him – despite his indispensability for me and his singular
> competence. Your scheme is all too simple.]

The Arendtian implication is that the relationships between the represented
and the representatives tend to cause the MPs to begin to resemble rulers, thus
rendering the voters politically powerless. From a Weberian perspective, it is
the bureaucratisation within the state, enterprises as well as parties and other
organisations, that tends to extend its powers over all others. Above all, parliaments
have the chance to serve as counterweights to the power of bureaucratisation, as
possible instruments of control on the behalf of those ruled (Weber 1918d: 226).

Arendt also refers to bureaucracy as the 'most social of all governments' and
as the rule of nobody (Arendt 1960: 41). Despite these formulations, which were
indebted to Weber, she appears to be less concerned than he about the potential
situation in which the everyday rule of the bureaucracy over the parliament and
the parliamentary government might develop into an uncontrollable form of
bureaucratisation. Judged retrospectively, Weber's fear of bureaucratisation was
perhaps exaggerated. Nonetheless, as compared with the democratically elected
parliaments, we might wonder what chances the Arendtian participatory local

councils would have against the bureaucratic tendencies within the state and indeed all organisations.

One of the major advantages of parliamentary regimes is that all *Herrschaft* is strictly limited in time, as regular elections offer an occasion to replace the incumbent government. Strangely enough, Hannah Arendt seems not to give to this any special significance, as is illustrated by the following quotation:

> For these evils there was no remedy, since rotation in office so highly valued by the founders and so carefully elaborated by them, should hardly do more than prevent the governing few from consulting themselves as a separate group with vested interests of their own. Rotation could never provide everybody, or even a sizeable proportion of the population, with the chance to become temporarily 'a participant in government'.
>
> (Arendt 1963: 238)

Here Arendt seems to miss the decisive distinction between the two forms of time limits, the ancient principle of rotation and the modern competitive principle of electoral choice, on which the struggle for power shares in parliamentary government is based. Making reference to Jefferson, Arendt even speaks of 'elective despotism' (Arendt 1963: 238). In contrast to this, Weber speaks about the election-based *Herrschaft* in terms of its being an antiauthoritarian reinterpretation of *Charisma*, because it is not the charismatic ruler but the electorate which can overthrow her who has the last word (Weber 1922: 155–6).

It is interesting to note that, for Arendt, time does not play a constitutive role in distinguishing between different types of regimes. In this context, Pierre Rosanvallon has indicated an obvious similarity between the authoritarian regimes and those longing for a direct or immediate form of democracy (Rosanvallon 2000: 409–14) The rule of a parliamentary majority for a limited period of time does not aim at minimising the damage done by governments, as was the central idea behind the old demand for frequent elections. The point is rather to give the parliamentary majorities a temporally limited chance that expires with the deadline of the next elections and the subsequent construction and implementation of their own new policy. If not all governments are a priori bad, they can be judged in terms of their performance, including their political use of time.

Councils and political representation

Arendt is no less critical of elections than she is of parties, which she considers to be a type of authoritarian organisation, similar to the monarchy and the nation:

> After the nation during the nineteenth century 'had stepped into the shoes of the absolute prince,' it became, in the course of the twentieth century, the turn of the party to step into the shoes of the nation. It is, therefore, almost a matter of course that the outstanding characteristic of the modern party – its autocratic and oligarchic structure, its lack of internal democracy and freedom,

its tendency to 'become totalitarian', its claim to infallibility – are conspicuous by their absence in the United States and, to a lesser degree, in Great Britain.

Arendt 1963: 263, (the quotations refer to Maurice Duverger's
Political Parties, English edition of 1954).

Arendt's critique is thus directed against the organisational form of the party, independently of the strength of the competition between them and their role in the parliament and government. Of course, the classical studies of Ostrogorski and Michels indicate similar trends that render party competition less crucial than its 'oligarchic' organisational form, strengthened by the fierce mutual party struggles. Independently of this, the difference between the monocratic power of a single party and the plurality of parties, based on voluntary membership and mutual competition, remains decisive (see Weber 1918d: 217).

The fierceness of Arendt's criticism indicates that she would in all likelihood never even have considered joining a party. She does, however, present an unconventional view on the difference between two- and multiparty regimes:

What distinguishes the two-party systems of these countries [USA and Great Britain], with all their differences, so decisively from the multi-party systems of the European nation states is by no means a technicality, but a radically different concept of power which permeates the whole body politic. If we were to classify the contemporary regimes according to the power principle upon which they rest, the distinction between the one-party dictatorship and the multi-party systems would be revealed as much decisive than that which separates them both from the two-party systems.

(Arendt 1963: 268)

The passage also allows us to gain a somewhat clearer insight into why she preferred the anglophone two-party systems, judged by Ostrogorski as those most liable to the rule of the bosses, to the continental multi-party systems. The chances for definite alternation in government are probably most explicit in the Westminster-style two-party regimes. Arendt's arguments on the weakness of the opposition, and particularly how easily coalition governments tend to give up their own policy profiles in the name of the unity of the nation, are, nonetheless, noteworthy.

If Max Weber were to come back to life today, he could resort to some of the recent scholarship in his polemics against the Arendtian view of representative democracy. Frank Ankersmit emphasises the legacy of the continental style of coalition governments as regimes in which the creative compromises between the coalition parties might legitimise this version of a parliamentary regime (Ankersmit 1996: 134–6; 2002: 99–104). Nicolas Roussellier's work (1997, 2000) sheds doubt on the conventional wisdom regarding the role of the short-lived governments in terms of the failure of the French Third Republic. As governmental changes were partial and concerned personnel rather than policy, the frequent falls of governments alone is not a sufficient criterion for political instability. And the ultra-parliamentary Third Republic regime has an advantage in terms of the role of the eloquence and argumentation of the individual MPs, which simultaneously tends to be lost in regimes with strong party discipline (Roussellier 2000: 260).

Arendt seems, in the final analysis, to defend a variant of the Rousseauvian thesis that the will cannot be represented:

> However, while it may be true that, as a device of government, only the two-party system has proved its validity and, at the same time, its capacity to guarantee constitutional liberties, it is no less true that the best it has achieved is a certain control of the rulers by those who are ruled, but it has by no means enabled the citizen to become a 'participator' in public affairs. The most the citizen can hope for is to be 'represented', whereby it is obvious that the only thing which can be represented and delegated is interest, or the welfare of the constituents, but neither their action nor their opinions.
>
> (Arendt 1963: 268)

Her conclusion is that what can be represented are 'interests', in other words, the pre-given and apolitical data of the persons. In this perspective, 'representation' is conceptually narrowed to the private law paradigm, in which the representatives are the agents representing the clients (see Pitkin 1967).

Drawing this type of conclusion regarding representation would be hasty and inexact. The Arendtian view corresponds to what Ankersmit calls the mimetic principle of representation, to the ideal that the parliament should be a miniature of the people. Ankersmit defends an 'aesthetic gap between the representatives and the represented as a condition of even speaking about representation (Ankersmit 1996: 46–7). From his perspective, the Arendtian view is based on the ethical principle of identity, as opposed to the inevitable selectivity of the aesthetic concept of representation (Ankersmit 1996: 49).

In Weberian terms we could, more specifically, insist on the politically crucial distinction between the voters and the parliamentarians when dealing with the subject matter of deliberations and decisions. Whereas the MPs deliberate and decide upon political issues, the voters are only able to do so indirectly, through their deliberations about candidates, as if they were the actual incarnations of the alternative policies and styles of politicking (Palonen 2004b; *see* Chapter Ten in this volume). Controversies and deliberations about what is valuable, desirable and realisable seem to be lacking entirely from the Arendtian concept of representation. For this reason, the parliaments do not play a prominent role in her conception, and she does not pay any attention at all to the politically crucial distinction between parliamentary and presidential regimes.

There is, however, a point in the Arendtian party critique, namely her critique of the parties' virtual monopoly over the nomination of candidates, which, according to her, actually means that 'representative government has in fact become oligarchic government' (Arendt 1963: 269). Her point is directed against the widespread and understandable tendency of the established parties to form a kind of cartel against potential newcomers. Arendt turns this tendency into an opposition between the principles of representation and power as such: 'Action and participation in public affairs ... obviously are not signs of health and vitality but of decay and perversion in an institution whose primary function has always been representation' (Arendt 1963: 271–2).

What is remarkable is her renunciation of representation and not power in this context. For her, power is an original source of action, whereas representation can only be derived from this source, although it can turn against it, as is the case precisely with the oligarchic party system in the representative regime.

All this refers to Arendt's distinctive concept of power, and here again the contrast to Max Weber is obvious. In order to delve deeper into this contrast we must take a closer look at Arendt's understanding of 'direct participation in public affairs'. Her somewhat surprising defence of the principle of revolutionary councils offers a key to her conception.

For Arendt, the opposition between parties and councils (*Räte*) is rooted in the German Revolution of 1918 and 1919, when in the aftermath, the Russian Soviets' debates surrounding the spontaneous powers of the Workers' and Soldiers' Councils briefly dominated the debate on the new German Republic and were opposed to parliaments elected by the entire citizenry. The *Rätebewegung* soon lost its momentum, except among the anti-Bolshevist extreme left, where the theorising continued (see Rühle 1924 on the workers' unions).

Hannah Arendt had no ideological links to the German *Rätebewegung*, but it is the spontaneity of the councils in revolutionary situations that appealed to her thinking. This was especially the case with the Hungarian 'Revolution' of 1956 (Arendt 1958), but in her later writings we can also find a distinct sympathy for the 1968 *événements* in Paris (Arendt 1971: 164–91, see also her letter to Daniel Cohn-Bendit, quoted in Young-Bruehl 1984: 412). As opposed to the anarchist or left-wing Communist council theorists, Arendt aims at rendering the councils respectable by including them in a 'bourgeois' version of direct democracy. The crucial reference here is to Jefferson's writings on the New England town hall meetings. According to Arendt, Jefferson intended to complete the foundation of the republic aiming mainly at ensuring the 'safety of the republic' (Arendt 1963: 254). The point is 'the power of "every one" within the limits of his competence' (Arendt 1963: 254).

Two views on power

The Arendtian view of the new American republic is based on the construction of power at various hierarchic levels. The role of political participation is thus, as noted above, less oriented toward the Arendtian idea of 'acting is fun' (1971: 166) than as a means of connecting the individuals into the community. Within this construction, the Weberian notion of politics as a struggle over power shares, the alternative modes of using them and contesting their current distribution (Weber 1919c: 36) does not play a constitutive role.

In other words, for Arendt, the councils are – as opposed to parliament and parties – not *loci* of deliberation and contestation, as paradigmatically expressed in the parliamentary procedure, but of co-operation. This idea is perhaps most explicitly outlined in her essay on the Hungarian Revolution:

> Under modern conditions, the councils are the only democratic alternative we know to the party system, and the principles on which they are based stand in sharp opposition to the principles of the party system in many respects. Thus, the men elected for the councils are chosen at the bottom, and not selected by the party machinery and proposed to the electorate either as individuals with alternative choices or as a slate of candidates. The choice, moreover, of the voter is not prompted by a program or a platform or an ideology, but exclusively by his estimation of a man, in whose personal integrity, courage and judgment he is supposed to have enough confidence to entrust him with his representation. The elected, therefore, is not bound by anything except trust in his personal qualities, and his pride is 'to have been elected by the workers, and not by the government' or a party.
>
> (Arendt 1958: 30)

The distinction between Weber and Arendt is perhaps even greater in her conception of power (*Macht*) than in her conception *Herrschaft*. The core of her conception lies in the figure of 'action in concert', which she already uses with reference to Edmund Burke in her *Origins of Totalitarianism* (Arendt 1954: 726). For the Weberian imagination, the question thus arises of against whom or what the joint action is directed. In the Weberian sense we could speak of chances for the joint action of parties in the parliaments in order to form counterweights against the overwhelming tendencies toward bureaucratisation (see esp. Weber 1918d: 221–37). Or we could invoke the figure of the spontaneous groupe-en-fusion in Jean-Paul Sartre's *Critique de la raison dialectique* (1960) which is directed against the everyday powerlessness of the 'serial' relationship between individuals.

This question is, of course, not one that Hannah Arendt herself asks. For her, action in concert, incarnated in the councils, appears valuable as such. In the essay *On Violence*, she emphasises that 'power' consists of rendering a common action possible, and she even regards power as the 'property' of a group (Arendt 1971: 113). The questions of adversaries and the criterion of the exclusion from the 'we' 'possessing' a power in its co-operative efforts remain outside the horizon. Referring to a footnote of Weber's, we could claim that the 'action in concert' resembles the reduction of politics to the level of the municipal self-government (Weber 1918d: 218).

How should we understand such a 'depoliticisation' of power in the work of Arendt? The contractarian legacy of Arendt's thinking is clear in *On Revolution*. The aim of establishing a *novus ordo saeculorum*, which Arendt traces back to the Mayflower Compact, serves to legitimate the vacuum of power characteristic of the state of nature (Arendt 1963: 167). Indeed, it seems that it is the spectre of the state of nature that serves as the tacit adversary. It is against reverting back to the state of nature that the contractarian assumptions of acting in unison and co-operation as a source of power appear more intelligible, and, for contractarians themselves, Arendt included, almost indisputable.

The point of *On Revolution* is, however, to break with the classical natural law version of contractarianism. Arendt instead joins the Roman tradition, as she also saw the founders of the US Constitution as having done. Contracts should retain their vigour through the active participation of the citizens. And it is precisely in this sense that Arendt's conception of councils is not harmful to the state, government and order, but, rather, aims at the 'foundation of a new state and the establishment of a new form of government' (Arendt 1963: 261).

The crucial question for all council theorists and advocates of direct democracy is thus how to deal with controversies and disputes. Arendt tends to consider them, in a Kantian manner, as something to be overcome by joint 'common sense' as manifested in the act of judgment (see the lecture in Arendt 2003: 138–42). From the Weberian perspective, it is here that the parliamentary procedure based on the rhetorical principle of speaking pro et contra allows us to question both the possibility and the desirability of such common sense (see Weber 1917f: 186–9; 1918d: 235–7).

Against the assumption of the contractarians that the longer we debate, the closer we come to each other, the history of parliamentary practice teaches exactly the opposite (see Hamilton's maxims from as early as the eighteenth century, 1927). The more time we get, the better our chances to construct counter-intuitive views or dispute that which has thus far appeared as acceptable to all. Any debate offers further occasions for the appearance of new nuances and individual profiles. The parliament is a political arena that is based on the procedural principle that in order to appropriately judge the merits and demerits of any proposal, opposing perspectives must be presented and deliberated. It is in this radical utilisation of both the controversy surrounding the issues and the adversity of the persons politely persuading each other that the political superiority of parliamentary regimes exists.

Final remarks

Weber and Arendt had a different relationship to practical politics. Max Weber was a passionate *homo politicus* from his early teens on (see the letters from his youth in Weber 1936). Even his academic correspondence contains comments on daily events and the political incompetence of various public figures to cope with them: for example, the remarks on the political dilettantism of his friends Professor Georg Jellinek and M.P. Friedrich Naumann from 1908 (Weber 1994a: 311, 698). Weber accepted the chances to stand as a candidate for the DDP in the Weimar Constituent Assembly elections of January 1919, and, while he was easily outmanoeuvred by the locals, he still participated actively in the campaign (see Weber 1919b and Mommsen's editorial comments 1991: 186–7, 224–31).

This kind of orientation as a *homo politicus* is quite exceptional among twentieth-century political theorists, including Hannah Arendt. Although her mother was a Social Democratic activist in Königsberg, the biographers indicate that in her youth Arendt had barely any interest at all in politics, and it was the experience of Nazism and her participation in the Zionist charities that slowly changed her attitude. In her emigrant life in the US, combined with annual month-long visits to Europe, she never had a chance to intimately acquaint herself with the practices of professional politicians. In other words, despite her admiration of politics, Arendt had no occasion to distance herself from the conventional academic *deformation professionelle* against professional politicians.

To sum up the *advocatus diaboli* game, despite all her praise for politics, action and novelty, Hannah Arendt joins the chorus of other contractarians from Hobbes (see Skinner 1996) to Habermas (see Skinner 1982) in their attempt to reduce and simplify the activity of politics, instead of celebrating à la Weber its controversial and contingent character. From her comments on elections, parliament and representation discussed above, we can also draw a more general conclusion: the contractarian theories are inherently unable to fully conceive the singularity of the parliamentary style of politics based on acting and speaking pro et contra.

The Weberian attitude corresponds better than the Arendtian to Quentin Skinner's thesis on the priority of 'political life' in the study of political thought (Skinner 1978: xi; see Palonen 2005). The academic search for *große Politik* (Nietzsche) is another expression of the contempt for parliaments and politicians and their daily practices. The Weberian approach acknowledges such practices and recognises their value and singularity, although he attempts to render them politically intelligible from an academic distance. A corollary of Skinner's point is also that political theorists should not leave the everyday politics in parliaments, parties and elections to narrow-minded empiricists but use all of these aspects in their own political theorising.

Chapter Nine

The State as a *Chance* Concept: Max Weber's De-Substantialisation and Neutralisation of the Concept

Max Weber's last lectures on 'Allgemeine Staatslehre und Politik' from spring 1920 – or rather, all that remains of them, namely the lecture notes of two students – have been recently published in the *Max-Weber-Gesamtausgabe* (Weber 2009). In his extensive 'Einleitung' [Introduction] (Hübinger 2009b) and 'Editorischer Bericht' [editor's report] (Hübinger 2009a) to the volume, Gangolf Hübinger has thematised the context of the lectures in terms of the 'Werkgeschichte' [history] of Weber's writings on the concept of the state and placed them in their political, intellectual, disciplinary and university historical contexts as well as in the life of Max Weber.

I have profited from Hübinger's introductions when I wrote this chapter. Nonetheless, my interest has a different focus, namely, the conceptual and rhetorical history of the Weberian concept of the state. Instead of setting Weber within well-established traditions of thought and debate, my point is to insist on Weber's break with them. His singular style of concept formation manifests itself also in his reconceptualisation of the state. Here, Weber's key move was his extraordinary use of the concept of *Chance*, a key figure that connects his political and methodological writings, as I have emphasised in *Das 'Webersche Moment'* (Palonen 1998).

As Hübinger points out, Weber had long planned a separate '*Staatssoziologie*' that would go beyond the categories of the state paragraph in *Wirtschaft und Gesellschaft* (Hübinger 2009b: 2–4). The students' notes of the lecture illustrate more clearly than Weber's own publications how crucial the concept of *Chance* was for Weber's empirical analysis of the state. In this chapter, I speculate on the political and methodological points of Weber *Chance*-oriented style of concept-formation and its singularity in the history of the concept of the state.

Weber and the German concept of the state

If we compare Weber's views with the prevailing interpretations of the concept of state in early twentieth-century Germany, it is evident that his vision differs from all the others. Indeed, although Weber frequently played down the originality of his views, this may have been part of a rhetorical tactic to render his own vision more acceptable. This tactic was also needed because Weber's discussion of the state took the concept to a new level, beyond the main traditions of the German *Staatslehre*, whether within the organic tradition (Gierke), in the idea of the state as an acting subject (Jellinek), or in the identification of the state with the legal order (Kelsen). By dissolving the substantial character and the legal personality of the state without committing himself to a juridical formalism, Weber introduces a new dimension to the debate on the concept. It is the concept of *Chance* that makes the difference.

In the introductory section of the article 'Staat und Souveränität' [State and Sovereignty] in the *Geschichtliche Grundbegriffe*, Reinhart Koselleck describes both the common assumptions and the internal differentiations in the German use of the concept 'Staat' after the French Revolution. His key thesis operates with the metaphor of an hourglass that gives to the specific history of the concept of the state a profile both similar to and different from other key concepts revised in the context of what Koselleck famously calls the *Sattelzeit* [time of conceptual transformation]. *Der Staat* also becomes a collective singular, that is, it subsumes its previously separate aspects under a more abstract concept, 'the state as such', around 1800:[1]

> The German history of concepts before and after the French Revolution is comparable with passing through the narrow neck of an hourglass. Before the year 1800 the word 'state' had a number of related meanings. ... Around 1800 the word 'State' wins a monopoly position and a claim to exclusiveness that swallows almost all of the related connotations. Now the history of our concept runs through a nozzle that concentrates all meanings into 'the state as such' (*Staat schlechthin*). The state was reconceptualised as 'the modern state'; it becomes an acting subject with a will of its own, an organism, also an organisation, to which society will be included as the people of the state (*Staatsvolk*). It transcends the institutional meaning and becomes the 'ideal state', a state *an und für sich*, against which all empirical states will be measured. The state as a new collective singular absorbs all the regulations of constitutional law: it is a result of a hypostating of all previous definitions of natural law into a philosophy of history, which – as with Hobbes and Pufendorf – had already regarded the state as a big personality, *persona moralis*. What was new, and in theory revolutionary, was that this self-founding state as such, as a reasonable state, was realisable only in the future (my translation).

---

1. 'Die deutsche Begriffsgeschichte vor und nach der Französischen Revolution läßt sich mit dem Durchlauf durch den Engpass einer Sanduhr vergleichen. Vor rund 1800 hatte das Wort "Staat" zahlreiche ständische Bedeutungen ... Um 1800 herum gewinnt "Staat" eine Monopolstellung und einen Ausschließlichkeitsanspruch, der fast alle ständischen Konnotationen verschluckt. Jetzt läuft die Geschichte unseres Begriffs durch eine Düse, die alle Bedeutungen zum "Staat schlechthin" konzentriert. "Staat" wird als "moderner Staat" auf einen neuen Begriff gebracht; er wird zum Handlungssubjekt mit eigenem Willen, zur real gesetzten großen Persönlichkeit, zum Organismus, auch zur Organisation, in denen die Gesellschaft als Staatsvolk aufgeht. Er wird über seine institutionelle Bedeutung hinaus zum "idealen Staat", zum "Staat an und für sich", an dem alle empirischen Staaten gemessen werden. "Staat" als neuer Kollektivsingular saugt alle staatsrechtlichen Verfassungsbestimmungen in sich auf: Ergebnis der geschichtsphilosophischen Transposition vorangegangener naturrechtlicher Definitionen, die "Staat"– seit Hobbes und Pufendorf – schon früher als große Person, als persona moralis zu sehen gelehrt hatten. Neu und in der Theorie revolutionär war, dass dieser sich selbst begrundende "Staat schlechthin" als "Vernunftsstaat" erst in der Zukunft zu realisieren sei' (Koselleck *et al.* 1990: 2).

Koselleck's point lies specifically, however, in the thesis that after this phase of abstraction – the narrow neck of the hourglass – the horizon of meanings again begins to expand, although now within the conceptual horizon of the new collective singular.[2]

> Conceptualised once and for all, it now became possible – as the neck of the hourglass opens up – that this eternally rational state with a unique history obtains qualification criteria for directing action. The modern state (*Staat der Neuzeit*) was turned into a universal concept applicable to the entire history, as well as to a concept to which varying aims could be given. It becomes an action concept, allowing party political colours, without losing its character as a reflective basic concept (*Grundbegriff*), referring to the one 'true state' or 'state as such'. This was something that could not have been possible before 1800 (my translation).

Max Weber equally wants to purge the concept from its feudal elements. Apart from this, his concept of the state has hardly anything in common with the modes of conceptualising the state seen in academic *Staatslehre* or in the daily political uses of the concept in nineteenth-century Germany. Consequently, the authors of 'Staat und Souveränität' only mention Weber's concept of *Machtstaat* as he used it in his 1916 article 'Deutschland unter europäischen Weltmächten' (Koselleck *et al*. 1990: 88–9), but remain silent on his more formal concept, as presented in *Wirtschaft und Gesellschaft* and elsewhere.

The original programme of the *Geschichtliche Grundbegriffe* was to deal with the *Sattelzeit* of conceptual change, *c*.1770 to 1850 (see its first formulation in Koselleck 1967). Although Koselleck later relativised the end of the period, it is clear that the conceptual changes which Weber initiated are of a different kind than those characteristic of the *Sattelzeit* (see Palonen 2003b). Nonetheless, Koselleck emphasises Weber's neutralisation of the concept of 'Herrschaft' to an analytical category (Koselleck 1979: 128) and his replacement of the idealistic term 'Geist' [spirit] with the nominalistic 'Kultur' (see Koselleck 1991: 134–8) demonstrates his clear recognition of Weber's innovative conceptual moves.

The state as a complex of actions and relationships

By combining several aspects into a single, coherent and abstract concept, Weber's concept of the state corresponds to the Koselleckian requirements of a *Kollektivsingular*. At the same time, Weber purged the state of all 'collective

---

2. 'Einmal auf diesen Begriff gebracht, wurde es jetzt möglich – und nun öffnet sich der Engpass der Sanduhr – daß dieser Staat der ewigen Vernunft mit geschichtlich einmaliger Zukunft handlungsanleitende Qualifikationsbestimmungen erhielt. Der Staat der Neuzeit wurde sowohl zum ontologischen Allgemeinbegriff, anwendbar auf die ganze Geschichte, wie auch zum variablen Zielbegriff. Er wird zum Aktionsbegriff, der sich parteipolitisch ausfächert, ohne deshalb aufzuhören, reflexiv auf den gleichen Grundbegriff eines wahren "Staates", des "Staates schlechthin" zu beziehen, was so vor 1800 unmöglich war' (Koselleck *et al*. 1990: 23).

agency', as he did with other concepts (see Weber 1904b: 210–12 for an extensive critique of *Kollektivbegriffe*).

For Weber, the state is neither an acting subject nor a normative or future-oriented concept. This aspect is evident already in his 'Objektivität' essay of 1904, in a passage illustrating the concept of ideal types. The state is for Weber a complex of 'active and passive human actions' (as Keith Tribe translates '*Handlungen und Duldungen*') and of 'partly unique, partly recurrent' relationships.[3]

> If we ask to what empirical reality the thought 'state' corresponds, we encounter an infinity of diffuse and discrete active and passive human actions, relations regulated factually and legally, sometimes unique, sometimes recurrent in character, all held together by an idea, a belief in actually or normatively prevailing norms and relations of rule of man by man. This belief is partly consciously held as a developed idea, partly dimly perceived, partly passively accepted and reflected in the most varied forms in the heads of individuals who, if they really did clearly think this idea through, would have no need of the 'general theory of the state' that they sought to elaborate. The scientific concept of the state, however formulated, is naturally only a synthesis that could be found in the heads of historical humans.
>
> (Weber 2004c: 394)

The point of this passage is that the state cannot be formed independently of the actual beliefs of historical persons, but only in a synthesising relationship with them. The nominalistic conceptualisation of the state that Weber presents *in nuce* in the quoted passage marks a real disenchantment with the German nineteenth-century concept of the state. For Weber, the other alternative to the subject concept, namely Kelsen's legalistic formalism, which identifies the state with the legal order (1911), follows the positivistic German tradition of state thinking that disconnects the concept from action and politics altogether.

In the quoted passage, the concept of *Chance* is not mentioned. Its presence is, nonetheless, evident in Weber's theory of action, constructed in the first pages of his 'Objectivity' essay. As is well known, *Chancen* and *Nebenfolgen* are the two key concepts through which Weber transcends the merely normative and teleological approach of ends and means (see Weber 1904b: 149–50). He, furthermore,

---

3. 'Wenn wir fragen, was in der empirischen Wirklichkeit dem Gedanken "Staat" entspricht, so finden wir eine Unendlichkeit diffuser und diskreter menschlicher Handlungen und Duldungen, faktischer und rechtlich geordneter Beziehungen, teils einmaligen, teils regelmäßig wiederkehrenden Charakters, zusammengehalten durch eine Idee, den Glauben an tatsächlich geltende oder gelten sollende Normen und Herrschaftsverhältnisse von Menschen über Menschen. Dieser Glaube ist teils gedanklich entwickelter geistiger Besitz, teils dunkel empfunden, teils passiv hingenommen und auf das mannigfaltigste abschattiert in den Köpfen der Einzelnen vorhanden, welche, wenn sie die "Idee" wirklich selbst klar als solche dächten, ja nicht erst der "allgemeinen Staatslehre" bedürften, die sie entwickeln will. Der wissenschaftliche Staatsbegriff, werde, ist nun natürlich stets eine Synthese, die wir zu bestimmten Erkenntniszwecken vornehmen. Aber er ist andererseits auch abstrahiert aus den unklaren Synthesen, welche in den Köpfen der historischen Menschen vorgefunden warden' (Weber 1904b: 200–1).

thematises the contingency of the past through 'objective possibilities', another key topic of the essays (Weber 1904b: 179, 192, 194) and even more in his defence of unrealised past possible where, in his 'Kritische Studien', he opposed the views of Eduard Meyer (Weber 1906a).

In other words, for Weber the concept of *Chance* and *Handeln* are interconnected: we cannot speak of actions in cases where there is no chances to act differently (see Palonen 1998: 133–42). Of course, Weber's concept of *Chance* has nothing to do with a positive and optimistic analysis of the situation but is purely formal: there is always a chances to act differently with regard to modes of encountering death or catastrophe. The concept of *Chance* is the most powerful sign of the radical contingency that shapes the entire thought of Weber.

Weber's contribution to the lexical project of *Wirtschaft und Gesellschaft* links action to relationships (*Beziehungen*), which allows Weber then to distinguish distinct types of complexes of chances, which serve as horizons of the possible for the agents in different situations. The entire set of '*Ordnungen und Mächte*', which Weber presents in the volume, is nothing less than an exposition of the different types of complexes of chances: excluding some, regularising others and rendering still others difficult and uncertain to realise. The orders and powers that Weber analyses differ in the profiles of chances which each of them enables as well as excluding agents from recourse to them.

More explicitly than before, Weber denies that the state is an acting, collective personality:[4] 'As far as sociology is concerned the object "state" is by no means necessarily constructed from legal components. And in any case sociology does not recognise the existence of "acting" collective personalities' (Weber 2004a: 321). His opposition to the nineteenth-century German tradition becomes clearer than ever. From this perspective, we can then also understand his famous 'definition' of the state:[5] 'A political institutional organization will be called state to the extent that an administrative staff can successfully exercise a monopoly of legitimate physical force in the executive of its orders' (Weber 2004a: 356).

In other words, the specific political chances of the institution of the state are connected to its chances to act successfully by using its monopoly of legitimate violence. The state exists for Weber only in relation to the actions and to the judgments regarding the relationships between the agents in the situation:[6] 'A "state", for example, ceases to "exist" sociologically with the disappearance of the likelihood (*Chance*) that particular forms of meaningfully oriented social action might occur' (Weber 2004a: 331). If legitimate violence cannot be monopolised

---

4. 'Für die Soziologie besteht der Tatbestand "Staat" nicht notwendig nur oder gerade aus den rechtlich relevanten Bestandteilen. Und jedenfalls gibt es für sie keine "handelnde" Kollektivpersönlichkeit' (Weber 1922: 6).

5. 'Staat soll ein politischer Anstaltsbetrieb heißen, wenn und insoweit sein Verwaltungsstab erfolgreich das Monopol legitimen physischen Zwanges für die Durchführung der Ordnungen in Anspruch nimmt' (Weber 1922: 29).

6. 'Ein "Staat" hört z.B. soziologisch zu "existieren" dann auf, sobald die Chance, daß bestimmte Arten von sinnhaft orientiertem sozialen Handeln ablaufen, geschwunden ist' (Weber 1922: 13).

in a given context, the agents in the situation cannot have the powers of the state at their disposal.

Similar to other Weberian concepts, the state refers to 'orders and powers' with certain types of chances, that is, to a horizon of the possible, not to a stable and fixed thing-like entity. There are degrees to the estimation of the realisability of orders and powers (see esp. Weber 1913); however, they are not calculable probabilities, but dependent on the actions of the persons relevant to the situation. From this perspective, it is clear that the state remains a political medium for certain types of action. Success in reaching the monopoly of legitimate violence is also 'merely' a chances, that is, something that is not guaranteed before the action, although some constellations tend to render success more plausible than others.

The political agents do not act 'as the state' or 'in the state', but through the specific chances made available through the medium of the state and present in the constellation of *Herrschaft* [rulership]. For Weber, *Herrschaft* is also a *Chance* concept (Weber 1922: 28) and, as he illustrates in a letter to Michels on 21 December 1910, though chances are asymmetrically available to different actors in a situation of *Herrschaft*, no actor is left without any chances (Weber 1994a: 761, *see* the quote and translation on p. 110). Accordingly, Weber does not subscribe to Michels's strict dualism between possessors of *Herrschaft* and those who lack it (see Michels 1910). Rather, he acknowledges that there always exist some chances to rule that are connected to the possibilities inherent in human action itself.

From this point of view, we can draw certain conclusions on how to understand the singularity of the Weberian concept of the state. In a manner similar to what he has done to the concept of *Herrschaft* (according to Koselleck), Weber also neutralises the concept of the state. Or, to put it in Skinnerian (1996) terms, Weber performs a paradiastolic redescription of the concept. This includes a demystification of the views of state worshippers as well as state demonisers. The chances bound up with the state are available for opposite purposes, and always remain uncertain in their effects.

Weber does not, however, identify the state with the state apparatus. Through 'the monopoly of legitimate violence' and the area (*Gebiet*), he provides the minimal necessary conditions for distinguishing the state from other types of *Verbände* [associations] or *Anstalten* [institutions], but he does not metonymically identify the apparatus necessarily used as a means by the state with the state itself. When, for example, Skinner writes, 'there has been a noticeably tendency in recent times to think of the state – usually with a nod in the direction of Max Weber – as nothing more than the name of an established apparatus of government' (Skinner 2009: 326), we can take this to be a polemic against the numerous unnamed interpreters of Weber rather than against Weber himself.

The lecture notes on Weber's concept of the state

Hübinger explains in his 'Einleitung' [Introduction] that, besides Weber's own preparatory notes for the lecture and some remarks in his correspondence, everything that has been found of Weber's eleven lectures of May 1920 consist of the lecture notes of two participants in the course, namely Erwin Stölzl and Hans Ficker, with the latter's notes written down by Margaret Haußleiter around 1931. As any university teacher might expect, the two series of notes differ both in what they picked up from Weber and in how the students formulated his diction. Nonetheless, the main points seem to follow similar lines.

Here I will concentrate on the first lecture, on the concept of the state itself. Above all, Weber emphasises a difference between the juridical tradition of *Allgemeine Staatslehre* [general theory of the state] (which in German universities never followed Georg Jellinek's programme of an independent *Soziallehre des Staates* [social theory of the state]) and his own empirical approach, which he calls *Staatssoziologie* [state sociology].

But I must pause to wonder why Weber chose 'sociology' as the disciplinary title for his own type of work. Was it not precisely sociology that, since Auguste Comte, was full of organic metaphors and collective concepts? Obviously what Weber wanted, for example, regarding the concept of 'objectivity' (see Palonen 2010a, b), was to capture this vague but fashionable discipline title rhetorically in order to make it compatible with his own 'methodological individualism'. Today we can see that Weber was not especially successful in this, but that sociology is still widely dominated by collective concepts of the kind about which Weber would have been horrified.

In opposition to the sovereignty assumption among the jurists, the Weberian 'sociologist' asks the question, what do acting persons think about the state? Stölzl's notes put it as follows:

Der Soziologe fragt, woran denken denn die Menschen, wenn sie vom Staat reden: (1) Schule: Prügelchancen, (2) Schutzmann: Die wollten, daß der Schutzmann kommt, (3) Militärdienst, (4) Steuer, (5) Gericht; Gesetze. Auch dieses Zusammentreffen ist nur eine Chance.

(Weber 2009: 68)

The sociologist asks, of what are people thinking when they speak of the state: (1) school, chances to be beaten, (2) policeman: they wanted the policeman to come, (3) military service, (4) taxes, (5) court, laws. Also this constellation is only a *Chance*.

Here Weber offers his class some paradigmatic examples of everyday uses of the state. At the same time, he notes that in the examples there is no necessary connecting link between them, 'only *Chance*', which does not indicate an accident, but the chances to connect diverse phenomena. Explicating this, Stölzl's notes continue:

Immer nur sind es Chancen einer bestimmten Art von menschlichen Handlungen. Die Gesamtheit dieser Chancen sind der Staat. Mit diesen Chancen rechnet man. An ihnen orientiert man sein Handeln. Wann besteht der Staat: wenn er die Chance hat, daß man ihm gehorcht! Räterepublik, Demokratie, Königtum nebeneinander in Bayern!

(Weber 2009: 68)

They are always merely chances of a definite art of human activities. The sum of these chances is the state. They are those chances that count. One's action is oriented to these chances. When does the state exist; when there is a chances that it will be obeyed! The Republic of Councils, democracy and monarchy parallel each other in Bavaria!

The notes of Hans Ficker give the same topic this formulation:

Soziologisch: woran denkt der Mensch bei 'Staat'? Immer nur Chancen einer bestimmten Art von Handlungen: Staat. An ihnen orientiert man sein Handeln. Soziologie: Wissenschaft vom Handeln. Existenz des Staates: Gehorsamschance. Widersprechende Normen tun dem Soziologen nichts. Soziologischer Rechtsbegriff: Vorstellung in den Köpfen des Publikums, das es für legitim hält. Soziologischer Staatsbegriff.

(Weber 2009: 69)

Sociologically: what is a person thinking of 'the state'? Always merely chances of a certain type of action: the state. One's action is oriented to these. Sociology: a science of action. Existence of the state: Chances of being obeyed. Mutually contradictory norms not disturbing for the sociologist. Sociological concept of law: imaginations in the heads of the public, what it holds as legitimate. Sociological concept of the state.

Common to both interpretations of the lecture is a recognition of Weber's strong insistence that his use of the state vocabulary involves 'only' the chances of human action. This is presumably in order to show once more that the state is not a fixed subject or a stable thing, but a concept of the possible. This corresponds to the way in which Ficker formulated sociology as a study (*Wissenschaft*) of action. The notes of both students thus claim that Weber's conception of knowledge and human sciences is based on the contingent element par excellence: human action.

All of this is opposed to the traditional view that sees in the contingent only residual traces, of which nothing definite can be said, and which are, accordingly, only accessible to a limited extent to 'science's' study of order or of stability which can be regulated by 'social laws'. In such a view, action is a merely passing and contingent phenomenon and as such is not intelligible by means of science. With its claim to render human actions intelligible, Weber's programme uses the concept of *Chance* for a different vision of the human sciences (Weber 1904b; see Palonen 1998, 2010b).

The state, for Weber, comprises an 'entire complex' (*Gesamtheit*, note the difference to *Totalität* and other holistic concepts) of a certain type of chances. In other words, the state does not refer to the totality of chances, but to a complete set of a distinct type. In order to understand the specific nature of the state, Weber goes beyond merely enumerating everyday thoughts on the state, and proposes instead a concept that connects state-related activities as such, namely obedience (*Gehorsam*). As Ficker puts it, the distinctive point for the existence of a state lies in chances of obedience (*Gehorsamschance*). In other words, insofar as there exists a chances to obey, a state exists. In both students' notes, we can detect a link to Weber's concept of *Herrschaft* as formulated in the *Soziologische Grundbegriffe*.

To interpret the state in terms of a chances to obey illustrates the character of the state as a special form of *Herrschaftsverband*. Illustrating his understanding of the existence of the concept of the state, Weber uses three alternative regime types, all of which coexisted and claimed to represent the Free State of Bavaria in the spring of 1919: the republic of councils, democracy and monarchy. The first 'anarchist' and subsequently 'communist' *Räterepublik* lasted altogether less than a month, from April to May 1919 in Munich and elsewhere (see the Bavarian library website: Revolution, Rätegremien und Räterepublik in Bayern, 1918/19). The governments of both Bavaria and the German *Reich* were legitimised by the general elections held in January 1919. It remains unclear what exactly Weber counts as the monarchist element – probably not the paramilitary *Freikorps*, but rather the remaining powers of the old bureaucracy, which contested the legitimacy of democracy and parliamentarism. For Weber, the crucial point is that the three regimes competed for their political legitimacy both in space (the Hoffmann government fled to Bamberg during the *Räterepublik*) and in time. Each simultaneously insisted on its chances to command the obedience of the citizens.

This is the major point of Weber's empirical analysis of the state: in a historical situation, competing regimes can exist simultaneously, each claiming before the citizenry the ability and competence to act with the powers of the state, though no guarantee exists that any candidate will be successful. The competition between regimes as candidate states is not necessarily a passing phenomenon, but whether it will endure remains an empirical question. In Weimar Germany, the contest between the republican and the monarchical elements lasted throughout the regime, being manifested in, for example, the academic debates of the constitutional lawyers, with many of the monarchists disputing whether the republic could be legitimised based on mere 'positive law' versus a 'more profound' idea of the state.

Weber regards the sovereignty criterion of the state, the claim that no more than one state can exist at a time in a given region, as mistaken. His Bavarian example illustrates how it is quite possible to find empirical situations where different regimes all have some degree of plausible claim to represent the state. This 'sociology' à la Weber can analyse all the types of normative claims to believe in obedience.

The lecture notes also illustrate how Weber formalised and neutralised the concept of the state. His critique of the sovereignty-centred juridical state was only partly due to this concept's failure to recognise the multiple empirical possibilities by which regimes can compete for the status of a state. His additional point was to neutralise the state by turning it into a concept that can be used independently of whether it is judged positively or negatively, accepted or rejected (thus corresponding to Koselleck's criteria for a *Grundbegriff*). Even the anarchists of the *Räterepublik* served as 'ministers' or, according to Soviet terminology, as 'people's commissars' (*Volksbeauftragte*), and would have been successful in commanding obedience only insofar as the citizens recognised its claim as a state or at least a state-in-the-making.

Weber's neutralisation of the state can be found in the 1917 version of his 'Wertfreiheit' essay, in which he parodies the view of some jurists in not accepting anarchists as university lecturers. For Weber, there is no need for professors, as officials of the state, to accept the state as such:[7]

> One of our foremost jurists has occasionally, while declaring himself to be opposed to the exclusion of socialists from the academic platform, stated that he, too, would at least not be willing to accept an 'anarchist' as a teacher of law, since [an 'anarchist'] denied the validity of law in general – an argument which he apparently regarded as conclusive. I hold precisely the opposite view. An anarchist can certainly be a good legal scholar. If so, then precisely that Archimedean point which he occupies by virtue of his objective convictions … and which lies outside the conventions and assumptions which are so self-evident to us, may enable him to see that the basic tenets of ordinary legal theory contain problems which will be overlooked by everybody who takes [those tenets] too much for granted. The most radical doubt is the father of knowledge. The jurist is no more responsible for 'proving' the value of the cultural goods whose existence is bound up with the existence of 'law' than the doctor is responsible for 'demonstrating' that the prolongation of life is desirable under any circumstances. Indeed, neither is at all able to do so with the means at his disposal.
>
> (Weber 2012: 308)

Of course, Weber was personally committed in favour of the state, although at the same time he was interested in anarchist political thought (for his links to the Ascona bohemians, see Whimster 1999). The point of his lecture series was rather to illustrate that a theory of the state, aiming at an abstract ideal based on the actual beliefs of citizens and rulers, was independent of defending or rejecting the state.

---

7.   'Einer unserer allerersten Juristen erklärte gelegentlich, indem er sich *gegen* den Ausschluß von Sozialisten von den Kathedern aussprach: wenigstens einen "Anarchisten" würde auch er als Rechtslehrer nicht akzeptieren können, da der ja die Geltung des Rechts als solchen überhaupt negiere, – und er hielt dies Argument offenbar für durchschlagend. Ich bin der genau gegenteiligen Ansicht. Der Anarchist kann sicherlich ein guter Rechtskundiger sein. Und ist er das, dann kann gerade jener sozusagen archimedische Punkt *außerhalb* der uns so selbstverständlichen Konventionen und Voraussetzungen… in den Grundanschauungen der üblichen Rechtslehre eine Problematik zu erkennen, die allen denjenigen entgeht, welchen jene allzu selbstverständlich sind. Denn der radikalste Zweifel ist der Vater der Erkenntnis. … Gerade die entscheidensten und wichtigsten praktisch-politischen Wertfragen sind heute von den Kathedern deutscher Universitäten durch die Natur der politischen Verhältnisse *ausgeschlossen*' (Weber 1917a: 496).

To speak of the state in terms of *Chancen* enabled him to form a concept that could be used by either adversaries or adherents of the state as well as by those who fitted neither of these categories.

An interesting question concerns the temporality of the state. For Weber, the state as a historical phenomenon is the most powerful contemporary form of a *politischer Verband*. The concept of *Chance* also refers to an analysis of time, to agents' experience of a horizon of the possible, which always refers to temporal concepts, such as a situation, a conjuncture or momentum. Thus Weber is able to raise the question of the historical duration of the state as well as the temporal prospects and limits on the legitimacy of specific states or candidate states and even to identify 'failed states'. A further specification of the state as a *Chance* concept lies in the analysis of the art of temporal duration of states, where their past or future success is dependent on this sense of *Chance*.

A comparison with Schmitt, Arendt and Skinner

With such an attitude, Weber could not find any friends among the revolutionaries of the *Räterepublik*, including his one-time student Ernst Toller. Someone else who attended his lectures and participated in his *Dozentenseminar* was from the opposite side of the political spectrum, namely Carl Schmitt (see Hübinger 2009a: 50). The effect of Weber's lectures on him, with their demystifying of the concept of the state into a complex of chances and its severing the link between the state and sovereignty, may perhaps be seen as one impulse behind Schmitt's militant defence of sovereignty in *Die Diktatur* (1921) and *Politische Theologie* (1922). As is well known, Schmitt's point was to rescue state sovereignty by connecting it to two other concepts: dictatorship and state of exception (*Ausnahmezustand*).

In these books, Schmitt never mentions Weber as the target of his polemics, and we may ask to what extent he understood his books as such. (Parts of *Politische Theologie* were included in the *Gedächtnisschrift* [dedication] to Weber). More than ten years later, however, Schmitt's *Legalität und Legitimität* (1932b) entered into a polemic against Weber's concept of *Chance*. His subtitle *Legalität und gleiche Chance politischer Machtgewinnung* includes a footnote,[8] which in a recent English translation reads:

> The word *Chance* remains untranslated here. It belongs particularly to the way of thought and speech of a liberal era of free competition and of expectation, and it concerns the mixture of fortunate occurrence and conformity with law,

8. 'Das Wort Chance bleibt hier unübersetzt. Es gehört eigentümlich zur Denkweise und Mundart eines liberalen Zeitalters, der freien Konkurrenz und der expectation und trifft die Mischung von Glücksfall und Gesetzesmäßigkeit, Freiheit und Berechenbarkeit, Willkur und Haftbarkeit, wie sie dieser Ära charakteristisch ist. Andere derartige Worte sind zum Beispiel Ideologie, Risiko, ferner das "Sollen" mit seiner sämtlichen "Bezogenheiten", sowie alle mögliche Arten des "Geltens". Solche Worte läßt man besser unverändert, damit der Stempel ihrer geistigen Herkunft sichtbar bleibt. In der Soziologie Max Webers kommt "Chance" besonders häufig vor' (Schmitt 1932b: 30).

freedom and calculability, arbitrariness and culpability, that is characteristic of this era. Other such words are, for example, ideology, risk, and, moreover, the 'obligation' with its collective 'implications', as well as all the possible types of 'validity'. Such words are better left unchanged, so that the mark of their intellectual origin remains visible. '*Chance*' occurs frequently in Max Weber's sociology.

(Schmitt 2004: 135–6)

Schmitt's rhetorical tactics are obvious. He rejects the concept of *Chance* as a sign of the past 'liberal' age and connects it to a number of other concepts, with which it does not necessarily have much in common. He identifies Weber's frequent use of *Chance*, and by this he consigns Weber to the museum of hopelessly outdated liberals. Nor does Schmitt see any grounds for discussing Weber's specific understanding of *Chance*. As his former student, he should have known that Weber never uses his key concepts '*im üblichen Sinne*' [in their normal sense] (see Weber 1910: 176), but always specifies their meanings and points for his own purposes. To rescue the state as an order concept par excellence, Schmitt turns against *Chance* as a concept that neutralises the state and against the concept of legitimisation based on the subjective legitimacy of the beliefs.

Another thinker who turns against Weber's concept of *Gehorsamschance*, but from a perspective opposite to Schmitt's, is Hannah Arendt. In a response to critics of *Eichmann in Jerusalem*, she writes:

Hence the question addressed to those who participated and obeyed orders should never be, 'Why did you obey' but 'Why did you support'. This change of words is no semantic irrelevancy for those who know the strange and powerful influence mere 'words' have over the minds of men who, first of all, are speaking animals. Much would be gained if we would eliminate this pernicious word 'obedience' from our vocabulary of moral and political thought. If we think these matters through, we might regain some measure of self-confidence or even pride, that is, regain what former times called dignity or honor of man: not perhaps of mankind but of the status of being human.

(Arendt 1964a: 48)

Without disputing her famous critique of the supporters of the Nazi regime, we can ask whether Arendt's proposal to eliminate the concept of obedience from the political vocabulary is also directed against Weber's concept of the state. The argument is based on her categorical distinction between *Macht* and *Herrschaft*, which enabled her to be an apologist for power and to reject rulership (Palonen 2008a, *see* Chapter Eight in this volume). For Arendt, obedience either exists or does not exist: she does not consider that it can have degrees of existence relating to its *Chance* aspects. In other words, if *Gehorsam* and *Herrschaft* are reinterpreted in the Weberian manner as *Chance* concepts, the Arendtian proposal to revise the vocabulary misses the point.

Gehorsamschance as Weber's key to the existence of a state equally contains the chances to act in a contrary way: through refusal to obey (*Gehorsamsverweigerung*). In empirical states, such chances may coexist with chances for obedience, and Weber gives the example in 'Politik als Beruf' of the Quakers, who rejected the state while at the same time finding some way to accommodate themselves to it (see Weber 1919c: 83). If the criterion of the existence of the state is not set in either/or terms – to obey or to disobey – but 'merely' in terms of the chances to obey, it also can render intelligible practices for finding a modus vivendi on the part of the disobedient.

Hannah Arendt supported institutionalised forms of 'civil disobedience' that did not require rejection of the state, but rather complemented it (Arendt 1964a: 47–48 and especially Arendt 1973). From this perspective, we could perhaps make Weber's opposition to pacifism more nuanced. It is well known that his colleague in Munich the professor of pedagogics F. W. Foerster represented for him the paradigmatic example of an apologist of the apolitical *Gesinnungsethik* [ethics of conviction] (see Weber 1919c: 81–2). Weber also had no sympathy for the scientistic 'organised pacifism' of A. H. Fried, who represented the main element of pre-war pacifism. A more action-oriented and consciously political pacifism was only formed around the time of Weber's death, with the institution of 'conscientious objection' providing conscripts with the chances to serve in non-military capacities (see the essays in Hiller 1981). Such a view can be compatible with Weber's concept of the state, in that it finds legitimate chances to accommodate oneself with the state, though rejecting conscription and the military dimension of the state.

Quentin Skinner has taken up the Hobbesian figure of the state as an artificial person, or as he puts it in a recent essay, a fictive *persona* (see Skinner 1999a, 2009). *Persona* is here understood in the Latin sense as a mask. Such a 'person' is of interest in how, while deconstructing the organic concept of person, Skinner upholds the person as a figure of state unity. How does this vision of the state relate to Weber's?

It might be difficult to conceptualise how the state as a *Chance* concept, instead of as a *persona ficta*, could, for example, take care of the public debt (Skinner 2009: 363–4). But the Weberian idea that the state itself forms a distinct type of *politischer Verband* also contains the notion of the state as an ideal concept that not only has moments of difference but also a unity that both transcends its constitutive elements and connects them together. The Weberian state as a complex of chances definitely contains aspects of political accountability, which might be enough to render the public debt intelligible.

For example, his insistence that Wilhelmine Germany was lacking political leadership for want of a politician responsible to the parliament (esp. Weber 1918d: 224) can perhaps be regarded as a claim to a political unity, which a bureaucratic regime with an irresponsible monarch as its nominal head could not achieve. Weber also repeatedly emphasises the superiority of the British parliamentary state in its foreign policy achievements in comparison to Germany (for example Weber 1918d: 237–8).

Can such a concept of the state be made compatible with the figure of a fictive *persona*? Or is the latter still an unnecessary metaphor, a step towards the substantive image of the state that Weber strove to get rid of? Does Weber's economic metaphor of monopoly bring him, after all, closer to the concept of sovereignty than he himself recognised? (See also the discussion in Kalmo and Skinner 2010.) I leave these questions open, as questions to be dealt with as empirical cases, where the *Chance* character of the Weberian state is connected to more detailed topics.

Concluding points

Weber's appeal to the human agents' everyday understanding of the state has the very difficult task of getting rid of the image of it as a hard, durable and tough reality, or '*General Dr. von Staat*', as Thomas Mann described his own image of the state in *Betrachtungen eines Unpolitischen* (1918: 239). Weber's image of the state as a *Chance* concept, a phenomenon of the possible, might at first sight be hard to justify among citizens, politicians and state officials.

Nonetheless, Weber's suggestion for re-thinking the state in terms of *Chance* may be well worth pursuing beyond the point at which he left it. It may allow us, above all, to see *Chance* as referring exactly to the reality of the possibilities that face acting persons, whereas the facticities of situations depend on interpretive perspectives and their horizons of chances. This relieves us from the illusion that the facts are something given and unalterable. The point is not to ask whether any chances are available, but rather, how do the chances profiles of various situations differ, and how do their 'orders and powers' differ.

Today, veneration of the state has largely disappeared in Western Europe, and the fate of the demonisation of the state looks equally unpromising, though remnants of it are still visible on the left and on the populist right of the political spectrum. Weber's neutralisation of the concept of the state has the advantage of not moralising about the political conflicts around the state by moving those conflicts from the terms of good and evil to ones of judging the openings and closures in the range of possibilities of state-bound politics.

Similarly, the success and failure of the state can be relativised when its ends and means are set in Weberian relation to chances and unintended consequences. We can then enter into a type of political judgement that weighs relative advantages and disadvantages of alternative actions (including the possibility of revising the criteria) attained through the medium of the state. Weberian methods would allow for the deconstruction of nineteenth-century dichotomies of progress and reaction, and of change and continuity, and would favour more specific temporal concepts, such as analysis of momentum, temporal durations and the calendar of politics (see Palonen 2008c). The question of the state as a medium of politics then turns to one of debating and judging the range and the forms of possibilities that can be practised by means of obedience to the *Chancen* of the state type of *Herrschaftsverband*.

We can, for example, ask whether Weber's concept of *Gehorsamschance* still retains heuristic value as a reference point for analysing the specific likelihood of a state continuing to exist. Does Weber's concept of the state still presuppose, as his writings against the Treaty of Versailles suggest (see MWS 1/16), a Westphalian balance between the great powers in inter-state relations? How might we think in Weberian terms of the relative blurring of borders between the state and other *Herrschaftsverbände*, such as in the *Chance* complexes of the European Union?

In short, there are plenty of possibilities beyond those used by Weber himself to expand his type of political imagination for rethinking the state and state-related concepts. Perhaps the main point is that, when we think about the state as a *Chance* concept, we should not imagine it as something beyond politics, but as a complex formed through political struggles themselves.

PART III

A PARLIAMENTARY VISION

Chapter Ten

Max Weber, Parliamentarism and the Rhetorical Culture of Politics

One of the remarkable differences between the British and German debates prior to and during World War I was the asymmetric relationship between parliamentary government and universal suffrage. In Britain, the parliament was accepted as the locus of high British political culture, while universal suffrage was regarded with suspicion. In Germany, the male suffrage of the Reichstag elections increasingly gained acceptance, whereas even liberals and socialists widely rejected parliamentarism.

Max Weber was one of just a few German proponents of parliamentarism during the war. In his pamphlet 'Wahlrecht und Demokratie in Deutschland', Weber also parodied those particularly fanatical 'democrats' who saw 'parliamentarisation' as leading to corruption and the perversion of democracy (Weber 1917f: 186). His view regarding the democratisation of suffrage and parliamentarism as complementary to one another was an exceptional position in the German context.

I will not enter into a dispute on the question of the extent to which we should regard Weber's late stance for a plebiscitary *Führerdemokratie* with a strong *Reichspräsident* as being a move away from parliamentarism (Weber 1919c: 72; 1919d; for comments, Mommsen 1959: 186–205; Beetham 1974: 96–102). Nor will I ask whether Marcus Llanque, with his thesis that prior to the July crisis of 1917 Weber had not yet spoken of 'parliamentary democracy' and was only radicalised after it (Llanque 2000: 183, 237–9, 248–52), overestimates the differences between the versions of Weber's texts.

My thesis is that an understanding of Weber's position requires a broader view on parliamentarism as an expression of an eminently rhetorical political culture. It was precisely this rhetorical culture of speaking for and against, seen as the crux of the British parliamentary tradition, that was so commonly despised in Wilhelmine politics, and it was this that Weber defended. In order to legitimate this view, I follow the procedure of Quentin Skinner (1978, 1996) and others who deny the distinction between major and minor works – in the case of Weber between his academic and his polemical writings. In reading Weber as a political theorist, the fragments on theorising that are contained in his polemic writings deserve closer analysis. They become more intelligible when linked intra-textually to each other and con-textually to the contemporary political events, practices and claims.

Parliamentarism as a rhetorical political culture

The parliament has its etymological origins in the Italian *parlare* and in the French *parler*. This aspect, a polity of speech par excellence, is neglected in the histories of parliamentarism (for example, von Beyme 1970; Kluxen 1983; Beranger 1999). Similarly, in terms of the histories of rhetoric, parliamentary speeches merely offer illustrations without providing any insight into the inherent link between the parliament and the speech as the paradigmatic mode of action. In recent years, however, the rhetorical dimension of parliamentary politics has attracted the interest of a number of scholars (Roussellier 1997, 2000; Goldberg 1998; Meisel 2001; Mergel 2002), and I will use this burgeoning literature in order to put forward a rhetorical revision of the concept of parliamentarism itself.

Among the critics of parliamentarism, there is no lack of accusations regarding the parliament as being a talk-shop dominated by *bavardage*, the critique of the priority of words over deeds, rhetoric over reality, eloquence over substance and so on. It is a common topos in conservative, nationalist, populist, socialist or anarchist variants of anti-parliamentarism alike. However, especially among nineteenth-century English politicians, we can identify some who are proud of the rhetorical dimension of parliamentarism. In an essay on William Pitt (1859), Thomas Babington Macaulay uses the expression 'government by speaking', and Walter Bagehot's *Physics and Politics* (1872) contains an eloquent chapter on 'government by discussion'. In his *Considerations on Representative Government*, John Stuart Mill expresses the view that the accusations waged against *bavardage* are utterly misdirected:

> Representative assemblies are often taunted by their enemies with being places of mere talk and 'bavardage'. There has seldom been more misplaced derision. I know not how a representative assembly can more usefully employ itself than in talk, when the subject of talk is the great public interests of the country, and every sentence of it represents the opinion either of some important body of persons in the nation, or of an individual in whom some such body have reposed their confidence.
>
> (Mill 1861: 117)

Mill also understands that the parliamentary procedure is based on the exchange of arguments and counter-arguments, the parliament being '[a] place where every interest and shade of opinion in the country can have its cause even passionately pleaded, [and] in the face of the government and of all other interests and opinions, can compel them to listen' (Mill 1861: 117). In the parliament, open and public controversy amongst adversaries is the most basic procedure for dealing with political questions. As such, for Mill, the parliament is the paradigmatic locus of rhetorical politics.

This rhetorical character of parliamentarism can be better understood when the history of the parliamentary procedure is taken into account. One excellent old study, that of the Austrian jurist Josef Redlich's *Recht und Technik des Englischen*

Parlamentarismus from 1905, is very illustrative in this respect. His main point is that parliamentarism is a regime of speech:[1]

> Without speech the various forms and institutions of parliamentary machinery are destitute of importance and meaning. Speech unites them into an organic whole and gives to the parliamentary action self-consciousness and purpose. By speech and reply expression and reality are given to all the individualities and political forces brought by popular election and the representative assembly.
>
> (Redlich 1908, vol. 3: 42)

Redlich insists on the co-presence of speeches for and against from the early phases of English parliamentary history (Redlich 1905: 46). He does not, however, mention the link between the parliamentary practice of speaking for and against and the lively rhetorical culture in the English Renaissance, as emphasised recently by Quentin Skinner (1996). By combining the independent insights of Redlich and Skinner, I claim that the parliamentary practices and procedures that mediate and accentuate aspects of this rhetorical culture were present in English politics well beyond the period in which the fame of rhetoric declined.

The principles of parliamentary procedure that Redlich excavates from the history of the English parliament become intelligible in terms of the rhetorical culture of speaking for and against. This is the case, for example, with the 'complete freedom of speech' as a special privilege of MPs (Redlich 1905: 37) and the parliamentary immunity of MPs, (Redlich 1905: 38) both of which were already accepted in the fifteenth century. In the struggle against the Stuart kings, the independence of the speaker, the establishment of specific parliamentary procedure, as well as documentation of the proceedings of the parliament strengthened the privileges of the parliament against attempts to extend the royal prerogatives (Redlich 1905: 55–6). The principle of equality between the MPs was directed against the attempt of the members of the Privy Council to obtain privileges in parliamentary debates (Redlich 1905: 66–7). The concern regarding minorities was another expression of the rhetorical understanding of parliamentary deliberations: it can be directly connected to the Protagorean principle of making a weaker case stronger through intra-parliamentary persuasion.

This rhetorical interpretation of parliamentary procedure can be contrasted to the view put forward, for example, by François-Pierre Guizot (1851: 14) and Jürgen Habermas (1962: esp. 127–45) that search for truth is the constitutive principle of parliamentarism. With an ironic nuance, Carl Schmitt parallels the truth-producing quality of parliamentary regimes to the ideology of a free market (Schmitt 1923: 45–6). Since rhetoric has fallen into disrepute in the academic

---

1. 'Die Rede ist es erst, die verschiedenen Formen und Institute des parlamentarischen Apparats mit Inhalt und Sinn erfasst, die sie miteinander organisch verbindet; durch die Rede erst wird die Tätigkeit des Parlaments zweckbewusst gestaltet. Rede und Gegenrede sind erst die Mittel, durch welche die gesamten individuell-psychischen und die politischen Kräfte, wie sie durch den Prozess der Volkswahl im Hause der Abgeordneten vereinigt sind, zum Ausdruck und zur Wirksamkeit gelangen' (Redlich 1905: 58–67).

world, the authors mentioned typically fail to recognise or understand the distinct rhetorical legitimation of parliamentary practices.

To sum up, neither 'government by speaking' nor 'government by discussion' refer to a kind of oratorical competition. A parliament in which political eloquence is assessed only in terms of artistic performance is pre-political, subordinated to the politics of the cabinet, the bureaucracy or the party apparatus. The claims of the independence of MPs from both parties and voters and the ideal that parliamentary speeches themselves should be crucial aspects of the decisions that are taken still allude to the parliament as a discussion club of gentlemen, not as a powerful political assembly. The rhetorical point of parliamentary politics can be specified instead in terms of both the systematisation of a procedure of speaking for and against and of the regularisation of the controversy to present opposing points of view regarding any item to be discussed in the parliament.

The formation of a specific parliamentary agenda of temporal items is intelligible only in the rhetorical terms of speech and counter-speech (for France, see Pierre 1887; for the rotation between speakers for and against in early German parliaments, see Botzenhart 1977: 472, 486; Grünthal 1982: 372). The institutionalisation of the opposition itself forms the next step in the creation of a political basis for criticising the government. The parliamentary style of politics is oriented toward the alteration of the views of an audience by means of speech. The number of adherents is the main *Machtanteil* [power share] of this kind of persuasive–dissuasive politics.

Parliamentary rhetoric is, above all, a deliberative rhetoric of elected assemblies. The extension of the parliamentary style of rhetoric to the elections through which the assembly is chosen, to assemblies with their popular audiences, as well as to analogical types of discussion and decision situations can be understood as extensions of the parliamentary style of politics, not as alternatives to it.

Weber's 'parliamentary' theory of knowledge

During the nineteenth century, the authority of science replaced heritage and monarchy as the main competitor of the parliamentary style of politics. Positivistic and other approaches longed to eliminate the rhetorical politics of controversy by means of the 'scientisation' of politics. An alternative view, indebted to ancient rhetoric and the sophists, rejected the search for a certain kind of knowledge. The most prominent proponent of the perspectivistic view of knowledge was Friedrich Nietzsche. His relationship to rhetoric has recently been analysed and his Basle lectures on ancient rhetoric have been published for the first time (Nietzsche 1995). Here, however, I will only briefly mention his famous figure of *Umwertung der Werte* [transvaluation of all values], which forms an exemplary case of a 'paradiastolic' rhetorical redescription of the normative dimension of concepts (see Skinner 1999b; Palonen 1999b).

Max Weber refined the Nietzschean perspective of knowledge and the human sciences in his famous 'Objektivität' article of 1904. By accentuating the rhetorical aspects of this article, we can better understand the significance of the political dimension in Weber's theory of knowledge and the human sciences. This is manifested in the following programmatic formulation of Weberian perspectivism:[2]

> *There is no* absolutely 'objective' scientific analysis of cultural life – or ... of social phenomena ... *independent* of special and 'one-sided' perspectives, on the basis of which such phenomena can be (explicitly or implicitly, consciously or unconsciously) selected as an object of research, analysed and systematically represented.
>
> (Weber 2004b: 113)

As in politics, there is neither authority nor neutral instances in science. Objectivity is only possible within the competition between perspectives, and the concepts are the key instruments in this struggle:[3] 'concepts are not the *objective*, but the *means* to the end, knowledge of relationships that are significant from individual viewpoint – *Because* the contents of historical concepts are mutable, they need in any given context to be as clearly formulated as possible' (Weber 2004b: 399). By rendering the analysis of the conceptual struggles an instrument of understanding the contestational character of academic research, Weber almost sketches a programme of *Begriffsgeschichte avant la lettre* (see Palonen 2000):[4]

> The thought apparatus developed by the past through the cognitive processing of immediately given reality – which in truth means cognitive *reconstruction* – and by ordering reality in terms of those concepts corresponding to the apparatus's state of knowledge and the tendency of its interest, is constantly challenged by new knowledge that we can and *wish* to draw from reality. In the course of this struggle cultural scientific work makes progress.
>
> (Weber 1904b: 398)

Academic controversies are indispensable to 'progress' in the human sciences. For Weber, expressions such as *Gesichtspunkte* [point of view], *Auseinandersetzung*

---

2. 'Es gibt keine schlechthin "objective" wissenschaftliche Analyse des Kulturlebens – oder ... der "sozialen Erscheinungen" unabhängig von speziellen und "einseitigen" Gesichtspunkten, nach denen sie – ausdrücklich oder stillschweigend, bewusst oder unbewusst – als Forschungsobjekt ausgewählt, analysiert und darstellend gegliedert werden' (Weber 1904b: 170).

3. 'die Begriffe [sind] nicht Ziel, sondern Mittel zum Zweck der Erkenntnis der unter individuellen Gesichtspunkten bedeutsamen Zusammenhänge: gerade weil die Inhalte der historischen Begriffe notwendig wandelbar sind, müssen sie jeweils notwendig scharf formuliert werden' (Weber 1904b: 208–9).

4. 'Der Gedankenapparat, welchen die Vergangenheit durch denkende Bearbeitung, das heißt aber in Wahrheit: denkende Umbildung, der unmittelbar gegebenen Wirklichkeit und durch Einordnung in diejenigen Begriffe, die dem Stande ihrer Erkenntnis und der Richtung ihres Interesses entsprachen, entwickelt hat, steht in steter Auseinandersetzung mit dem, was wir an neuer Erkenntnis aus der Wirklichkeit gewinnen können und wollen. In diesem Kampf vollzieht sich der Fortschritt der kulturwissenschaftlichen Arbeit' (Weber 1904b: 206).

[controversy] and *Kampf* [struggle] are not metaphors but indicators of the presence of a rhetorical and political dimension within the research process itself.

Weber's view on conceptual change is analogous to the alternation in government through the shifting of electoral or parliamentary majorities. With an 'einseitige Steigerung' [one-sided accentuation] (Weber 1904b: 191), we could speak of Max Weber's 'parliamentary' view on the human sciences as an extension of the parliamentary politics of controversy. This is the rhetorical message of the above-quoted Weberian paragraph.

Weber's defence of the *Wertfreiheit* [value freedom] of academic research has a double edge. It is, of course, directed against the patronage-cum-exclusion system of the Prussian universities. More crucially, however, he emphasises that it is up to the political agents themselves to choose the normative principles. The Schmollerian appeal to the authority of 'science' is illusory, but, above all, it denies the freedom of political agents. Weber expresses this idea in the first pages of the 'Objektivität' article:[5]

> no person behaving reflectively and responsibly cannot avoid balancing the ends of an action against its consequences. ... Therefore, any person who acts responsibly and reflects on [his action] has to weigh the goal of his action against its consequences ... Turning an assessment of this kind into a decision is certainly *not* the business of science, but of the desiring person: he weights and chooses between the values concerned according to his conscience and personal viewpoint. Science can help him to a *consciousness* that *all* action – naturally in some circumstance a *lack of action* – has its consequences of *endorsement* of particular values, but today that this also involves the consistent *rejection of other values* is too often readily overlooked. Making a choice is his own affair.
>
> (Weber 2004b: 361–2)

On the performative level of activities, Weber sees research as more reminiscent of politics than is commonly acknowledged due to the key role of controversy in the scholarly activity itself. Of course, the scholar is relieved from the existential commitments of the politician and is not bound by parliamentary majorities, which renders him or her much freer to conduct thought experiments than the politician, who is obligated to worry about the lives of other persons. But in a broader sense, both research and politics, at least in parliamentary regimes and universities

---

5. 'so kann an der Abwägung von Zweck und Folgen des Handelns gegeneinander keine Selbstbesinnung verantwortlich handelnder Menschen vorbeigehen ... Jene Abwägung selbst nun aber zur Entscheidung zu bringen, ist freilich *nicht* mehr eine mögliche Aufgabe der Wissenschaft, sondern des wollenden Menschen: er wägt und wählt nach seinem eigenen Gewissen und seiner persönlichen Weltanschauung zwischen den Werten, um die es sich handelt. Die Wissenschaft kann ihm zu dem *Bewusstsein* verhelfen, daß *alles* Handeln, und natürlich auch, je nach den Umständen, das *Nicht*-Handeln, in seinen Konsequenzen eine *Parteinahme* zugunsten bestimmter Werte bedeutet, und damit – was heute so besonders gern verkannt wird – regelmäßig gegen andere. Die Wahl zu treffen, ist seine Sache' (Weber 1904b: 150).

respecting the principles of *Lernfreiheit* and *Lehrfreiheit* [freedom of learning and teaching], are practices carried out within a context that is appreciative of open controversy. Both are opposed to bureaucratic rule, and we may also regard the parliamentary view of knowledge as an instrument of the struggle against bureaucracy in the academic world.

Weber's critique of anti-parliamentarism

The parliamentary government was a key element of Weber's idealisation of British politics. He repeatedly used Britain as a model example of a well-functioning and effective parliamentary regime. It served as point of contrast for the quasi-parliamentary politics of the German Empire. In 1904, he entered into a polemic against Eugen Jagemann's call for the elimination of the parliamentary element from the imperial constitution. Weber saw this as a fashionable attempt to rejuvenate the old form of anti-parliamentarism (against Schmoller's critique of *Parlamentsgerede*, see Weber 1905b: 96):[6]

> The rumination of subordinate minds regarding the possibility of an extra-parliamentarian regime belongs to the system of pinpricks by which, year after year, certain courtly and agrarian circles produce propaganda about our parliamentary institutions. It is undeniable that the belief in the out-datedness of the parliament and the like – something one might have heard in the same way in England 250 years ago – nowadays among us belongs to such an extent to 'good form' that it practically requires a certain level of courage to strictly oppose this fashionable babble.

Weber's second point was directed against the German system of government in the name of the efficiency of the parliamentary regime (Weber 1904a). Why did he consider a parliamentary regime to be more efficient than a constitutional monarchy? Evoking the 'Objektivität' article from the same year, we could suggest that the lack of discussion surrounding the alternatives and the corresponding arbitrariness of the governmental decisions appear to him as weighty grounds for the decline of German efficiency and prestige. This was also the point of Weber's critique of Wilhelm II in a footnote from 1906, in which he referred once again to the antiparliamentary *Gerede* [talk] characteristic of 'personal regimes', in contrast to parliamentary democracies: 'Dieses Gerede ist zurzeit schon deshalb deplaziert, weil es zu kritischer Vergleichung der gegenwärtigen Leistungen der Länder mit parlamentarisch-demokratischem und denjenigen mit "persönlichem"

---

6. 'Das Spintisieren subalterner Geister über die Möglichkeit eines außerparlamentarischen Regimes gehört in jenes System von Nadelstiche, mit denen von gewissen höfischen und agrarischen Kreisen gegen unsere parlamentarischen Institutionen seit Jahren Stimmung gemacht wird. Es ist nicht zu leugnen, dass ... der Glaube an die "Überlebtheit" des Parlamentarismus und dergleichen – Dinge wie man übrigens vor 250 Jahren in England ganz ebenso hören konnte – bei uns jetzt derart zum "guten Ton" gehört, dass fast ein gewisser Mut erforderlich ist, diesem Modegeschwätz überhaupt entgegenzutreten' (Weber 1904a: 17).

Regiment auffordert' (Weber 1906c: 19). Weber inverts the old accusation that parliamentarism, as a 'demagogical' regime, has a tendency toward arbitrary rule, against the 'personal regime' of a monarch. The latter is extremely arbitrary, whereas the deliberation between competing perspectives has the potential to reduce this arbitrariness, to lead to moderate and balanced results, not least in the sphere of foreign policy.

Weber's seemingly modest writings on Russia are key to his political theorising, which is always linked to an historical analysis of the situation. The rural *zemstvos* [Russian form of local government] were not parliaments: their powers were highly limited, although they did allow for political practice from below, and their national congress was experienced in 1904 as a threat to the Czarist regime. Following the revolutionary events of 1905 and the summoning of a national Duma, Weber saw the basis of the *zemstvos* as undermined. He saw in the *zemstvos* precursors of a parliamentary style of politics as suppressed by the bureaucratically controlled Duma. The political point of individual rights as the counterweight to bureaucratic and centralist rule and the defence of the 'individualistic' notion of 'inalienable human rights' was better realised in the *zemstvos* than in the Duma (Weber 1906c: 98).

In Weber's second article on Russia, one of the main chapters is dedicated to the '*Konstitution*' and the Duma as the first Russian '*Parlament*', both in quotation marks (Weber 1906c: 172). According to him, many of the key principles of West European parliamentary procedures were severely limited in the Russian 'constitution', primarily the parliamentary immunity of the members of the Duma and the decisions regarding irregularities in elections (Weber 1906e: 172). The parliamentary principles were violated even more gravely in the Reichsrat (Upper House), which was controlled by the Czar, in the merely consultative character of the Duma, its limited budgetary powers, the parliamentary rights of initiative and interpellation, as well as in the extraordinary powers left to the Czar (Weber 1906e: 174–88).

A monarchist and bureaucratic regime is so arbitrary that it can neither allow for even modest parliamentary control nor follow the procedures and practices of a parliamentary regime. The lack of self-government in the internal agenda of the Duma gave it far fewer powers than the *zemstvos* to serve as a counterweight to the Czar and his bureaucracy. The concern surrounding the lack of a counterweight against bureaucratic rule (for Germany, see Weber 1909b: 128) serves as a further expression of Weber's recourse to the parliamentary model, in the sense of the establishment of the possibility to argue both for and against.

In a debate in Heidelberg that opposed Weber to his own successor to the *Nationalökonomie* chair Eberhard Gothein, he reiterated his insistence on the superior results of parliamentary regimes, including the stronger influence (*Einfluss*) of the king in 'England'. He remarked that we do not need any restraints on parliamentarism – 'it's already bad enough that this tree has failed to grow to its proper height' – and demanded the removal of the obstacles to parliamentarism. 'Bremser brauche man also dem Parlamentarismus gegenüber nicht; dass seine Baume in Deutschland nicht in den Himmel wachsen, dafür sorge man schon' (Weber 1908: 134).

In other words, Weber admits that perhaps parliamentarism does indeed also have a shadowy side (for the critique of *Parlamentspatronage*, see Weber 1905b: 96), but the obstacles are all currently unsurpassable, and there is no time to be concerned with such shadows. Weber clearly uses the Protagorean argument in order to strengthen the weaker *logos*, thus illustrating the link between his pro-parliamentary politics and the parliamentary theory of knowledge (for a similar argument, see Weber 1906a: 99). At the end of his intervention against Gothein, he affirms the need for parliamentarism by alluding to the 'Daily Telegraph Affair', which is a reference to an 'interview' with Wilhelm II:[7]

> All things considered, Germany needs parliamentarism because she is ripe for it. And when a certain quarter up in Freiburg said recently that an extension of parliamentary rights would be destructive, it is incomprehensible that the German nation could submit to this.

The introduction of a parliamentary regime was not unproblematic within the federal structure of the German empire, and Weber did not propose any distinct models of this type of regime. It is obvious that his sympathies lay with the English 'parliamentary sovereignty', with its two-party system and clear alternation in government, rather than with the French practice of a coalition government, which tended frequently to be dismissed by the parliament during the electoral term (Weber 1906c: 20; for a reappraisal of the Third Republic practice, see Roussellier 1997, 2000).

The parlamentarisation of German political culture

The preceding sections serve as a *Verfremdungseffekt* [distancing effect] that enables me to broaden both the conceptual and contextual references in the analysis of Weber's late detailed writings on parliamentarism in terms of the rhetorical paradigm. His essay 'Das preussische Wahlrecht', published in April 1917, ends with an apology for the ideal type of the leading parliamentary politician, whose source of power is election by universal suffrage: 'Today a free stage for universal popular election (*Volkswahl*) is needed in order to bring to light the specific political talents, which ... are obstructed from appearing'.[8]

The open competition in democratic elections forms the only possible counterweight to the rule of officialdom and their narrow *Fachwissen* [factual knowledge]. It is precisely the indispensable nature of this factual knowledge that causes the need for counter-knowledge to arise. The leading politician, elected by

---

7. Alles in allem: einen Parlamentarismus braucht Deutschland, denn es sei reif dafür. Und wenn von bestimmter Seite jüngst droben in Freiburg gesagt wurde, eine Erweiterung parlamentarischer Rechte führe Zersetzung herbei, so sei es unbegreiflich, wie sich die deutsche Nation so etwas gefallen lassen kann (Weber 1908: 134).

8. 'Heute bedarf es der freien Bühne der allgemeinen Volkswahl, um jene spezifisch politischen Begabungen an das Tageslicht zu bringen, die ... gehindert werden, in die Hohe zu kommen' (Weber 1917b: 100).

the citizens, whose daily life was dominated by the *Fachmenschen*, is the only type of human being that can effectively counter the rule of officialdom, due to the specific competences created by the experiences of electoral competition and parliamentary deliberation (Weber 1917b: 100–1).

According to Weber's historical analysis, the expansion of bureaucracy is an overwhelming tendency which requires political counterweights. The construction of such a counterweight is analogous to the construction of a competing theoretical perspective to a hegemonic viewpoint. The very notion of competing views on knowledge and, analogously, competing sources of power, is incompatible with bureaucratic rule. This is based not only on the *Fachwissen* but also on the *Dienstwissen* [knowledge from office] and *Amtsgeheimnis* [official secrets], as Weber puts it the same year (Weber 1917d: 119–20).

In *Parlament und Regierung im neugeordneten Deutschland*, he formulates in explicit terms the link between this form of knowledge and the claim of uncontrolled power and insists that the powerlessness of the Reichstag is due to the lack of control over bureaucratic knowledge:[9]

> Only someone who can procure this knowledge of the facts, independently of the good will of the official, can control the administration effectively in individual cases. Depending on circumstances, this may require access to files, on-the-spot examination, and again, in extreme cases, the *cross-examination* under oath of those involved as witnesses before a parliamentary examination commission.
>
> (Weber 1994b: 179)

The core of bureaucratic rule lies in official secrecy, *Dienstgeheimnis*, a means of protecting the administration from control (Weber 1918d: 236). For the Weberian 'parliamentary' theory of knowledge, the coalition of *Fachwissen*, *Dienstwissen* and *Geheimwissen* is a way of immunising a definite viewpoint against the control of competing perspectives. Bureaucratic claims tend to doom any competing forms of power to inferiority and to regard the perspective of those offices as the only legitimate view, as a view based on facts as opposed to speculation. This is diametrically opposed to the Weberian ideal of a parliamentary style of competition in both politics and science. The bureaucratic perspective also tends to reduce politics to administration, and its absolutisation of factual knowledge devalues the constitutive role of opportunities, decisions and judgements for politics. For Weber, the main difference between the politician and the official concerns their responsibility. Similar to the responsibilities of entrepreneurs, the politicians' responsibilities are based on the struggle with competitors (Weber 1918d: 223: *see* quote and translation on p. 49.)

---

9. 'Nur wer sich diese Tatsachenkenntnis unabhängig vom guten Willen des Beamten beschaffen kann, vermag im Einzelfall die Verwaltung wirksam zu kontrollieren. Je nach den Umständen kommen Akteneinsicht, Augenscheineinnahme, äußerstenfalls aber wiederum: das eidliche Kreuzverhör der Beteiligten als Zeugen vor einer Parlamentskommission in Betracht. Auch dieses Recht fehlt dem Reichstag' (Weber 1918d: 236).

From this perspective we can also understand better why, for Weber, not only bureaucratic but also academic knowledge can serve as a source of power. A further criterion for the priority of the parliamentary and electoral sources of power over those based on factual or academic knowledge can be seen in their publicity, one of the main points of Weber's claim in favour of the parliamentary control commissions in the Reichstag (see Weber 1917d: 119–22).

A second main link between parliamentarism and rhetoric in Weber's later writings concerns the relationship between the principles of numbers and compromise, as exposed in his pamphlet 'Wahlrecht und Demokratie in Deutschland'. Weber describes the various contractual compromises that characterise the old estate regimes and concludes that it is here that we can detect a major break between the constitutional and parliamentary forms of government:[10]

> Even in today's constitutional state there are crucial points … where state action still rests, legally and politically, on compromise. But this is not *logically* the case with elections, nor with the transactions of a parliamentary body, nor can it be the case without destroying their foundations.
>
> (Weber 1994b: 102)

This difference could also be described as concerning various forms of rhetoric. The regimes of compromise practise a kind of rhetoric of negotiations between given partners. The parliamentary and electoral regimes are based on persuasion and voting, as a final deliberative move, both in the assembly and in elections. Negotiation and compromise exist in parliamentary regimes, but they are subordinated to the principle of numerical majority, to the 'ultima ratio des Stimmzettels im Hintergrund' (Weber 1917f: 169). The competence of a parliamentary and electoral politician is based on her ability to count and anticipate votes, as shares of power, and those who are too romantic to want to engage in this practice should stay well away from politics (Weber 1917f: 169).

The majority principle and the *Zifferndemokratie* [democracy of numbers] (Weber 1917f: 169) also express the individualist basis of parliamentary regimes. The partners and parties involved in the negotiations are constituted by elections and parliamentary deliberations, and the majorities are performative, that is, dependent upon the speeches and votes of individuals. This is also expressed by Weber's concept of the *Staatsbürger*, who is constituted into a political unit by means of her equal right to vote and an abstraction from her social being (Weber 1917f: 169).

The rhetoric of parliamentary deliberations presupposes that MPs are not mere delegates of the voters. Weber, in a sense, extends the parliamentary model to elections, particularly in his concept of the occasional politician (*see* the quote and

---

10. 'Im konstitutionellen Staat ruht in entscheidenden Punkten auch heute noch das staatliche Handeln … im Rechtssinn und politisch, auf dem Kompromiss … Nur als das Kompromiss die rechtliche Grundlage politischen Handelns war, war auch die ständische Berufsgliederung ihrem Wesen nach am Platze. Nicht aber da, wo der Stimmzettel regiert: für eine Parlamentswahl' (Weber 1917f: 169).

translation on p. 48.) Voting in elections is an individual act par excellence, and it is analogous to the decisions that are made through voting in the parliament.

The deliberative activity of weighing and ranking the alternatives forms one of the main focuses of Weber's description of the performance of parliamentarians. In the 'Wahlrecht' pamphlet he emphasises the distinctive achievement of the parliament:[11]

> *This* is the specific achievement *(Leistung)* performed by parliament: to make it possible to achieve the 'best' solution (relatively speaking) by a process of negotiation and compromise. The price to be paid for this achievement is the same sacrifice as that made by the voter in a parliamentary election when he has to vote for the party which is *relatively* the most acceptable to him. Nothing can replace this purely technical superiority of parliamentary legislation.
>
> (Weber 1994b: 128, translation modified)

The rhetorical point is that there are no pre-conceived alternatives in parliamentary politics. The items discussed and voted on ought to be judged in terms of their political weight, on which Weber writes: 'das … ein Parlamentarier im Kampf der Parteien zu lernen vermag, die Tragweite des Wortes zu wägen' (Weber 1917f: 187). The assessment of the political 'weight' of words presupposes a detailed ranking of one's own aims in relation to those of adversaries, as well as a preparedness to alter standpoints and priorities during the parliamentary deliberations. The above-quoted paragraph helps us to understand why Weber extends the situation of the parliamentarian to the voter – and not vice versa – and why he attempts to 'teach' voters to act in the ballot box as if they themselves were MPs.

Not all of Weber's comments on parliamentary practices and conventions are positive at the outset. In the *Parlament* volume he distinguishes between *Arbeitsparlament* and *Redeparlament*. The lack of power cannot be compensated for by oratorical qualities. The aim of Weber's advocacy of a British-style working parliament focused on the control of administration, 'solches, welches die Verwaltung fortlaufend mitarbeitend kontrolliert' (Weber 1918d: 234), is again to create a counterweight to bureaucracy. The power of bureaucracy is indispensable and cannot be replaced by the parliament, but it is precisely for this reason that the power shares of parliament should be extended to the control of bureaucracy.

Weber by no means underestimates the power shares created by speech. On the contrary, in his discussion of the types of politician, particularly of the advocate and the journalist, he emphasises the decisive role of speech as a mark of the

---

11. 'Das ist die spezifische Leistung des Parlaments: dass es ermöglicht, durch Verhandlung und Vergleich das relativ Beste zustande zu bringen, und diese Leistung wird mit dem gleichen Opfer erkauft, welches der Wähler bei der Parlamentswahl in der Form zu bringen hat, dass er nur für die ihm relativ genehmste Partei optieren kann. Diese rein technische Überlegenheit parlamentarischer Gesetzgebung ist durch nichts zu ersetzen' (Weber 1917f: 188).

competence of the politician, for example in this passage commenting on the changing styles of parliamentary eloquence:[12]

> How, then, is this leadership selected? Firstly, on the basis of what ability is the selection made? Here what matters most … is of course the power of demagogic speech. Its nature has changed since Cobden's time, when the appeal was to reason, via Gladstone, a master of the technique of seeming soberly to 'let the facts speak for themselves' down to the present, where pure emotive means, like those of the Salvation Army, are often deployed in order to stir the masses.
> (Weber 1994b: 343)

Oratorical competence appears to Weber as a common characteristic of the ideal type of politician. The criteria for a brilliant speech may vary greatly, but it is clear that it is impossible to become a leading politician without possessing a certain degree of eloquence. Weber speaks of demagogy in both a derogatory and appreciative sense. When he denounces Wilhelm II as a demagogue, he is referring to a demagogue in a negative sense (see Weber 1918d: 210), although this does not prevent him from appreciating advocates as politicians precisely because of their demagogical competence (Weber 1919c: 53). Any politician must be a demagogue before a popular audience. He formulates this idea in 'Politik als Beruf' by accentuating the historical link between the ancient *demagogos* and the modern politician, even as an important aspect of the occidental *Sonderweg* [path that is distinctive for the occident] (Weber 1919c: 38).

Weber makes a direct connection between the figure of Pericles, the strategist whose power was based on elections, unlike other officials in ancient Athens, and the modern leading politician. The demagogic qualities are now extended by his emphasis on either speech or writing as a decisive instrument of the political leader, and especially that of a journalist as politician (Weber 1919a: 54).

Max Weber's writings are characterised by a provocative attitude toward the antipolitical mood of his listening and reading audiences. This is, however, necessary for his project of rehabilitating politics and politicians. Such an *Umwertung der Werte* did not only concern the rhetorical qualities of politicians, journalists and so on, but also the rhetorical style of thinking itself, as it is paradigmatically represented by the parliamentary mode of acting politically (see Palonen 2002).

A provocative formulation on the real audience of parliamentary speeches is contained in the 'Parlament' pamphlet:[13]

---

12. 'Wie findet nun die Auslese dieser Führerschaft statt? Zunächst: nachelcher Fähigkeit? Dafür ist – … natürlich die Macht der demagogischen Rede vor allem maßgebend. Ihre Art hat sich geändert von den Zeiten her, wo sie sich, wie bei Cobden, an den Verstand wandte, zu Gladstone, der ein Techniker des scheinbar nüchternen Die -Tatsachen-sprechen-lassens war, bis zur Gegenwart, wo vielfach rein emotional mit Mitteln, wie sie auch die Heilsarmee verwendet, gearbeitet wird, um die Massen in Bewegung zu setzen' (Weber 1919c: 65).

13. 'Reden, die ein Abgeordneter halt, sind heute keine persönlichen Bekenntnisse mehr, noch viel weniger Versuche, die Gegner umzustimmen. Sondern sie sind amtliche Erklärungen der Partei, welche dem Lande "zum Fenster hinaus" abgegeben werden (Weber 1918d: 230).

Speeches given by a member of parliament are no longer statements of his personal convictions, far less are they attempts to persuade the opponent. Rather, they are official declarations by the party, which are addressed to the country at large 'through the window'.

(Weber 1994b: 170)

Here again we see that Weber is by no means an admirer of French parliamentarism, in which speeches had the potential to alter the fate of governmental coalitions (Weber 1918d: 259, 273), but instead prefers the British style, in which party discipline is taken for granted and parliamentary speeches seldom, if ever, change the entire political constellation. The perspectivistic controversy in the parliament does not require that governments be overthrown by the rhetorical qualities of parliamentary speeches. Weber's illusionless view was, rather, that it was through elections that parliamentary majorities were created and altered. The second point of the above-quoted passage focuses on the situation that, in a parliament with a stable governmental majority, speeches are held for the electorate rather than for the other MPs. This by no means diminishes the value of the parliamentary paradigm of politics, but instead even accentuates it by extending the parliamentary-style audience to the electorate. Perhaps this requires more than Weber seems to assume, for the auditory and visual presence of the MPs, especially of adversaries, should be regarded as a crucial condition of the parliamentary style of politics.

Toward a rhetorical redescription of parliamentarism

In his *Reason and Rhetoric in the Philosophy of Hobbes* (Skinner 1996: esp. ch. 4), Quentin Skinner suggests the procedure of rhetorical re-description in order to facilitate the understanding of conceptual changes (see also Skinner 1999b and the analysis in Palonen 2003a: ch. 6). The scheme *paradiastole*, in which virtues are devalued and vices are perhaps not simply revalued but rendered harmless, allows us to understand the changes in the normative colour of concepts.

I have practised here a rhetorical redescription of the very concept of parliamentarism in order to reinterpret Weber's relationship to it. I have extended its 'range of reference' (see Skinner 1979) by shifting its focus from constitutional law to rhetoric and from the mere statement of a majority to the procedure of persuading the audience by means of speaking for and against. This also allows for the extension of the range of parliamentary styles of politics from the national parliament to elections, party conferences and to public debate in general. In this perspective, parliamentary politics appears as both the paradigmatic manifestation of a culture of controversy and a rhetorical style of politics par excellence.

Within the Weberian *oeuvre*, this rhetorical extension of the concept of parliamentarism also allows us to specify the political point of his search for the counterweights to bureaucratisation. It is not so much the legal rule of officialdom as the tendency of officialdom to monopolise and render their factual knowledge secret that he is against. What I have referred to as Weber's 'parliamentary theory of knowledge' rehabilitates the value of competition and deliberation in the formation and assessment of knowledge. The parliamentary politician is an ideal–typical figure who is competent to use such knowledge against the bureaucratic tendencies and toward monopoly and secrecy.

In the German context, it is this rhetorical concept of parliamentarism that Max Weber revaluates. In his wartime writings, this revaluation is expressed in the form of a conscious attempt to rehabilitate the British political culture as a culture of conducting controversies by speaking. He does not affirm the aesthetic value of parliamentary speaking but, rather, the efficiency of a rhetorical procedure in which questions are examined and dealt with from opposite sides. This also appears as his specific defence of the superiority of the government by politicians of the rule of officialdom.

Chapter Eleven

'Objectivity' as Fair Play: Max Weber's Parliamentary Redescription of a Normative Concept

Few concepts enjoy a better reputation than 'objectivity'. However, when we consider the rhetorical force of the speech acts appealing to 'objectivity', their oxymoronic character becomes clear. They are simultaneously attempts to support one's own standpoint and to surpass partisan standpoints.

To scholars of academic rhetorical practices, 'objectivity' thus appears as a rather dubious concept. Why, for example, does Max Weber use quotation marks when he refers to the 'objectivity' of knowledge in social science in his 1904 essay 'Die "Objektivität" sozialwissenschaftlicher und sozialpolitischer Erkenntnis'?

The quotation marks allude to the fact that he clearly seems to be well aware of the oxymoronic character of 'objectivity'. In his essay, Weber offers a rhetorical redescription of the concept of 'objectivity', through which he revises its conceptual point and range of reference. What steps did Weber follow in constructing his new concept? My thesis is that the Weberian concept of 'objectivity' alludes to dealing with the treatment of scholarly controversies, as he explicates in this passage:[1]

> No one can evade the fact that the problem exists ... this is clear for anyone who observes the struggle over method, 'basic concepts' and presuppositions, the constant change of 'viewpoints' and the continual redefinition of 'concepts' – it is evident that theoretical and historical deliberations still seem to be separated by an unbridgeable chasm: 'two sciences of economics!' as a bewildered Viennese examinee once peevishly complained. What does objectivity mean in this context? The following discussion is devoted solely to this question.
>
> (Weber 2004b: 367–8)

The background to this view lies in Weber's rhetorical reinterpretation of the concept of knowledge itself, which is mediated through the work of Friedrich Nietzsche. However, Nietzsche had a high degree of academic contempt for day-to-day politics, whereas Weber, a life-long *homo politicus*, connects his regulative idea of objectivity, namely fair play, to a definite historical paradigm of rhetoric,

---

1. 'Daß das Problem als solches besteht und ... kann niemandem entgehen, der den Kampf um Methode, "Grundbegriffe" und Voraussetzungen, den steten Wechsel der "Gesichtspunkte" und die stete Neubestimmung der "Begriffe", die verwendet werden, beobachtet und sieht, wie theoretische und historische Betrachtungsform noch immer durch eine scheinbar unüberbrückbare Kluft getrennt sind: "zwei Nationalökonomien", wie ein verzweifelnder Wiener Examinand seinerzeit jammernd klagte. Was heißt hier Objektivität? Lediglich diese Frage wollen die nachfolgenden Ausführungen erörtern' (Weber 1904b: 160–1).

to the parliamentary mode of dealing with political struggles, as it was exemplified by the English Parliament. How could he plausibly argue at the beginning of the twentieth century that his revised concept was still that of 'objectivity'?

'Objectivity' – what is it not?

Weber replied to one of the critics of his *Protestantische Ethik* by saying that he was not concerned with the conventional meaning of his key concept: 'Was der "übliche Sinn" des "kapitalistischen Geistes" ist, kümmert mich nicht …' (Weber 1910a: 176). The same can be said about his concept of 'objectivity'; the quotation marks should warn Weber's readers to direct a careful attention to the concept and to be prepared to reconsider its meaning and point. By analysing the twenty-four singular uses of 'objective' and 'objectivity' in the essay, we are able to gain a clear insight into what Weber does not mean by them. The analysis of Weber's reinterpretation of the concept should start with his demarcations of the concept from its conventional meaning.

There still exists a textbook view that scientific objectivity may be reached by eliminating all subjectivity, by extinguishing everything personal from the research process. For Weber, it is, however, clear that the 'objectivity' of knowledge is not the inherent property of the 'object' under analysis: 'Die Qualität eines Vorganges als "sozialökonomischer" Erscheinung ist nun nicht etwas, was ihm als solchem "objektiv" anhaftet' (Weber 1904b: 161; 2004: 368). Weber is a sworn adversary of the so-called mirror theory of knowledge, which insists on the emanation of knowledge from the object to the subject. He defends a perspectivistic view that is clearly indebted to Nietzsche's concept of 'perspectivistic Erkennen' in his *Zur Genealogie der Moral* (Nietzsche 1887: 860–1; for a closer analysis of his concept and Weber's debt to Nietzsche, see Palonen 2010b: 22–4).

Accordingly, Weber not only follows Nietzsche in putting 'Objektivität' into quotation marks, he also militantly denies that the 'objectivity' of knowledge is independent of the perspective of the scholars in question (Weber 1904b: 170; 2004: 374, *see* quotation and translation on p. 141).

However, for Weber, 'objectivity' is not a quality possessed by scholars themselves. No scholar can ever be in the position of a 'neutral' judge or referee of academic disputes. Weber is even less willing to accept the Hegelian ideal of a state official as representing the 'objective spirit' of the historical period. Against the objectivity claims of one of his most prominent colleagues, the leading neocameralist professor of national economy Gustav Schmoller, Weber insists that such claims are ways to escape from the personal responsibility of the scholar: 'By "morally" endorsing all possible cultural ideals one did away with the specific virtue of ethical imperative without gaining anything with respect to the "objective" validity of such ideals' (Weber 2004b: 360–1).[2]

---

2. 'Indem man die Gesamtheit aller möglichen Kulturideale mit dem Stempel des "Sittlichen" versah, verflüchtigte man die spezifische Dignität der ethischen Imperative, ohne doch für die "Objektivität" der Geltung jener Ideale irgend etwas zu gewinnen' (Weber 1904b: 148).

For Weber, scholars are necessarily involved in the research process, and are thus in a constant situation of competition and controversy with all other scholars. A precondition for the understanding of Weber's point regarding 'objectivity' lies in the insight that it is the research process itself, in particular the human aspect of presenting opposing and contesting perspectives, which is the focus of his essay. It might be conceivable to attempt to search for an Archimedean point as regards the controversy itself, which could be referred to as 'objectivity'. The scholarly disputes would then be resolved by a criterion beyond the reach of its participants. However, nothing could be farther from Max Weber's intention.

In his essay, Weber parodies all conceivable candidates for such a bird's eye view. Weber cannot expect from the scholarly language itself any 'objective' criteria for judging scholarly disputes. The appeal to scientific 'laws' or the concept of 'system' refers to nothing more than some occasionally applicable but by no means indispensable heuristic instruments that are at the disposal of scholars (Weber 1904b: 178–80; 2004b: 380–1).

Weber definitely rejects the combination of 'objectivity' with the middle way as being 'not one jot closer' to it than the extreme ideals. The middle way refers to a kind of zero-option which enables the avoidance of committing to a definite perspective[3] (Weber 2004b: 364). For Weber, on the contrary, boldness of consciously presenting a one-sided perspective, its 'einseitige Steigerung' [onesided accentuation] (Weber 1904b: 191; 2004b: 388), is to be judged as a major strength of a scholarly work.

It is equally clear that the Weberian concept of objectivity has nothing to do with the inter-subjective consensus among scholars. The young Carl Schmitt, writing some years after Weber's essay, spoke of an assumed consensus among jurisprudence-schooled lawyers as a criterion of the 'right' (*richtig*) judgment in a court (Schmitt 1912: 71).

In terms of academic disputes, we cannot imagine the existence of any pool of trained scholars who could set themselves apart from the competition in their own field. No such agenda exists in the sphere of academic controversies. It is impossible to determine the 'objective' weight and significance of an issue for the scholarly world. On the contrary, Weber claims that agenda disputes are inherently dependent on the perspectives that are part of the controversy itself:[4]

A system of cultural sciences – even if only in the sense of a definitive, objectively valid, systematic final determination of questions and spheres with which it would henceforth deal – would be an absurdity. All that can

---

3. 'Die "mittlere Linie" ist um kein Haarbreit mehr wissenschaftliche Wahrheit als die extremsten Parteiideale von rechts oder links' (Weber 1904b: 154).

4. 'Ein System der Kulturwissenschaften auch nur in dem Sinne einer definitiven, objektiv gültigen, systematisierenden Fixierung der Fragen und Gebiete, von denen sie zu handeln berufen sein sollen, wäre ein Unsinn in sich: stets kann bei einem solchen Versuch nur eine Aneinanderreihung von mehreren, spezifisch besonderten, untereinander vielfach heterogenen und disparaten Gesichtspunkten herauskommen, unter denen die Wirklichkeit für uns jeweils "Kultur", d.h. in ihrer Eigenart bedeutungsvoll war und ist' (Weber 1904b: 184–5).

emerge from such a project is the listing of several, particularized, mutually heterogeneous and disparate viewpoints through which reality is for us a given 'culture', that is, whose specific character was or is significant.

(Weber 2004b: 383)

Weber's use of 'objectivity' alludes instead to the need to regulate the disputes which arise among scholars in the research process itself. How, thus, do we organise and systematise the process of dealing with scholarly disputes in a formal and not a priori partisan manner?

In academic jargon, the appeal to 'objectivity' is most frequently used as one of the rhetorical means aimed at indicating that scholarly disputes will ultimately be settled over the course of 'scientific progress'. For Weber, nothing could be more misleading. Nothing is farther from the realities of the research process: controversies on theories, concepts and the disputes between schools and approaches are a permanent part of the research process. Every phase of the research process contains 'subjective' elements. For Weber, this subjectivity is a heuristically invaluable part of the process of making scholarly innovations.

There are no grounds for assuming that scholarly disputes would diminish over the course of an intense and thorough research process. For Weber, a consensus among scholars could even be seen as a sign of ossification, of 'Chinese stationariness', as Weber (1904b: 184; 2004b: 383) puts it with an expression borrowed from John Stuart Mill's Bentham essay (1838). For Weber, the value of an open discussion with opposing points of view on all levels of the research process lies in the fact that controversies keep scholarly activity alive. All claims that an end to history can be reached through scientific progress are misleading and dangerous:[5]

Attempts to determine the 'genuine', 'true' meaning of historical concepts recur incessantly, but are always incomplete. As a consequence the syntheses with which history continues to work either remain imperfectly defined or, as soon as an unambiguous conceptual content is sought, the concept becomes an abstract ideal type and stands revealed as a theoretical, therefore 'one-sided' perspective capable of illuminating the reality to which it is related. But this concept also of course proves itself to be unsuitable for use as a schema within which reality can be completely *integrated*.

(Weber 2004b: 398)

---

5. 'Stets wiederholen sich die Versuche, den "eigentlichen", "wahren" Sinn historischer Begriffe festzustellen, und niemals gelangen sie zu Ende. Ganz regelmäßig bleiben infolgedessen die Synthesen, mit denen die Geschichte fortwährend arbeitet, entweder nur relativ bestimmte Begriffe, oder, sobald Eindeutigkeit des Begriffsinhaltes erzwungen werden soll, wird der Begriff zum abstrakten Idealtypus und enthüllt sich damit als ein theoretischer, also "einseitiger" Gesichtspunkt, unter dem die Wirklichkeit beleuchtet, auf den sie bezogen werden kann, der aber zum Schema, in das sie restlos *eingeordnet* werden könnte, sich selbstverständlich als ungeeignet erweist' (Weber 1904b: 206–7).

Weber's point in calling for 'objectivity' must be seen in relation to the value of the struggles and confrontations between scholars over the course of the research process itself. The core of the 'Objektivität' essay lies in shifting the problem of 'objectivity' to the question of how to properly deal with scholarly controversies. Weber reformulated his key problem almost in passing in my first mentioned extensive quote from his essay (*see* note 1 and translation). He alludes to the internal disputes on the 'national economy' in German-speaking countries around 1900. The two schools in question are, of course, the historical school and the marginal utility school, nowadays frequently referred to as 'Austrian economics'. In this specific passage, however, Weber defines in more general terms the regulation of struggles between competing perspectives as the key problem of the objectivity essay.

Behind Weber's reformulation of the problem of 'objectivity' lies his criticism of academics' general lack of willingness to accept that controversies on theories and concepts are an inherent part of the research process itself. In practice, controversies are dealt with in an unregulated fashion. Nothing prevents academic institutions from 'solving' scholarly disputes by the simple recourse to the institutional authority of the existing academic hierarchies, using the scholars in the lower ranks as the applauding audience. In practice, this can easily exclude many of the dissenting and innovative voices within the academic profession. (See Weber's statements on professorships in his letters from 1906 to 1910 in Weber 1990 and 1994a.)

Weber's response to this unsatisfactory situation is to search for a model of how to fairly deal with controversies outside the academic world itself. He recognises that 'objectivity' toward alternative proposals is much more prevalent in the political context, in which controversies are not only allowed but directly encouraged. The British parliament, in particular, has extensive experience with the practices and procedures of dealing with parliamentary disputes as the main component of its modus operandi (see, for example, Redlich 1905). Weber's tacit point in the essay is to extend the application of the parliamentary paradigm to the equally omnipresent yet much less recognised scholarly controversies.

Scholarly activity as an incomplete form of politics

Among the professors in Wilhelmine Germany, it is fairly safe to say that only Max Weber could have even suggested discussing academic struggles on theories and concepts in the rhetorical terms of parliamentary politics. He only hints at what he considers to be the correct procedure of how to deal with the scholarly disputes by borrowing practices from politics.

If we look at the vocabulary of the 'Objektivität' essay, we notice that Weber does not hesitate to apply concepts such as struggle (*Kampf*) and controversy (*Auseinandersetzung*) to the research process and scholarly institutions. The vocabulary refers to the performative character of the activities themselves and the processes and institutions that regulate them. At this level, *Wissenschaft* and *Politik* are not opposite concepts. On the contrary, Weber's vocabulary can be taken as a sign of the inclusion of the scholarly activity into the activity of politics itself.

Compared with the parliamentary paradigm of politics, the academic process is, nonetheless, both incomplete (crucial decisions regarding the life of other persons are largely missing) and simplified (the constant competition for votes in the electoral, partisan and parliamentary arena is lacking in the 'meritocratic' academic world of appointments). Both the limits of academic, as opposed to parliamentary, politics and the similarities in their performance are clearly expressed in the 'Objektivität' essay, for example when Weber speaks on the necessity to make decisions in the situation of weighing the ends and consequences of action against each other. (*See* the quote and translation in Chapter Ten in this volume.)

In the research process, scholars must also make decisions on subject matter, research strategy, the mode of interpreting results and so on. As such, the research process itself can also be understood as an activity (*Handeln*).

Weber's commitment to an action perspective offers us yet another example of the performative similarity between politics and research as activities. It is not the results of research but the scholarly activities themselves that serve as the point or reference for Weber's discussion of the human sciences and their 'objectivity'. The passage on human action is equally indispensable to the understanding of Weber's vision of politics as an activity. The perspective of activity is shaped by contingency and contestation, which is what gives it its inherently political dimension, which, accordingly, also concerns the scholarly version of human activity:[6]

> All thoughtful reflection on the ultimate elements of meaningful human action turns first of all on the categories 'means' and 'ends' ... Taking into account the prevailing bonds of our knowledge, we can determine *which* means are either suitable or not for a given end. We can also estimate the chances of achieving a particular end with the given available means, and so in this way indirectly determine whether the ends themselves, given the prevailing historical situation, are practically meaningful, or criticize them as meaningless in the given circumstances. Furthermore, *if* the conditions of attaining a given end

---

6. 'Jede denkende Besinnung auf die letzten Elemente sinnvollen menschlichen Handelns ist zunächst gebunden an die Kategorien "Zweck" und "Mittel". ... Da wir (innerhalb der jeweiligen Grenzen unseres Wissens) gültig festzustellen vermögen, *welche* Mittel zu einem vorgestellten Zwecke zu führen geeignet oder ungeeignet sind, so können wir auf diesem Wege die Chancen, mit bestimmten zur Verfügung stehenden Mitteln einen bestimmten Zweck überhaupt zu erreichen, abwägen und mithin indirect die Zwecksetzung selbst, auf Grund der jeweiligen historischen Situation, als praktisch sinnvoll oder aber als nach Lage der gegebenen Verhältnisse sinnlos kritisieren. Wir können weiter, *wenn* die Möglichkeit der Erreichung eines vorgestellten Zweckes gegeben erscheint, ... die *Folgen* feststellen, welche die Anwendung der erforderlichen Mittel *neben* der eventuellen Erreichung des beabsichtigten Zweckes, infolge des Allzusammenhanges alles Geschehens, haben würde. Wir bieten alsdann dem Handeln den die Möglichkeit der Abwägung dieser ungewollten gegen die gewollten Folgen seines Handelns und damit die Antwort auf die Frage: was "*kostet*" die Erreichung des gewollten Zweckes in Gestalt der voraussichtlich eintretenden Verletzung *anderer* Werte? (Weber 1904b: 149–50).

seem to be present ... we can determine the *consequences* that the application of the requisite means within the total context of the events will have *besides* the attainment of the intended end. In this way we offer to the actor the possibility of weighing the intended consequences against the unintended, and hence an answer to the question: what does the attainment of the desired end '*cost*' in the context of the foreseeable injury to *other* values.

(Weber 2004b: 361)

Weber's thinking in terms of action transcends any simple ends–means scheme. He refers to the omnipresent unanticipated consequences, *Nebenfolgen*, which are not mere side effects but components of the situation which may actually render the significance of the action as something entirely different to that which the ends and means alone would indicate. Weber's point is to render the role of consequences intelligible. Furthermore, the ends, means and consequences refer to his key concept, *Chance*, in the interpretation of the situation. In Weber's work, we can only speak of ends, means and effects in relation to a certain interpretation of the chances available to the agents in a given situation, their horizon of the possible and their use as occasions for acting differently (see also Palonen 1998).

The decisive role of *Chancen* in the Weberian conceptual horizon renders action in general and politics in particular contingent. For Weber, unlike the hazardous contingency of the *fortuna*, the contingency of *Chancen* is a condition of the intelligibility of action itself. There are always some chances, catastrophic ones included, and speaking about them does not require any optimistic interpretation of the situation at hand. Choosing ends and means must always be related to the interpretation of the specific profile of the chances available – or lack thereof – in the situation. The *Nebenfolgen* are also a contingent product of a situation that nobody acting in the situation can properly judge. Individual agents can only thematise a section of the horizon of the possible, which does not necessarily represent the most important aspects of the analysis of the situation (see Weber 1919c: 80–1).

In terms of the understanding of scholarly activity itself, this Weberian revision of the ends–means scheme in terms of chances and consequences is a first rank move. The research process also requires deliberations and choices, the assessment of the chances in various situations, as well as the connection of the ends, means and the expected yet unknown *Nebenfolgen* to these chances. Moreover, all of these aspects must be compared with the possible action of others, particularly one's scholarly critics and adversaries.

Politicians have more experience than scholars in dealing openly with controversies and making an approximate judgment on them (*Augenmaß* [sense of distance] in Weber 1919c). Scholars have to admit that they have a lot to learn from politicians when it comes to engaging in disputes. The performative aspects of struggles, academic controversies – including theoretical, personal and institutional power shares – can best be analysed as a micro-level version of politics.

The parliamentary paradigm

For Weber, the political element is, of course, always present in the subject matter of the human sciences:[7]

> The social and political character of a problem is distinguished by the fact that it cannot be resolved by the application of mere technical considerations to fixed ends, that argument can and must arise over the regulating standards of value, and because the problem reaches into the region of general cultural questions.
>
> (Weber 2004b: 363)

For him, the parliament is the locus in which everything 'can and must be disputed'. The parliamentary procedure is built on the rhetorical assumption that a proper judgment of any proposal can only be made if it is confronted with opposing views, as is the case in the parliamentary process of discussing pro et contra, both in the plenum and in the committee stage. What types of objections arise spontaneously? Which objections and advantages can be detected or constructed when viewed more carefully when the proposal is confronted with alternatives? If one has no pre-prepared objections, one can always come up with new ones and possible grounds for contesting other aspects of the government proposals. The parliamentary conflict between government and opposition as well as a number of other dividing lines among MPs will both serve as an impetus to construct objections and alternatives and enable the discussion of their merits and demerits.

This idea of speaking pro et contra has a long history in British parliamentary procedure. In the sixteenth century, Sir Thomas Smith expressed this idea in (the English translation of) *De republica anglorum*:

> For all that commeth in consultation either in the upper house or in the neather house, is put in writing first in paper, which being once read, he that will, riseth up and speaketh with it or against it: and so one after another so long as they shall thinke good. That doone they goe to another, and so an other bill. After it hath bin once or twise read, and doth appeare that it is somewhat liked as reasonable, with such amendment in wordes and peradventure some sentences as by disputation seemeth to be amended.
>
> (Smith 1583)

In the first decade of the twentieth century, Max Weber was almost the only contemporary German academic to defend parliamentary regimes (see Weber 1904a, 1908; see Palonen 2004b, *see* also Chapter Ten in this volume). In his 1917 'Wahlrecht' essay, he described the specific advantages of the parliamentarian in

---

7. 'Das Kennzeichen des sozial*politischen* Charakters eines Problems ist es ja geradezu, daß es nicht auf Grund bloß technischer Erwägungen aus feststehenden Zwecken heraus zu erledigen ist, daß um die regulativen Wertmaßstäbe selbst gestritten werden kann und muß, weil das Problem in die Region der allgemeinen Kulturfragen hineinragt' (Weber 1904b: 152).

terms of the comparative political judgments of the merits and demerits that an MP learns better than anyone (Weber 1917f: 187). A parliamentarian must learn to judge in ambiguous situations and assess the relative political weight and range of competing proposals.

The parliamentary analogy between government and opposition can also be applied to a certain degree to the scholarly world, as we can see from the following formula on the relationship between the scholar and the 'ruling ideas of the time': 'was Gegenstand der Untersuchung wird ... das bestimmen die den Forscher und seine Zeit beherrschenden Wertideen' [the subject of the enquiry is determined by the researcher and the ruling ideas of the time] (Weber 1904b: 184; 2004b: 383). There is a kind of analogy with a parliamentary majority, backed by government and administration, to which the scholar must rhetorically address herself in order to be able to dispute the 'ruling ideas' themselves.

The 'normal scientist' who subscribes to the conventions of the time is like a *Realpolitiker* who is content to strive for whatever is possible or attainable within the existing conditions. In his early letters, Weber refuses to accept this kind of *Realpolitik* (see a letter to Hermann Baumgarten from 1887 in Weber 1936: 232). He later came to see politics as a *Kunst des Unmöglichen* [art of the impossible], in which we have to set bold aims from which the horizon of chances also looks different to that of an adaptative *Realpolitik*, or, as he also puts it, *Bureaukratenmoral des Konfuzianismus* [bureaucratic ethics of Confucianism] (Weber 1917a: 514–15).

This problematisation of the basic assumptions of the ruling schools and trends in the scholarly world is explicit in Weber's interpretation of the history of economics in Germany. In this context, he proposes an approach that recognises the historicity of the human sciences to a degree that his programme might be called a conceptual history of the human sciences *avant la lettre* (see Palonen 2000). In a passage quoted in Chapter Ten in this volume, Weber emphasises the necessity of the continuous revision of concepts. The passage continues with the characterisation of the history of social sciences as a constant shift between the construction and dissolution of concepts:[8]

The outcome is a constant process of reconstruction of these concepts within which we seek to grasp reality. The history of the sciences of social life is, and thus remains, a constant shift from the attempt to order facts in thought through conceptual construction – the dissolution of cognitive constructs so realized in the extension and displacement of the scientific horizon – to the reformation of concepts in this changed foundation.

(Weber 2004b: 398–9)

8. 'Ihr Ergebnis ist ein steter Umbildungsprozeß jener Begriffe, in denen wir die Wirklichkeit zu erfassen suchen. Die Geschichte der Wissenschaften vom sozialen Leben ist und bleibt daher ein steter Wechsel zwischen dem Versuch, durch Begriffsbildung Tatsachen gedanklich zu ordnen, – der Auflösung der so gewonnenen Gedankenbilder durch Erweiterung und Verschiebung des wissenschaftlichen Horizontes, – und der Neubildung von Begriffen auf der so veränderten Grundlage' (Weber 1904b: 207).

In other words, the scholarly activity consists of the continuous rebuilding of its conceptual apparatus. This change is not 'progress' in any definite direction, but rather a break with the past that opens up a new horizon of action that can be used in many different ways. This break is not a mere shift in unintentional and ever-changing trends. The triad between the formation, dissolution and reformation of concepts can be clearly viewed against the politics of the alternation of parliamentary majorities and governments as a key aspect of democratic politics. Similarly to the political struggle, the academic dispute is not only a dispute between theories and concepts but also between those who subscribe to them and consciously advocate them.

The procedures and mechanisms by which the concepts and theories change in scholarly activity can be understood in parliamentary terms. The rhetorical struggle which is built into the parliamentary procedure offers a paradigm for the recognition of the historical and controversial character of academic knowledge. The procedures of parliamentary deliberations are much more comprehensively institutionalised than the introduction and acceptance of changes in the scholarly world. The parliamentary paradigm allows scholars to use controversies not only to prevent stagnation but also to transfer the task of dealing with scholarly disputes from the periphery to the core of the research process itself.

Fair play as the regulative idea of scholarly controversies

The parliamentary procedure of speaking pro et contra serves as the conceptual and historical paradigm of the rhetorical principle of fair play. The fair parliamentary game, as a regulative idea, refers to the equality of the chances that are available for a broad number of conceivable perspectives on a given phenomenon, particularly for alternative proposals for action.

In our present understanding, the concept of fair play is most commonly connected to sports and the newfound popularity of sports in nineteenth-century Britain. The ideal of fair play refers, however, to a broader context which Quentin Skinner (1996) has referred to as the rhetorical culture of the English Renaissance. Although there are still quite few detailed studies on parliamentary procedures and practices from the rhetorical perspective (see Mack 2002), it is clear that the parliament was a new type of political arena with its own specific procedures and practices of deliberation (see Redlich 1905; Hexter 1992). During the scholarly decline of rhetorical culture since the second half of the seventeenth century, this culture was upheld and further cultivated in the parliament, as we can see, for example, in William Gerald Hamilton's maxims for parliamentary speakers from the late eighteenth century, published as *Parliamentary Logick* (1808).

Today, many of the practices and procedures inherited from the early modern English Parliament may seem quite anachronistic. Some scholars also regard the parliamentary immunity and free mandate of MPs in modern party-based parliamentary regimes as anachronistic (see Leibholz 1957). From a rhetorical point of view, however, such 'individualistic' elements of the parliamentary regime are indispensable to the understanding of its singularity. Parliamentary debates and votes are based on the deliberation between individual members and not on quasi-diplomatic negotiation between parties (see Weber 1917f: 169 on the opposition between the parliamentary principle of the majority vote as the last resort and compromise as the principle of feudal assemblies). At every stage of the parliamentary process, the 'individualistic' basis of activities is indispensable for provoking objections and revisions, as well as for adding new items to the agenda, despite the need for compromise in parliamentary practice. (For a proposal in favour of invigorating the parliamentary powers by forbidding the whips of parliamentary groups and similar reforms, see Tomkins 2005).

The acceptance of the parliamentary paradigm in scholarly controversies demands the recognition that all innovations, revisions and breakthroughs are also short lived in the scholarly world. Novel theories and the revision of concepts may gain a momentum that can be evoked well before it will be turned into an element of stagnation. It is for precisely this reason that Weber strongly opposes the 'middle way' and opts for the one-sided accentuation of a particular point of view. Just as the parliamentarian knows that no elections will be won twice with the same election strategy, the scholar should not rely on their past merits, but should always be ready and willing to change.

However, Weber also turns against the hunt for novelty for novelty's sake alone, 'eine stete Hetzjagd nach neuen Gesichtspunkten und begrifflichen Konstruktionen' (Weber 1904b: 214; 2004b: 403). Here we can also detect an analogy to the formal equality between standpoints and alternatives in parliamentary procedure. The rhetorical principle of speaking pro et contra about all items on the agenda is a guarantee against vested interests and over-eager enthusiasm for the new. Similarly, in the academic world, the resistance of trends is well founded and the recourse to older and even overthrown theories and concepts is frequently a clever strategy. It allows scholars to stick to their position in the face of novelties and even claim a *Verfremdungseffekt* [distanciation effect] in order to relativise the alleged innovations.

The parliamentary style of politics is inherently incompatible with the one-dimensional opposition between progress and reaction. When examined through the Weberian *Umbildungsprozess* [process of re-conceptualisation], the recurrent events of unexpected breaks and turns at more or less regular intervals, it becomes clear that all standpoints and proposals in the scholarly debate should be given a fair chance, as is the case in the parliamentary process. In a more radical sense, speaking pro et contra, which characterises the parliamentary procedure, operates by devaluing virtues and attenuating vices, according to the classical schema of *paradiastole* (see Skinner 1996).

The rhetorical vision of parliamentary deliberation is much more radical than that which Jürgen Habermas and his adepts refer to as 'deliberative democracy'. Indeed, we can detect a debt to the rhetorical tradition even in Habermas's insistence on the constant deliberation between 'Argument und Gegenargument' against fixed commitments (Habermas 1962: 252). For him, however, this rhetorical moment of deliberation and debate remains nothing more than a passing phase in the process toward a higher consensus. In other words, the debate serves as a moment of catharsis that will be superseded by the superior moment of consensus.

In contrast to this instrumental role of deliberation, the ideal of fair play corresponds to the rhetorical principle that is characteristic of political situations, namely that good grounds can always be offered in defence of either side. It may even be wise to attempt to make the weaker *logos* stronger, in the sense of the Sophist Protagoras, for whom '[o]n every subject there are two *logoi* [speeches or arguments] opposed to one another' (Diogenes Laertius in Gagarin and Woodroff 1995: 187). The singularity of the parliamentary procedure lies in an institutionalisation of the fair play principle.

The Weberian parliamentary vision of the research process is not completely free of the pathos of truth either. This is, for example, the case when he writes: 'Denn wissenschaftliche Wahrheit ist nur, was für alle gelten will, die Wahrheit wollen' [Because scientific truth is only important to those who want the truth] (Weber 1904b: 183–4; 2004b: 383). Upon closer examination it becomes clear, however, that, for Weber, judgements on truth are related to perspectives as opposed to judgements about facts. As such, all factual judgments remain controversial and momentary agreements on them among scholars are not a sign of the superiority of consensus. Weber insists that an academic journal should be a place to search the truth, independently of the background or standing of the scholar, 'wo Wahrheit gesucht wird, die ... auch für den Chinesen die Geltung einer denkenden Ordnung der empirischen Wirklichkeit beansprucht' (Weber 1904b: 156; 2004b: 365). His claim is directed against the relativism of fixed standpoints that are essentially incompatible with one another. In other words, Weber turns against the arbitrary fixation of standpoints as the 'truth'.

Moreover, Weber uses this move as a rhetorical redescription of the concept of the truth. For him, the search for truth appears, above all, as a metaphor for the idea that the dispute should be maintained and everyone should be ready to alter her or his standpoint in the course of debate. This is clearly compatible with speaking *in utramque partem* and by no means requires abolishing opposing standpoints or setting an increased consensus as the aim of deliberations.

No less rhetorical is Weber's revision of the understanding of 'scientific progress'. For Weber, *Fortschritt* is not a kind of march 'forward'. Rather, it refers to breaking with established beliefs, conventions, long-term trends and so on, taking steps away from something but leaving the future direction open. Again, we can detect at least certain analogies with the parliamentary vote of no confidence or the alternation in government due to the electoral defeat of the current majority. Any such shift contains opportunity, openness and novelty that can be used in various ways, including the new strength that a party may gain in opposition.

This priority of a break with the past as a moment of change is famously illustrated by the 'eternal youthfulness' of all historical sciences:[9]

---

9. 'es gibt Wissenschaften, denen ewige Jugendlichkeit beschieden ist, und das sind alle *historischen* Disziplinen, alle die, denen der ewig fortschreitende Fluß der Kultur stets neue Problemstellungen zuführt. Bei ihnen liegt die Vergänglichkeit *aller, aber* zugleich die Unvermeidlichkeit immer *neuer* idealtypischer Konstruktionen im Wesen der Aufgabe' (Weber 1904b: 206).

But there are sciences destined to eternal youthfulness, and that includes all *historical* disciplines, all those disciplines to which the eternally advancing flow of culture poses new problems. Here the transience of *all* ideal–typical constructions, *but* at the same time the inevitability of constantly forming *new* constructions, is central to their task.

(Weber 2004b: 398)

The shifting character of the problems related to standpoints as a means of altering them can also be seen as an analogy to parliamentary politics. New items on the agenda either arise spontaneously from the changing constellations in the world around them or are more intentionally set as an issue to be debated in the parliament. The situation corresponds to the shift in political controversies from that between different answers to the same questions to the struggle over which issues should be debated, in what order and why, i.e. their status on the parliamentary agenda. Similarly, the academic world has also experienced the increased diversification of issues and the vanishing of a wide range of allegedly common grounds within individual disciplines. The one-sided construction of new perspectives marks the recognition of this situation as early as Weber's lifetime.

The parliamentary opposition to expert rule

Weber differs from his German contemporaries in his open idealisation of the British style of parliamentary government as early as the beginning of the twentieth century (see Palonen 2004b; *see* Chapter Ten in this volume). Weber insists on the procedural superiority of the parliamentary regime over a monarchy whose foreign policy is not under the control of a parliament. He defends parliamentarism against the possibility of the Emperor intervening in German foreign policy (Weber 1908: 134; *see* quote and translation on p. 144).

In his wartime essay 'Parlament und Regierung im neugeordneten Deutschland' (1918d), Weber describes the parliament above all as a counter-power against bureaucracy. An efficient bureaucracy is indispensable in every modern state. In the German Empire, however, the rule of officialdom, *Beamtenherrschaft*, prevailed without real counter forces in terms of parliamentary power and a government that was responsible to the parliament. Weber saw this as fatal, because he considered officials to be dilettantish politicians (Weber 1918d: 235; *see* the quote on p. 55).

Weber sees a monocratic understanding of knowledge as inherent to officialdom. He confronts it with a parliamentary view which corresponds to the rhetorical vision he sketched in the 'Objektivität' essay more than ten years earlier. The 'possession' of knowledge is the main power share available to officials. Their power is based primarily on factual knowledge. Furthermore, the officials gain a *Dienstwissen* [knowledge from office] in carrying out their tasks within the state apparatus (Weber 1918d: 236; 1994: 178). The decisive form of knowledge lies, however, in the secrecy of the knowledge they possess: 'Officialdom's most important *instrument of power* is the transformation of official information into *secret information* by means of the infamous concept of 'official secrecy', which ultimately is merely a device to *protect* the administration *from control.*'[10]

The power of officialdom is inherently linked to its expert knowledge, to which not even the parliament had access in Germany. The link between Weber's defence of the parliamentary regime and his rejection of the monocratic view of knowledge lies in his numerous proposals to form parliamentary counter-powers in order to limit officialdom's monopoly on knowledge as a source of uncontrollable power. In other words, Weber wants to alter the procedures of the Reichstag in order to allow it to control officialdom, just as the British Parliament had.

Weber's proposals for reforming Reichstag procedure refer to the rhetorical practice of speaking pro et contra. One example of this is the oath-based cross-examination of experts in the parliamentary commissions (*see* the quote and translatsion on p. 196 below). By opposing officials' specialised *Sachwissen* with one another, the parliamentarians are able to see that the knowledge of officials is inherently bound to the perspective of their offices. Parliamentary deliberation must overcome the perspectives of these offices by judging the work of the ministries from a political point of view. The control of the *Dienstwissen* also requires measures such as access to files, on-the-spot examination and hearings before a parliamentary examination commission (*see* the quote and translation in Chapter Ten in this volume). For the control of secrecy, Weber proposes a stronger measure, namely parliamentary enquête commissions, which he considered to be an English practice:[11]

> This is only possible, because parliament, without the so-called '*right of inquiry*' (*Enqueterecht*), is denied the means of acquiring the knowledge of the facts and of technical and specialist considerations which alone make it possible for parliament to participate in and influence the direction taken by the administration on a continuous basis.
>
> (Weber 2004b: 179)

All these measures allude to the rhetorical view that 'facts' and 'knowledge' can be seen as such only in relation to a certain perspective. In such situations, the parliamentary paradigm of knowledge is the surest guarantee against an uncritical belief in given facts. The powers of the parliament are decisively dependent on the systematic character of the use of opposing perspectives in the parliamentary and governmental process (see also Palonen 2004b; *see* also Chapter Ten in this volume).

Weber's defence of the English style of *Arbeitsparlament* over the French style of *Redeparlament* also corresponds to this view. Only through the work of the commissions' members on substantial issues can they become conscious of the

---

10. 'das wichtigste *Machtmittel* des Beamtentums die Verwandlung des Dienstwissens in ein Geheimwissen durch den berüchtigten Begriff des "*Dienstgeheimnisses*" bildet: letztlich lediglich ein Mittel, die Verwaltung *gegen Kontrolle zu sichern*' (Weber 1918: 236).

11. 'durch Handhabung des sogenannten "Enqueterechts" jederzeit jene Kenntnis der Tatsachen und der technischen Fachgesichtspunkte zu verschaffen, welche allein ihm fortlaufende Mitarbeit und Einfluß auf die Richtung der Verwaltung ermöglichen würde' (Weber 1918d: 236).

need to control and the means of controlling expert powers (Weber 1918d: 234–7). This vision is no less rhetorical than the French emphasis on speeches in the plenary sessions, which tend to increase the powers of the parliament at the cost of the government, in particular by shortening their life-span; the parliamentarians tended to misjudge that Weber's discussions in the 'Parlament' pamphlet on *Fachwissen*, *Dienstwissen* and *Geheimwissen* are relevant to the understanding of the tendencies of closure in the academic world. The monopolistic tendencies, the exclusion of competitors, students, amateurs and outsiders, the processes of co-optation and so on are also behind the inherent threat of stagnation in the use of theories and concepts. The need and chances to gain external parliamentary control of the research process itself is not as evident here as it is in the case of bureaucratic knowledge. For this reason, internal procedures analogous to those of parliaments should be applied to deliberation and debate in universities.

This presupposes, however, that scholars not only acknowledge that they must learn the procedures related to their internal disputes from politicians but that they are prepared to turn themselves into figures reminiscent of parliamentarians in the context of academic controversies.

Why does Weber speak of 'Objectivity'?

Max Weber himself seems not to use the expression 'fair play' in his methodological or political writings. Attributing it to Weber, as a regulative principle allowing us to gain a better understanding of the very singular and distinctive point he is making in the essay, is, of course, conjecture. Nonetheless, my intention here is to answer my initial question of why he claimed the controversial concept of 'objectivity' as his own.

My interpretation applies the principle of one-sided accentuation to Weber's own work. A minimum condition for making this kind of interpretation is shifting one's emphasis to the research process itself, to the controversial character of its results, to the conflicts between scholars and the chances to regulate the relationships between scholars offering contrasting interpretations. Regulations are needed precisely because the controversies on theories and concepts, as well as conflicts between scholars, are always present in scholarly activities. Those who adhere to a religion of science remain extremely reluctant to recognise this situation, whereas the life-long *homo politicus* Max Weber understood the inherent political element in scholarly activity better than any of his contemporaries.

This concept is no longer complexly unrecognised among some recent Weberologists. Joachim Vahland (2001) writes on the priority of dissent over consensus, that for Weber, dissensus is prior to consensus and therefore he recognises science as one manifestation of the political among others.[12] Despite

---

12. 'der Dissens, nicht der Konsens, der die Wissenschaft wie alle anderen Lebensbereiche bestimmt und vorantreibt ... Weber hat keinen Zweifel daran gelassen, daß für ihn Wissenschaft in letzter Instanz Manifestation des Politischen ist – wie alle anderen kulturellen Objektivationen auch: Alle Kulturarbeit ist zweckbestimmtes Stellungnehmen' (Vahland 2001: 113).

this, Vahland does not discuss the Weberian concept of 'objectivity' in terms approaching my perspective.

One of the programmatic aims of Weber's essay was to present the *Archiv* neither as a party organ in the academic world nor as a journal in which anything goes. He wanted to offer the academic world a neutral playground for debate, 'die Möglichkeit, mit politischen Gegnern sich auf neutralem Boden – geselligem oder ideellem – unbefangen zusammenzufinden' (Weber 1904b: 158; 2004: 367). He saw the *Archiv* itself as a forum analogous to the British parliament, with civilised deliberation and the debate between opposing perspectives as its *raison d'être*.

This passage is perhaps as close as Weber comes to offering us an explicit analogy with parliamentary politics and its rhetorical vision of knowledge and action. He uses it to indicate the model of parliamentary politics that should be applied to scholarly disputes. Examples of Weber's vocabulary and his spontaneous use of political analogies for scholarly controversies support this.

According to Weber, there were no satisfactory regulations for engaging in scholarly disputes on theories and concepts in his day. Convinced of the omnipresence and heuristic value of such disputes, he intended to transfer regulations from the institutionalised and reasonably well-functioning parliamentary context to scholarly disputes. Weber was not interested in the details of constructing an exact alternative for such a conceptual transfer. For him, it was sufficient to point out that there was indeed a parliamentary paradigm for a thorough discussion of objections and alternatives in a civilised manner that could also be applied in the scholarly world.

Referring to the application of a parliamentary paradigm for scholarly conflicts as 'objectivity' made the idea more acceptable. Before an audience of German academics, Weber's most provocative move was to claim that 'objectivity' was in fact more applicable in political than academic conflicts. This was part of Weber's comprehensive programme of reinterpreting the very concepts of knowledge and the human sciences in rhetorical terms, for which the English Parliament served as the historical paradigm. Such terms turned the scholarly activity of research itself into an activity of politics.

Chapter Twelve

Max Weber's Rhetoric of 'Objectivity': The Parliament as a Paradigm for Scholarly Disputes

My thesis in this chapter is that 'objectivity' has a better chance of succeeding in parliamentary than scholarly disputes. My aim is to challenge the widespread assumption that science is inherently more valuable than politics. One of the main justifications for this view is the belief that scientific research is 'objective' while politics is not. By disputing the basis of this assumption, I am practising what Friedrich Nietzsche referred to as the 'transvaluation of values' (*Umwertung der Werte*). Referring to the terms 'objective' and 'objectivity' in quotation marks alludes to Max Weber's famous 1904 essay 'Die "Objektivität" sozialwissenschaftlicher und sozialpolitischer Erkenntnis'. In this chapter, I refer to 'objectivity' exclusively in the sense in which it was used in the article Weber published as a member of the new editorial team (Edgar Jaffé, Werner Sombart, Max Weber) in the first issue of the newly renamed journal *Archiv für Sozialwissenschaft und Sozialpolitik*.

The reader should interpret Weber's use of quotation marks when referring to 'objectivity' as a kind of warning (see also Drysdale 2007). Contrary to what some Weber scholars seem to believe (e.g. Tenbruck 1959), Weber's point was not to reject 'objectivity'. Rather, his goal was to interpret the concept from a fresh perspective that challenged all other meanings assigned to the concept at that time. In what sense, then, does Weber defend 'objectivity'? In what sense does 'objectivity' remain a positive value? Why does he continue to cling to this ambiguous concept despite the fact that his interpretation of it differs so significantly from that of his contemporaries?

Readers of *Max Weber Studies* may recall the article I wrote on the 'Objectivity' essay some years ago (Palonen 2004b; *see* Chapter Ten in this volume). My main claim in that article was that, in order to understand Weber's defence of the parliamentary style of politics, we must reconsider its rhetorical dimensions as expressed in both the British nineteenth-century works on parliamentary government and Weber's 'parliamentary theory of knowledge', which he formulated in his essay on 'objectivity'. This time I will focus more specifically on how the rhetorical tradition and its links to British parliamentary politics can help us to understand better Weber's concept of 'objectivity' itself. The best example of the political consequences of his revision of the concept of 'objectivity' can be found in Weber's critique of the bureaucratic view of knowledge in his 1918 'Parlament' pamphlet.

'Objectivity' in scholarly controversies

It does not make sense simply to invert the commonly held view that science is an inherently more valuable activity than politics. Increasing the plausibility of Weber's standpoint requires indirect rhetorical moves that shatter the presuppositions of such commonly held beliefs. Quentin Skinner refers to this procedure as rhetorical redescription, and he sees its historical origins as lying in scheme of *paradiastole*, as it was used in Roman and Renaissance rhetoric (see esp. Skinner 1996: Ch. 4; 2002c: Ch. 10; 2007, 2008a). Skinner is particularly interested in the *paradiastolic* de- or re-valuation of the normative tone of concepts, i.e. in the idea that no value concept can possibly exist beyond the dispute and that negative concepts can indeed be extenuated or neutralised.

The *paradiastolic* demand for the revaluation of concepts in Roman and Renaissance rhetorical literature was understood as highly controversial. The ability to alter the normative tone of concepts through rhetorical redescription was frequently regarded as dangerous. Machiavelli's *Il Principe* was perhaps the most notorious example of both the devaluation of virtues and the revaluation of vices at that time (Skinner 1996: 162–80).

Many scholars, including Thomas Hobbes, found strong grounds for rejecting what Skinner refers to as the rhetorical political culture of the Renaissance and its inherent possibility of arguing *in utramque partem* ('in each and every view'). Hobbes's aim was to establish a *scientia civilis* on grounds similar to those upon which he assumed Euclidian geometry was based. Hobbes, however, was himself a learned rhetorician, and he utilised many of his rhetorical skills in his polemic against rhetorical culture. In the context of the English Civil War, Hobbes's political point of speaking against rhetoric was turned against the parliamentary style of politics based on the rhetorical principle of speaking pro et contra. He was particularly sceptical as to 'whether large assemblies can ever be safely entrusted with the conduct of government' (Skinner 1996: 287).

The polemic against the concept of rhetoric in the name of science that is prevalent today is very similar to that presented by Hobbes. However, the belief in the stable normative order in science is part of the anti-rhetorical rhetoric found in textbooks, not in the scholarly practices common to the human sciences. Since at least the 1980s, the rhetoric of the human sciences is a recurrent topos that cannot be denied simply by declaring one's belief in the value and dignity of science (see Nelson *et al.* 1987). Following the example of Nietzsche and Skinner, we can claim that the rhetorical practices of the transvaluation of values are part and parcel of the research process itself.

As every scholar with vast experience in the field of human sciences knows, disputes are not at all as rare and extraordinary as the names of some of the most famous controversies (*Methodenstreit, Positivismusstreit, Historikerstreit*, just to name a few of the German examples) would have us believe. The Weberian view of considering disputes as crucial to scholarly activity as such is probably more widely accepted today than it was in Weber's day.

One of the intellectual traditions that have assigned heuristic value to the omnipresence of disputes is conceptual history (*Begriffsgeschichte*). Reinhart Koselleck, for example, acknowledges that the key concepts of political language which are used by everyone are inherently contested and controversial (see for example Koselleck 1996 and his 'last words' on the issue in Koselleck 2006: esp. 67–70, 99–102, 533–38). From a point of view explicitly indebted to the rhetorical tradition, Quentin Skinner also recognises the inherently controversial character of concepts (see for example Skinner 2002c: Ch. 10). More explicitly than Koselleck, however, he also extends this view to academic debates, referring quite ironically to 'those moral and political philosophers of our own day who present us overarching visions of justice, freedom and other cherished values in manner of dispassionate analysts standing above the battle' (Skinner 2002c: 7).

In other words, scholars of rhetoric and conceptual history have reinforced the insight that, even when it comes to scholarly disputes on concepts, there are no 'higher' scholarly authorities or impartial judges. Rather, disputes are to be conducted among the scholars themselves. This is also the key message of Weber's essay on 'objectivity'. If we are to understand this essay better, we must also examine the nature of the rhetorical moves Weber makes when he reinterprets the concept of 'objectivity' so as to render it compatible with the continual controversies in academic practice, though without attempting to solve them.

Before delving any deeper into the analysis of Weber's essay, I shall take a closer look at the procedure of rhetorical revaluation. In the fourth chapter of his *Reason and Rhetoric in the Philosophy of Hobbes*, Quentin Skinner refers to two opposing styles and two different practices of the *paradiastolic* redescription of concepts. The styles are the renaming and reinterpretation of concepts, and the practices consist of altering the range of reference and normative tone of political concepts.

Weber limits the renaming move to the use of quotation marks, and he definitely retains the high valuation of 'objectivity'. All that remains, in Skinnerian terms, is to alter the range of reference of 'objectivity' and to reinterpret the 'core' of the concept. Weber is very clear about what he does not mean by 'objectivity' (see the discussion in Palonen 2008b; *see* also Chapter Eleven in this volume), but he offers no explicit constructive alternative. It is my thesis that Weber's alternative interpretation of 'objectivity' might be understood in terms of the metaphor of fair play. In order to render such an interpretation plausible, he must alter the range of reference applied to 'objectivity' regarding its relationships to other key concepts, such as knowledge, science (*Wissenschaft*), truth, subjectivity and politics. According to my interpretation, this is precisely what Weber is doing in his 1904 essay.

It is a well-known fact that Weber wrote this essay while slowly recovering from a severe illness (which is analysed in a detailed, albeit controversial, and psycho-historical manner by Radkau in 2005). Weber's illness forced him to permanently relinquish his professorship in political economy in Heidelberg in 1903. The long period of respite, however, also gave new direction to his thoughts. At the same time as he was working on the 'Objectivity' essay, Weber was also writing a three-part essay on the history of the older historical school in German economics (Weber 1903/06) as well as his *Protestant Ethic* essay (Weber 1904–05/20).

The immediate context of the 'Objectivity' essay refers to the contemporary disputes within the sphere of German-speaking economics, especially between Gustav Schmoller and his 'ethical' version of historical economics and Carl Menger and the 'Austrian economics' of the marginal utility school, which idealised the natural sciences. Weber defends both the historical approach – although not Schmoller's 'ethical' commitments to the Prussian state – and the theoretical intentions of economics minus Menger's naturalistic ideal of science. Weber identifies himself in the 'Objectivity' essay as an economist, and most of his arguments are related to the history and current state of that discipline. When Weber speaks of 'objectivity', he is referring directly to the *Methodenstreit* between Schmollerians and Mengerians, although he does so with the broader aim of discussing the modes of conducting scholarly disputes in general.

The key paragraph of the essay is that, according to Weber's thesis, the entire issue of 'objectivity' should be discussed in relation to the treatment of scholarly controversies. Anyone who speaks about 'objectivity' must also discuss the modes and procedures of treating scholarly disputes. Weber's point is that disputes cannot be solved or overcome in the name of 'scientific progress'. On the contrary, he seems to assume that scholarly controversies are an omnipresent and ongoing part of any scientific practice. Weber subscribes to the old rhetorical insight that the more intensively an issue is discussed, the more new and unconventional points of view the participants tend to construct (see Weber 1904b: 160–1; 2004b: 367–8, *see* full quote and translation on p. 153).

In other words, academic criticism cannot be seen as a mere cathartic phase that can be overcome by a shared consensus, but should be seen instead as part of an ongoing debate that lacks a neutral judge or arbiter. Progress is possible in the sense of the problematisation of an issue. Weber's main point is that each and every standpoint should be discussed fairly, critically and thoroughly. There is no 'objectivity as such', as no ideas or thoughts can exist independently of the perspectives of the scholars who present them. We can only speak of the 'objectivity' of the struggle between perspectives as regards their interpretations of reality (Weber 1904b: 170–1; 2004b: 374; *see* the quote and translation on p. 141).

What views of 'objectivity' does Weber exclude in these two quotations? He vehemently rejects the passivity of the scholar in the sense of the 'mirror theory of knowledge' (see for example Weber 1904b: 161, 181; Weber 2004b: 368, 377). No less obvious, although never explicitly stated in the essay, is the idea that 'objectivity' is something that can never be possessed by an individual, but, rather, is a process that not only contains the relationship between the scholar and her subject matter but also the relationships between scholars. In other words, Weber disputes the view that 'objectivity' is the polar opposite of 'subjectivity'. On the contrary, as opposed to denouncing 'subjectivity' as arbitrariness, in the manner that the 'method' teaching that is commonly practised within the social sciences tends to do, the quote indicates that 'subjectivity' is an inherent condition of the 'objectivity' that exists in the relationships between opposing points of view and the debates on them between scholars.

Similarly to the case of political struggles, Weber acknowledges that it is impossible to eliminate the personal dimension from academic disputes. In addition to the now generally recognised appreciation of the heuristic role of personal experiences in scholarly work, Weber is willing to acknowledge that personal rivalries are a source of innovation and originality in major intellectual controversies between scholars. Accordingly, he also disputes the value of the 'middle line' as a kind of surrogate for the truth (Weber 1904b: 154; 2004b: 364). In addition, intra-scientific termini such as 'laws' or 'system' are not seen as neutral arbiters of scholarly disputes (Weber 1904b: 179–80, 184; 2004b: 376, 383). These concepts neither have priority over other alternative analytic tools nor are 'inexpugnable' in the Hobbesian sense (quoted in Skinner 1996: 300).

As for the value of controversies themselves, Weber is adamant in the 'Objectivity' essay about the similarity between the human sciences and politics. Accordingly, he insists that the value of the struggle between opposing standpoints and their supporters, widely accepted both in politics and the cultural sphere, also be accepted in scholarly disputes (Weber 1904b: 153; 2004b: 363; *see* quote and translation on p. 160).

Accordingly, the point of 'objectivity' is not the termination of scholarly disputes but the open-minded and fair discussion of them. The tacit assumption of Weber's essay is that there is a keen lack of recognition of both the omnipresence and the heuristic scholarly value of academic controversies in the current academic world. This applies not only to the actual situation in the discipline of German-speaking economics but also to the general practice of minimising or ignoring the disputes within universities and other fora of scholarly controversies.

One consequence of this is that academic scholars have not instituted proper procedures for the continuous and omnipresent fair debate between different perspectives, approaches and theories.

How to deal with scholarly disputes?

Weber views the refusal to recognise the heuristic value of scholarly controversies, whether manifested in hiding them behind the academic scenes, as is the case with professorial appointments and so on, or in the repeated declarations of distinct academic schools, as a sign of stagnation. Referring tacitly to the concept of Chinese stationariness presented by John Stuart Mill in an essay on Bentham (Mill 1838), Weber speaks of the danger of a *chinesische Erstarrung* (Weber 1904b: 184; 2004b: 383). He sees the combination of academic politeness and the disgust with controversies as indicating a lack of willingness to change and to move in the direction of scholarly 'progress'.

The humanistic reform of the German universities after 1800 had in principle created a more debate-friendly intellectual climate. Immanuel Kant proposed one of the main ideas behind the university reform in his essay *Der Streit der Fakultäten*, namely the inversion of the ranks between the faculties. In the old university hierarchy, the philosophy faculty was in the lowest position and was therefore not affected by external interests as the teaching in the faculties of law, medicine and theology was. Kant's rhetorical move was to turn the free and unbound character of the philosophy faculty into the value that characterised the spirit of the entire university as an open field of arguments. He rejected the illegitimate (*unrechtsmäßig*) intervention of the bound faculties in the faculty of philosophy, but accepted that there are also legitimate (*rechtsmäßig*) contests between the faculties. His idea was to propose, just a few short years after the French Revolution, that the hierarchy of university faculties be reversed and treated analogously to the parliament.[1]

Although Kant's essay only concerns inter-faculty disputes and makes no mention of the substantial scholarly controversies within the faculties and disciplines, it does contain the idea of replacing the reliance on tacit solutions from academic authorities and their hierarchies with the principle of open argument. As such, he also takes up the problem that Weber would later refer to as 'objectivity'.

Kant's characterisation of the free faculty of philosophy as analogous to both the parliamentary opposition and the left wing indicated the need to transform the ranks between the faculties. His point is not to associate the faculty of philosophy automatically with the opposition. Rather, his intention is to present a rhetorical argument in favour of improving the chances to argue *in utramque partem*, i.e. ensuring that each and every view is heard in the *république de lettres*, just as the parliamentary procedure contains the rhetorical principle of arguing *pro et contra* on every issue on the parliamentary agenda (see Skinner 2008a: 138–40). We cannot properly understand the content, point and significance of a parliamentary proposal without hearing the arguments against it. This is the key point of Weber's perspectivistic theory of knowledge, and it clearly illustrates its link to the rhetorical tradition of discussing scholarly controversies, which Kant also takes up in his essay on the contest between faculties.

Of course, scholarly controversies and their implicit or explicit personal parallels are dealt with in some way or another. They may be discussed openly or hidden behind closed doors; added to the agenda of debates or removed from it; brought to the fore or pushed to the background; resolved by the institutional or positional authority or simply ignored. Unlike in the parliament, there is no established procedure regarding how to institutionalise controversies, which makes them more ambiguous and their outcome potentially hazardous, particularly since they are often the product of personal sympathies, shifting trends or actual constellations within faculties and departments.

---

1. 'Die Classe der obern Facultäten (als die rechte Seite des Parlaments der Gelehrtheit) vertheidigt die Statute der Regierung, indessen daß es in einer so freien Verfassung, als die sein muß, wo es um Wahrheit zu thun ist, auch eine Oppositionspartei (die linke Seite) geben muß, welche die Bank der philosophischen Facultät ist, weil ohne deren strenge Prüfung und Einwürfe die Regierung von dem, was ihr selbst ersprießlich oder nachtheilig sein dürfte, nicht hinreichend belehrt werden würde' (Kant 1798: 42).

In the context of the individual disciplines within a university, there exists an implicit hierarchical model that corresponds to Aristotle's epideictic rhetoric. The classical situation of a professor speaking to an audience corresponds to the epideictic rhetoric of the festivity speakers. The audience can only respond with praise and blame, i.e. by either hailing or rejecting the standpoint presented to them *ex cathedra*. We can also use the analogy of a referendum or plebiscite, to which voters can only answer 'yes' or 'no'.

In Weber's time, strong parallels could still be drawn between professors and the ancient festivity speakers or a Bonapartist president standing before the plebiscite. The plebs, i.e. the students, could 'vote with their feet' for the professors they wanted to listen to, as they had free access to all professors, disciplines, faculties and universities. Professors competed with each other for students. The number and quality of the students that professors were able to attract in lectures and in supervised dissertations boosted their reputation often more or less independently of their scholarly qualities and involvement in the controversies surrounding the theories and concepts in their discipline. Of course popularity among students alone was not enough to make a *Privatdozent* a professor (*Ordinarius*).

In today's more closed academic environment, the competition between scholars for students on the epideictic basis of praise and blame has been marginalised. The models of forensic and negotiation rhetoric have gained ground, but they too are unrelated to the fair treatment of theoretical disputes in the research process itself. Their existence and persistence are more broadly recognised today than they were in Weber's time, and aspects of regulating the disputes between scholars may exist in specific contexts, but a more systematic procedure analogous to that of the parliament is still a desideratum.

The rhetoric of fair play and its parliamentary paradigm

The historical role of rhetoric in Weber's thought warrants closer inspection. His youthful polemic against Cicero's 'schwankende und unsichere Politik' [vacillating and uncertain politics] gegen Catilina (letter to Fritz Baumgarten, 9 September 1878, in Weber 1936: 14) illustrates his classical education, to which the study of rhetoric was integral. This classical education also justifies looking for the rhetorical background to Weber's discussion of the fair treatment of academic disputes.

Weber's primary interest is in the role of the rhetorical arena par excellence, namely the British Parliament. Today's mainstream parliamentary scholars tend to marginalise the role of 'government by speaking' (Macaulay 1859). What is more, even the 'new rhetoric' scholars tend to diminish, if not ignore, the role of the parliament as a rhetorical arena (see for example the essays collected in Perelman 1989 or the depreciating remarks on the US senate deliberations in Nelson 1998: 188–92).

This was, however, not the case in the time of Max Weber. On the contrary, many nineteenth-century anglophone rhetorical works by parliamentarians, rhetoric teachers and scholars of parliamentary procedure warrant closer inspection. My main focus in this chapter is the rhetorical and parliamentary background of the ideal of fair play.

Thanks to the current online availability of books from this period, we are able to gain better insight into this forgotten genre and its link to parliamentary politics. Parliamentary politics featured prominently in many introductory anglophone works on rhetoric, and the dissensual character of parliamentary rhetoric was frequently praised. Although Weber was probably unfamiliar with most of this literature, it highlights many of the aspects of British parliamentary political culture that he so strongly admired.

The last decades of the eighteenth century saw the significant revaluation of British parliamentary eloquence. The publication of parliamentary debates was legalised in 1771 and soon after a wave of parliamentary speech collections celebrating the master speakers, such as William Pitt Sr (Lord Chatham) and Jr, Edmund Burke, Charles James Fox and Richard Sheridan, were published (see in particular the multi-volume collections of Chapman 1807–8, Browne 1808–10 and Hazlitt 1809–10). Representing a different genre, William Gerard Hamilton's collection of maxims from his long parliamentary career (1754–96), published posthumously as *Parliamentary Logick* (1808), serves as a kind of parliamentarian's handbook. This work is explicitly indebted to classical rhetoric and makes ample use of the leading Renaissance rhetorical concepts of *in utramque partem disputare* and *paradiastole* (for a summary discussion of his views, see Palonen 2008c).

The main focus of these speeches was, however, aesthetic rather than political. Famous British parliamentary speakers were compared to the ancient oratorical masters rather than associated with the parliamentary government that they were in the process of introducing. The editors were still more interested in the parliamentary 'set piece' speeches than in the debates themselves. This genre also barely mentions Hamilton's maxims other than with contempt.

In the second half of the nineteenth century, some professional rhetoric scholars included parliamentary oratory or eloquence as a part of their overviews or introductory works on rhetoric. For example, the US professor William Mathews referred (indirectly) in his *Oratory and Orators* to the principle that there are always two sides to every question, which is the single greatest advantage of modern parliaments over the ancient style of rhetoric à la Demosthenes:

> Speaking on questions upon whose decision hung the very existence of his country, the orator could not be expected to speak temperately; he could not believe that there were two sides to the question, and that conflicting views were equally reconcilable with patriotism in those who held them.
>
> (Mathews 1879: 35)

The origins of the parliamentary oratory in Westminster and its dissensual character are well documented by the Canadian professor, James De Mille, in his *Elements of Rhetoric* (1878). He distinguishes the singularity of the parliamentary as opposed to the mere 'controversial' debate (De Mille 1878: 473; *see* the quote on p. 66).

This passage expresses the precise conceptual and historical link between parliament and rhetoric, between the political form of parliamentary debate and a rhetorical view on knowledge. In the parliament, the dissensus between perspectives and the corresponding debate between members on the items on the agenda or the analysis of the political situation is a methodical principle of its activities. The debate is assumed to be a mode of understanding an issue from opposing points of view and judging the pros and cons of the proposals at hand. De Mille describes the paradigmatic character of the parliamentary debate for the understanding of the civilised dissensus as follows:

> A parliamentary debate, when carried on by able men, is one of the finest exhibitions of the powers of the human mind that can be witnessed. We see well-informed and well-trained intellects turning all their powers to the discussion of a subject from many points of view, in which two opposite forces struggle for the victory. In such a struggle all the highest intellectual forces are put forth.
>
> (De Mille 1878: 473)

De Mille also attributes to the parliamentary debate a paradigm status for the press debates. In more specific terms, the British cooperative activist George Jacob Holyoake, for example, favourably compared parliamentary debate to the platform oratory of public assemblies (Holyoake 1897: 148–9). In short, while there were numerous for a debate at the time of Weber's essay, the parliament was clearly the most important and the standard against which all other were measured.

The link between parliament and rhetoric is most explicit in the principles of parliamentary procedure. The rhetorical literature makes it clear that parliamentary procedure is indebted to the rhetorical culture of the Renaissance, although it only really began to be codified and institutionalised over the course of the eighteenth century.

The editor of the first codifying volumes originally published in the 1780s John Hatsell already spoke against 'unfair proceeding', opposing it to 'good sense' (Hatsell 1818, vol. 2: 132–3). The idea of fair play can also be detected in Jeremy Bentham's programmatic *Essay on Political Tactics*, which was originally written for the French revolutionary assemblies. The work is full of references to classical rhetorical authors. The presence of the notion of fair play can already be detected in the opening passage on the negative character of parliamentary procedure:

> In this branch of government, as in many others, the end is, so to speak, of a negative character. The object is to avoid the inconveniences, to prevent the difficulties, which must result from a large assembly of men being called to deliberate in common. The art of the legislator is limited to the prevention of everything which might prevent the development of their liberty and their intelligence.
>
> (Bentham 1791: 15)

In his classical study on British parliamentary procedure, published one year after Weber's 'objectivity' essay, the Austrian legal scholar Josef Redlich speaks explicitly of fair play as being a parliamentary principle inherent to British political culture:

> This is an instance of the application of a general principle that a recognized formula for the advancing of a piece of parliamentary business by one of the stages through which it has to pass can only be met by an acknowledged formula of amendment. The provisions thus established form a striking group in which the characteristic parliamentary mark of 'fair play' is plainly to be seen.
>
> (Redlich 1908, vol. 2: 231)[2]

Generally speaking, procedural literature refers quite rarely to rhetoric, eloquence or oratory. Redlich's words, however, clearly express the principles that the rhetoric of fair play is built deeply into the procedure of the parliament and that parliamentary speaking is characterised by the debate pro et contra:

> Speech in parliament is not monologue: speech and reply, the struggle between different sets of facts and views stated by different orators, are needed to elucidate the opinions of the members individually and of the body as a whole. There must be rules and standards before a succession of speeches becomes Debate, the characteristic form in which speaking appears in parliamentary proceedings.
>
> (Redlich 1908, vol. 3: 44)[3]

Although the ideal of fair play is quite rarely mentioned in the procedural or rhetorical literature, the quotes presented in this chapter illustrate its strong presence as a kind of regulative ideal for parliamentary procedure. The debates on procedure, for example during the crisis related to the obstruction tactics used by Charles Parnell and other Irish MPs in the 1870s and early 1880s, were also conducted in the name of fair play. In the procedural reforms responding to the obstructive uses of speeches, the principle of fair play was extended to include also the fair distribution of parliamentary time (see Redlich 1905: 162–220; 1908 vol. 1: 133–86).

---

2. 'Hier wirkt ein allgemeines Prinzip dahin, daß bestimmten Formen, in denen das Fortschreiten eines Parlamentsgeschäftes zum Ausdruck gelangt, auch nur mit ganz bestimmen Formen als Ausdruck der Bekämpfung des betreffenden Gegenstandes entgegengetreten werden darf. In solchen Bestimmungen tritt besonders stark das dem ganzen Parlamentsverfahren charakteristische Merkmal des "fair Play" hervor' (Redlich 1905: 500).

3. 'Die Rede im Parlamente ist kein Monolog, sondern auf Rede und Gegenrede, auf dem Wettbewerb der rednerisch vorgebrachten Tatsachen und Anschauungen beruht die Klärung der Meinung der Einzelnen und der Versammlung als eines Ganzen. Aber erst durch bestimmte Regeln und Normen wird aus der Wechselrede das, was für alle parlamentarische Redetätigkeit die charakteristische Erscheinungsform vorstellt, nämlich die Debatte' (Redlich 1905: 588–9).

The ideal of fair play

My analysis of Weber's essay has thus far identified the treatment of scholarly controversies as the problem of 'objectivity', highlighted his disqualification of the existing uses of this notion as irrelevant, as well as specified the intellectual context in which he claims that the discussion of 'objectivity' requires a formal procedure that did not exist at that time. In other words, according to my interpretation, Weber sees 'objectivity' as referring to a situation in which scholarly controversies are treated according to the principle that every proposal in an intellectual controversy is discussed in a fair manner from opposing points of view.

The notion of fair play is barely present in the textual corpus of Max Weber. Nonetheless, it is a part of his anglophile orientation to politics. The fair play principle was not, however, a new invention born out of the rhetoric of English sportsmanship during the nineteenth century. On the contrary, it was the manifestation of much older strains of thought, such as the tradition of medieval chivalry[4] and the Renaissance rhetorical culture. Expressions of this principle can be found, for example, in the works of William Shakespeare, who has recently been more closely associated with the rhetorical tradition than ever before (see Adamson *et al.* 2007, including Skinner's essay on *paradiastole*, and Armitage *et al.* 2009).

If the principle of fair play is seen as more than the minimum requirement of not violating the rights of others, it refers above all to the deliberative genre of rhetoric. In it there is no arbiter or judge as in forensic rhetoric, no limitation of the alternatives to yes and no as in epideictic rhetoric, and no permanently established partners as in negotiation rhetoric. Deliberation pro et contra is open-ended, and anyone has the potential to both persuade others and be persuaded by them. The ability to present fairly and weigh alternatives is the main precondition of deliberative rhetoric. The fair chance for all points of view – both those already in existence and those constructed over the course of the deliberations – to be heard in scholarly debates creates an occasion for change; the chances to present new perspectives in the face of existing ones, without, however, giving them any special priority over those already in existence. This concept can also be found in Weber's discussion of the process of conceptual revisions (*Umbildungsprozess der Begriffe*) (see Weber 1904b: 207; 2004b: 398–9; *see* quote and translation in Chapter Eleven in this volume).

The lack of any procedural model guiding the use of deliberative rhetoric in scholarly disputes is a good point of departure in attempting to understand Weber's defence of 'objectivity'. Weber suggests the duplication of a rhetorical paradigm from a context in which such a model exists, namely the parliamentary style of politics. As a lifelong *homo politicus*, he, unlike most of his German colleagues, had no difficulty reading scholarly practices as analogous to political practices without denying the existence of the differences between them.

---

4. See Weber's discussion of the concept of Spiel in the relationships between medieval knights in Weber 1922: 651.

The passage indicates the use of an analogy to the alternation of parliamentary majorities, although in the scholarly world there is seldom any clear division between 'government' and 'opposition'. The analogy applies to the parliament, in which there is a flexible majority that can be constructed and deconstructed on the basis of speaking in plenary and committees, as was the case in the French Third Republic (see Roussellier 1997). Although Weber idealised the British style of cabinet government in his view on parliamentarism (Weber 1918d: 259; 1994b: 230), the quote implies that in the academic world he favoured a situation with no strong government vs opposition divide, or strict party discipline. Such a constellation was a precondition of preventing stagnation and enabling the conceptual process of construction, deconstruction and reconstruction in scholarly disputes, as presented in the above quoted passage.

The Parliament pamphlet: bureaucratic vs rhetorical knowledge

Weber never explicitly discusses either parliamentary eloquence or the procedural paradigm of the parliament. Nonetheless, he occasionally refers to it as a well-established and widely accepted practice, and he hints at the fact that he not only appreciated its role in British parliamentary culture but also acknowledged its links to the rhetorical style of thought (see in particular Weber 1918d: 237; 1994b: 180–1).

Due to Weber's stand in favour of a strong *Reichspräsident* in 1919, his defence of parliamentarism has sometimes been seen as instrumental, i.e. as related to the formation of a strong political leadership (see Mommsen 1959). If, however, we consider his entire *oeuvre*, there is no doubt about Weber's strong parliamentary commitments. In some minor essays from the first decade of the twentieth century (Weber 1904a, 1908), he explicitly opposes the imperial Reichstag to the British Parliament and takes a vehement stand in favour of the parliamentarisation of German politics according to the broad lines of the British practice. He sees the resistance to parliamentarism in Germany as analogous to that which had taken place in Britain 200 years earlier. He uses Britain as an example of the fact that parliamentarism had indeed not had the feared result, but had instead proven its superiority over the German-style bureaucratic regime with its space for dilettantish political interventions by the monarch (for a more detailed discussion, see Palonen 2004b; *see* also Chapter Ten in this volume).

The link to both the deliberative genre of rhetoric and its historical paradigm of the parliamentary style of politics is explicit in Weber's pamphlet *Parlament und Regierung im neugeordneten Deutschland*, published in early 1918. Because it was merely a pamphlet, the theoretical discussions contained in it have largely been undervalued. However, with the help of this pamphlet, particularly its passages on the parliamentary control of bureaucracy and the bureaucratic vision of knowledge, we can better understand both the target of Weber's criticism in the 'Objectivity' essay and his vision of deliberating in scholarly controversies.

Weber characterises the political regime in the German Empire as one of the 'rule of officialdom' (*Beamtenherrschaft*). He acknowledges the indispensability of the daily rule of bureaucracy in the modern state, which is also precisely why he is searching for counterweights to it. The parliamentarisation of the government and the formation of well-equipped professional parliamentarians are the most obvious choices. In addition, he discusses the aspect of bureaucracy that is most difficult to control, namely the superiority over politicians in knowledge.

Here Weber distinguishes three types of knowledge: factual knowledge (*Fachwissen*), official knowledge (*Dienstwissen*), and secret knowledge (*Geheimwissen, Dienstgeheimnis*). How can parliamentarians control knowledge they do not actually 'possess'? Weber's answer to this question provides clear insight into the value of the rhetorical tradition. He demands that parliamentarians have access to files (*Akteneinsicht*), that they should be allowed to carry out on-the-spot inspections (*Augenscheineinnahme*) and cross-examinations of both experts and officials, and that they be granted the chances to create parliamentary commissions of inquiry (*Enqueterecht*) (Weber 1918d: 236–7; Weber 1994b: 179–80). None of these chances existed in the Reichstag of the German Empire.

The first two measures give parliamentarians access to the factual basis of the knowledge to which only officials are privy. The latter two measures illustrate the inherent inconsistencies or ambiguities in the character of bureaucratic knowledge itself, which means that it is not the facts presented by officials but the political point or significance of their knowledge that is disputed. Procedures such as cross-examination and the parliamentary commission of inquiry illustrate that both the interpretation of situations and the deliberations surrounding the proper course of action should be the responsibility of parliamentarians as opposed to officials. In all the cases mentioned, Weber relies on the concept of parliamentary procedure and its principle of discussing every item on the agenda pro et contra.

As Weber considers all knowledge to be perspectivistic and controversial in principle, the knowledge of officials is also bound to the perspectives of their respective offices and, if not controlled externally, to their status as officials. This situation is liable to lead to a *déformation professionnelle* of the rule of officialdom. Political control over officialdom is necessary in order to avoid this type of situation, and parliamentary procedure contains models for disputing their allegedly uncontested knowledge. In other words, the parliamentary principle of discussing every item pro et contra allows for the reduction or neutralisation of the knowledge privileges of officials in favour of deliberations and decisions based on broader political judgment. The seemingly factual questions of knowledge thus become rhetorical and political questions of interpretation, judgment, deliberation and decision.

Regarding the rhetorical style of thought, Weber shares the insight that knowledge and understanding can never be a possession that can be turned into a privilege or even a monopoly, whether by scholars or officials. When 'objectivity' refers to scholarly disputes, the monopolisation and exclusion tendencies of bureaucratic knowledge present a paradigmatic case of intellectual stagnation.

In Germany, Hegel and his followers considered bureaucracy to be the incarnation of 'objectivity'. For Weber, radical measures had to be taken to struggle against such a powerful tradition. He identified them in the 'Parlament' pamphlet as the political tradition of parliamentary government complemented by resources from the rhetorical tradition of parliamentary procedure. My thesis is that this discussion fourteen years later also allows us to better understand his essay on 'objectivity', not only in terms of the rhetorical ideal of fair play but also of its distinct underlying parliamentary paradigm of a procedure dealing with all opposing points of view.

Science as an imperfect form of politics

In his two lectures published in 1919, 'Wissenschaft als Beruf' (Weber 1919e) and 'Politik als Beruf' (Weber 1919c), Max Weber is adamant that a clear distinction be made between science and politics. In the 'Objectivity' essay, in which his emphasis is on the deliberation of scholarly enterprises, he highlights the similarities between the practices of scholars and politicians. Unlike what most of his colleagues believed and what continues to be the textbook view of science to this day, the activities of both are always related to that of their colleagues, to the struggles, controversies, disputes and debates within their fields. Science (*Wissenschaft*) and politics are by no means polar opposites (see also Palonen 2008b).

The point of Weber's essay can thus be seen as the thesis that, while 'objectivity' refers to intellectual controversies, the activities of scholars are much closer to those of parliamentarians than most of them would like to admit. For both, the key element of their work is the willingness and competence to argue pro et contra and to listen to opposing arguments.

Of course, the activities of scholars and politicians are not identical. Even if knowledge (*Erkenntnis, Wissen*) requires action, it still differs from politics proper. In particular, some of the key elements of politics are missing from the sphere of scholarly activity, for example the necessity to make binding decisions that concern the lives of other people. In addition, the majority principle tends to have much more limited value in scholarly than in political disputes.

Two of Weber's three criteria for being a politician, namely *Leidenschaft* [the passionate commitment to a cause], and *Augenmaß* [detached approximate judgment], are equally important to scholars. They have less need, however, for the *Verantwortungsgefühl*, which is the sense of responsibility, particularly for the fate of other people, and scholars are thus freer to speculate on and contemplate seemingly unrealistic alternatives than politicians (Weber 1919c: 75–6; 1994b: 352–3).

In this sense, I see the scholarly activity as an incomplete form of politics. As such, we can better understand why Weber advocates that the fair play ideal of deliberative rhetoric and its paradigm of parliamentary procedures and rhetorical practices should also be regarded as an ideal for fair and open discussions in scholarly controversies. How this ideal can and should be realised in the procedures and practices of the academic world remains an open question. As such, it is just as important for us, the scholars of the early twenty-first century, as it was in Weber's time.

But let us end this chapter by focusing on the similarities between activities of scholars and parliamentarians. The justification for drawing analogies between their activities is that both are engaged in debates. In a recent interview, Quentin Skinner expressed the parallel succinctly: 'I now say to my students on Hobbes's "Leviathan"... think of it as a speech in Parliament; all of these great works of political philosophy are recognizably contributions to a debate; interpreting them is uncovering what that contribution was...' (Skinner 2008a).

Unlike what Hobbes himself thought, no scholarly work can be accepted without dispute, and the better the work is, the more it is worth being debated. The problem is that even today's scholars seem to be reluctant to debate with their colleagues. In this respect it is high time for us to learn from the parliamentarians, to learn both how to read parliamentary debates as moves within rhetorical political cultures and to present scholarly concepts, theories and arguments in a manner analogical to debating parliamentarians.

Chapter Thirteen

Was Max Weber Wrong about Westminster?

In a famous article title, Guenther Roth (1987) called Max Weber 'the would-be Englishman'. The characterisation can be extended to Weber's admiration for the Westminster Parliament and its political practices. Later German scholars have disputed the soundness of Weber's interpretation of British parliamentarism in his 1918 pamphlet *Parlament und Regierung im neugeordneten Deutschland*, claiming his view was coloured by his critique of the contemporary German situation. Weber's distinction between 'working' and 'talking' parliaments (*Arbeitsparlament* vs *Redeparlament*) (Weber 1918d: 234, 238) has generally been understood only in the revised sense used by his critics within the German political science profession since the 1960s.

The thesis in this chapter is that Weber well understood the singularity of Westminster practices, its committee system in particular. German political scientists of the post-war era, on the contrary, have ignored the specific point of the Westminster tradition of parliamentary committees and reduced parliamentarism to a system of government. By understanding this, Weber's original point on the difference between the two types of parliaments can also be understood: every working parliament always also includes a talking parliament. For Weber, parliamentarism refers to a wider concept: a political culture of debate. However, Weber's manner of naming parliaments is not straightforward, and this chapter ends with a discussion of other types of parliaments mentioned by the critics in order to highlight Weber's conceptual pair against a broader set of alternatives.

Critiques of Weber's understanding of Westminster parliamentarism

In a letter of 26 August 1917, Max Weber characterised his book *Parlament und Regierung im neugeordneten Deutschland* as an academic pamphlet (*akademische Streitschrift*) (Weber 2008: 745). The book is seldom analysed in detail among Weberologists or parliamentary scholars. Wolfgang Mommsen, in his well known dissertation from 1959 *Max Weber und die deutsche Politik (1890–1920)*, devalued Weber's defence of parliamentarism to a mere mechanism for the selection of political leaders, which Weber himself had given up in early 1919 when he moved to defend the strong, directly elected character of the office of *Reichspräsident* (see Mommsen 1959: esp. 186–205 and 355–441; compare the critique of Beetham 2006: 345–6). Many scholars have followed Mommsen's authoritative interpretation and Weber still does not enjoy the best reputation among German parliamentary scholars. Nonetheless, Marcus Llanque (2000), for example, has done valuable work analysing the differences between Weber's

Frankfurter Zeitung articles from the spring of 1917 and the book version of his 'Parlament' pamphlet in relation to the crisis preceding the fall of Chancellor Bethmann Hollweg in July 1917.

The West German *Grundgesetz* (constitution) of 1949 adopted the parliamentary examination commissions which Weber had proposed as a constitutional reform to the liberal *Fortschrittliche Volkspartei's* parliamentary group in spring 1917 as well as in his pamphlet (see Weber 1917a: 116–22; 1918d: 236–8). In the Federal Republic, the parliamentary examination commissions serve as an extraordinary tool for the opposition. Winfried Steffani, however, claims that, contrary to Weber's assumptions, such commissions did not serve as instruments for the opposition in British parliamentary practice. Steffani, on the contrary, finds the idea of parliamentary control commissions incompatible with the notion of parliamentary government founded on the principle of majority rule. He regards Weber's views as an expression of the situation in non-parliamentary Wilhelmine Germany, which he maintains led Weber to misinterpret the British variant of parliamentary government (Steffani 1960).

Weber insisted that the British Parliament was an *Arbeitsparlament* and the German Reichstag a 'mere' *Redeparliament* (Weber 1918d: 234, 238; see also 1917b, d). Ernst Fraenkel, a German lawyer who emigrated to the US and later became a political scientist and leading professor at Berlin Free University, reinterpreted Weber's distinction by regarding the US Congress as the prototype of a working parliament. In point of fact, Fraenkel does not refer to Weber at all in this context, but emphasises the contrast to Westminster by claiming that the congressional budget is not debated in political, but merely administrative, terms. The US budget is analysed 'nicht unter politischen Geschichtspunkten im Plenum der beiden Häuser, sondern unter administrativen Gesichtspunkten in deren Ausschüssen' (Fraenkel 1960: 317). This also provides the background for his assertion that the Congress is a 'working parliament': 'Im Gegensatz zum House of Commons ist der Kongress primär nicht ein redendes, sondern ein arbeitendes Parlament' (Fraenkel 1960: 317).

Steffani supports Fraenkel's view of the paradigms of the two types of parliament and offers an interpretation of the concepts that radically deviates from the Weberian one. For him the talking parliament is above all a forum of public opinion for discussing the great political questions of the nation, which takes place above all as a confrontation between government and opposition parties, 'das wichtigste Forum der öffentlichen Meinung, die offizielle Bühne aller großen, die Nation bewegenden politischen Diskussionen' (Steffani 1965: 236). As opposed to this, in the working parliament the fundamental locus of power is the committees, which he interprets as the proper forum for the confrontation between the government's and the opposition's experts, a *Spezialbürokratie* (Steffani 1965: 236). Steffani clearly prefers the British to the American system, but at the same time continues his polemics against Weber by giving the working parliament a connotation that Weber would not have endorsed.

In two reference-work articles, Steffani further develops his views, using F. Schneider's alternative designations for the two types – *Diskussionsparlament* (discussion parliament) and *Ausschußparlament* (committee parliament) – to make it clear that it is Fraenkel's and not Weber's concept he is using (Steffani 1967a: 33). The confrontation between government and opposition leaders, or ministers and shadow ministers, is now the decisive criterion of Steffani's discussion of parliament. In addition, he repeats his view that a parliament of committees turns parliament into a special form of bureaucracy for the two groups of experts, and maintains that the German Bundestag is a parliament that combines both types (Steffani 1967b: 418–20).

In German political science, the terminology of Fraenkel and Steffani has become dominant; for example, Stefan Marschall (2005: 188–90) refers only to Steffani (see also the 'Parlament' article in the German Wikipedia). Philip Dann refers to the Bagehotian view of a 'fusion' between the legislative and executive powers and sees this as emblematic of the parliamentary system corresponding to what he calls 'debating parliaments'. Dann himself applies this designation to the European Parliament in order to emphasise its special features and proposes for it a further name, the 'controlling parliament' (Dann 2003).

Against this *communis opinio*, which rejects Weber's original distinction, it is nonetheless clear that Weber understood the Westminster committee system and, based on that understanding, his distinction between *Arbeitsparlament* vs *Redeparlament* can be defended against the later interpreters. In support of this argument, I shall focus on Weber's own formulations, their contexts and their point, to which Fraenkel, Steffani and later scholars have never dedicated close attention. For them 'parliamentarism' is 'defined' as a regime based on the government's responsibility to the parliament and which necessarily results in the confrontation between government and opposition parties in parliament, elections and elsewhere. Their views on Westminster parliamentarism of the late nineteenth and early twentieth century are anachronistic inasmuch as they fail to consider that the standard, post-war political-science view of parliamentarism cannot simply be projected back on to what Weber was doing when he defended British parliamentary practices. My study, in contrast, is part of the historical and conceptual reading of Weber's work, for which Wilhelm Hennis with his *Max Webers Fragestellung* (1987) was pioneer, and Peter Ghosh (2001, 2008) for example is a fine contemporary exponent.

Weber and the Westminster committees

As my point of departure, I take the concept of committee. The Westminster committee has not merely a different range of references: its very conceptual core differs from the committee paradigms of the French Assembly and the US Congress. This difference is crucial for a precise understanding of Weber's distinction between two types of parliament, and it also contributes to his central thesis concerning parliamentary control of the knowledge of administration and officialdom. Finally, Weber shares the conception of parliament as a deliberative assembly and the British political culture as a parliamentary one. In short, my point is to challenge the widespread view that would reduce parliamentarism to a mere governmental technique instead of extending the concept to a deliberating political culture. This also allows me, with Weber and older British parliamentary scholars such as Ernest Barker, who characterises parliamentary democracy as a 'process of discussion, or a method of collecting views and taking decisions on the views so collected' and emphasises the role of parliamentary rules of procedure for this purpose (Barker 1942: 210), to reconnect parliamentary studies to the studies of political thought, rhetoric and parliamentary procedure.

The most eloquent argumentation for the English[1] committee system and its link to a parliamentary culture of politics can be found in a passage of Weber's 'Parlament' pamphlet. He relates the integrity of English officialdom and the high degree of political education among the British people to the reporting of parliamentary committee deliberations by the press as a measure of political maturity. He opposes this parliamentary practice to the 'unorganised parliamentarism' of the French–Italian variety and emphasises how, in Britain, citizens can leave the daily management of their affairs to officials insofar as the parliament exercises continual control and influence over the bureaucracy. The key to this control is the power of parliament and the committee system, and therein consists their contribution to the political education of both parliamentarians and citizens.[2]

> The integrity of the English officials and the high level of political education among the English public rests essentially on this practice (among other things), and it has often been stressed that the best criterion of political maturity is to be found in the way the proceedings of these committees are followed by the English press and public alike. Political maturity is not expressed in votes of no confidence, denunciations of ministers and similar spectacles of *unorganised* parliamentary rule in France and Italy, but rather in the fact that the nation is well informed about how its officials are *conducting their affairs*, so that it constantly controls and influences their work. The committees of a powerful parliament are the only possible places from which that educative influence can be exerted.
>
> (Weber 1994b: 179–80)

---

1.   Weber mostly speaks of 'English' instead of British. When referring to his views, I frequently stick to his vocabulary.

2.   'Die Integrität des englischen Beamtentums und der hohe Stand der politischen Erziehung des englischen Volkes beruhen wesentlich mit darauf, und man hat oft betont, daß in der Art, wie die Komiteeverhandlungen von der englischen Presse und deren Leserkreis verfolgt werden, der beste Maßstab für den politischen Reifegrad gegeben ist. Denn dieser äußert sich ja nicht in Mißtrauensvoten, Ministeranklagen und solchen Spektakelstücken des französisch-italienischen *unorganisierten* Parlamentarismus, sondern darin: daß eine Nation über die *Art der Führung ihrer Geschäfte* durch das Beamtentum orientiert ist, sie fortlaufend kontrolliert und beeinflußt. Nur Ausschüsse "eines mächtigen Parlaments sind die Stätten und können sie sein, von wo jener erzieherische Einfluß ausgeübt werden kann". (Weber 1918d: 236–7)

In order to understand this passage, we have to clarify what Westminster parliamentary committees are. Scholars of today tend to assume that 'committee' simply denotes a subsection of a parliament, with a membership smaller than a plenum and comprised mainly of those who, due to previous training or parliamentary experience, are experts or specialists in a distinct field of politics. However, none of these claims necessarily holds for what is understood as a committee at Westminster.

The historical paradigm of the Westminster committee is the 'Committee of the whole House', a term that goes back to the seventeenth century (for the origins of distinguishing between 'grand committees' and the 'Committee of the whole House', see Lambert 1980: 765–7). The name indicates that it is not a subsection of the Houses of Parliament, but rather the House itself in the form of a Committee, to which a bill or motion has been sent – that is, 'committed' – from the plenum of the House. The US scholar A. Lawrence Lowell commented on this in the early twentieth century as follows: 'The most important committee, the Committee of the Whole, is not in this sense a committee at all. It is simply the House itself acting under special forms of procedure' (Lowell 1908: 265).

In other words, British parliamentarians and past parliamentary scholars have articulated a specific understanding of the concept of committee as well as of the reasons why this name can be used for 'the House itself acting under special forms of procedure'. Gilbert Campion, the author of the last comprehensive tract on Westminster procedure, writes on its origins:

> But the Committee of the Whole House seems also to have had a more deliberately intellectual origin, which seems to indicate a desire on the part of the ordinary Members to deal in open House with the arcana which had hitherto been reserved for the 'Grandes'.
>
> (Campion 1958: 27)

With this type of committee, the members also have the chances for examination and oversight of government and administration, and are expected to add this duty to their own parliamentary activities and competences.

For Westminster we can thus distinguish two states of House of Commons sittings: the 'House' and the 'Committee'. The House and the Committee of the whole House have the same membership, although they deal with motions – including bills – that are at different stages of the parliamentary journey, being first put on the House's agenda, then 'committed', and then returned after having been deliberated in detail by the Committee. The two stages correspond to the principle of subjecting every motion to two types of debate, for the difference between the House and the Committee also concerns different modes of agenda setting and of conducting debate. The crucial distinction is that in the House a member can, barring certain exceptions, speak to a motion only once, whereas in the Committee no such limits exist. The difference is explained by Thomas Erskine May, author of the most famous and now canonical tract on Westminster procedure and later Clerk of the Parliament, in the first edition of his Treatise:

The main difference between the proceedings of a committee and those of the house is, that in the former a member is entitled to speak more than once, in order that the details of a question or bill may have the most minute examination; or, as it is expressed in the standing orders of the lords, 'to have more freedom of speech, and that arguments may be used pro et contra'. These facilities for speaking are not often abused so as to protract the debates; but are rather calculated, in ordinary cases, to discourage long speeches, and to introduce a more free and conversational mode of debating. When a member can speak only once, he cannot omit any argument that he is prepared to offer, as he will not have another opportunity of urging it; but when he is at liberty to speak again, he may confine himself to one point at a time.

(May 1844: 226)

In other words, the difference in the character of debate between the House and the Committee is intentional. The aim of the House is to receive diverse views and opinions from a wide spectrum of members in order to broaden the debate and incorporate different perspectives on the pros and cons of the motion. In contrast, the aim of the Committee is to exchange views and opinions, focusing more on the details of the items, as to both their content and formulations. In Lowell's words:

The fact that a member can speak more than once makes it a real convenience for the purpose for which it is chiefly used, that is, the consideration of measures in detail, such as the discussion and amendment of the separate clauses of a bill, or the debates upon different items of appropriations.

(Lowell 1908: 265)

When Weber speaks of Westminster committees, he is definitely referring to the Committee of the whole House, in which every member was expected to participate. The distinction between House and Committee representing different stages of assembly, each holding their own type of debates and regulations, underlies his view of committees. Every member of an *Arbeitsparlament* receives political training in administration because he – if we stick to the pronoun of that time – must, precisely in order to be able to participate in both plenary and committee debates, master both of the main genres of parliamentary debating.

Weber's point also refers to the Westminster committee system as an ingenious arrangement to avoid dividing parliamentarians into generalists who debate in the plenum and specialists who speak only in committees in their fields of speciality. The Committee of the whole House system obliges every parliamentarian to participate in detailed committee debates on government legislation, administrative matters or motions from the members. This is the specifically Westminster method of controlling the government and administration, i.e. through submitting them to intensive as well as extensive parliamentary control by non-specialist parliamentarians. This was one of Walter Bagehot's main points in his defence of the parliamentary over the presidential form of government: 'A Parliamentary statesman will be a man of quite sufficient intelligence, quite enough various knowledge, quite enough miscellaneous experience, to represent effectually general sense in opposition to bureaucratic sense' (Bagehot 1867: 137–8).

After the 1832 parliamentary reform, the Committee of whole House paradigm became too crude an instrument, at a time of a sharp rise in both the number of agenda items and the expectation of the constituencies that their members participate in debate. The reform of the committee system was a major project in the nineteenth-century attempts to revise the procedure. One of the main reformers was Erskine May, who wanted to put an end to the excessive use of the Committee of the whole House. He knew well the French system of *bureaux* and the US system of specialist committees, but favoured instead a system of grand committees, consisting of about eighty members each, thus every member of the House being included in one of them, but working in a similar manner to the Committee of the whole House.

Although this system was never fully adopted (see the discussion in the Whittaker Committee, 1914), it illustrates an adherence to the Westminster principle that, even in face of ever scarcer parliamentary time, the committee members are treated as generalists. Campion rightly insists on the difference between the standing committees of Westminster and the US or French committees:

A standing committee in the House of Commons has no permanence or individuality; its members are constantly changing; it is distinguished only by a letter of the alphabet; and it does not receive one type of bill more than another. It is a miniature committee of the whole House.

(Campion 1953: 158–9)

In other words, the entire system reflects the priority given to the broad political judgment of generalists, and this is also true regarding the detailed questions dealt with in the parliamentary committees.

Weber's concept of the 'working parliament'

Weber never speaks of the details of the Westminster committees. Still, there is no doubt that the Westminster type of committee is a necessary condition for understanding Weber's vision of a working parliament. For Weber, too, the committee is characterised more by its mode of deliberations than as a small group of specialists in certain fields. Nowhere is this more obvious than in Weber's defence of the *Arbeitsparlament*. For him, the opposition between a talking and a working parliament is illustrated by the different types of politicians they tend to advance. The talking parliament fosters merely demagogic competences, a quality that Weber definitely respects and sees as inherently connected with democracy (1918d: 265), but does not regard as sufficient for the formation of genuine political leadership. The strength of a working parliament to control the administration lies in its ability to support the formation of a parliamentary leadership that transcends merely demagogic competences (Weber 1918d: 234; 1994b: 176–7; *see* quote and translation in Chapter Five in this volume).

Of course, the working parliament is not a silent parliament in the manner of the *Corps législatif* in the Napoleonic constitutions (see Garrigues 2005: 102–22). Weber's working parliament is a parliament that conducts pro et contra debates on the items on its agenda. In other words, for Weber the two types of parliament are not polar opposites. On the contrary, their relationship is to be understood as one in which the talking parliament is simpler, the working parliament a more complex case, since it is vested with a wider range of powers and activities than merely giving a voice to various issues.

When Weber contrasts the two types of parliament, his aim is not merely to try to make an analytical distinction, but to try to make a polemical point against the declamatory style of plenary speaking, as characteristic of the powerless Reichstag, or perhaps also the French Assembly. This view is most explicit in reports of two of his speeches from 1917 (1917b: 343; 1917d: 346). Weber's demand for an *Arbeitsparlament* refers to the practice of deliberating in the Westminster style, based on non-specialised committees that deal with items in a detailed manner and exercise efficient control over the administrative apparatus.

Weber insists on this aspect with his emphasis that, in the modern state, the everyday exercise of power lies in the hands of officialdom: 'Im modernen Staat liegt die wirkliche Herrschaft, welche sich … in der Handhabung der Verwaltung im Alltagsleben auswirkt, notwendig in den Händen des Beamtentums' (Weber 1918d: 212). Parliaments can, accordingly, be considered to represent those who are ruled by the bureaucracy (Weber 1918d: 226), which allows us to understand better Weber's special emphasis on the controlling power of parliaments.

Only a parliament based on extensive member participation in committees can provide the necessary political schooling in serious parliamentary 'work', as has been illustrated through the formation of Britain's parliamentary leaders. Through the parliamentary committees, members gain the knowledge and ability to control the bureaucracy. The committees also support the transparency and publicity of the bureaucracy. Thus Weber regards the committees as necessary for promoting the type of serious (*sachlich*) working politicians that the British Parliament has excelled at fostering.[3]

Only this school of intensive work with the realities of administration which a politician goes through in the committees of a powerful *working* parliament, and in which he has to prove his worth, turns such an assembly into a place

---

3. '*Nur* jene Schule intensiver Arbeit an den Realitäten der Verwaltung, welche der Politiker in den Kommissionen eines mächtigen *Arbeits*parlamentes durchzumachen hat und in der er sich bewähren muß, machen eine solche Versammlung zu einer Auslesestätte nicht für bloße Demagogen, sondern für sachlich arbeitende Politiker, als welche das englische Parlament (was ehrlicherweise niemand verkennen darf) bis heute unerreicht dasteht. Nur diese Art des Zusammenwirkens von Fachbeamtentum und Berufspolitikern garantiert die fortwährende Kontrolle der Verwaltung und durch sie die politische Erziehung und Schulung von Führern und Geführten. Durch effektive *Parlamentskontrolle* erzwungene *Publizität der Verwaltung* ist das, was als Vorbedingung jeder fruchtbaren Parlamentsarbeit und politischen Erziehung der Nation zu fordern ist. – Der Weg dazu ist auch bei uns beschritten' (Weber 1918d: 238).

for the selection of politicians who work objectively [*sachlich*] (as opposed to mere demagogues). No one could honestly deny that the English parliament is the best example we have ever seen of this process. Only this kind of cooperation between specialist officials and professional politicians can guarantee continuous control of the administration and thereby the political education and training of both the leaders and the led. An efficient system of *parliamentary supervision and control* which forces the administration to work *publicly* must be demanded as a prerequisite of the political education of the nation and of any fruitful parliamentary work. We, too, have already started down this path.

(Weber 1994b: 181–2)

A concern with efficient parliamentary control of administration is a key feature of nineteenth-century British writings on parliamentary politics. Although Weber in his 'Parlament' pamphlet never mentions the name of Walter Bagehot or *The English Constitution*, the latter is perhaps the best specimen of British parliamentary tracts in that it realises that efficient parliamentary control of administration is one of the key advantages of parliamentary government over the US type of presidential system. Bagehot speaks of politically responsible heads of ministries, who should be changed frequently in order that they might be able to speak the language of parliamentarians and not be swallowed up by the ministerial administration, and to be able to defend their ministries in the face of parliamentary scrutiny (Bagehot 1867: 122–40). Weber's promotion of 'cooperation' between professional, non-specialised politicians and efficient administration is indebted to this Bagehotian view.

To understand the notion of a working parliament better, we need to identify what kind of 'work' is done in a Westminster-type parliament. In the nineteenth century, the committees were engaged in multiple activities related to the agenda of the plenary debates. The members of a committee were required first to read the motions or documents that the government or other members had set on the agenda as well as any related background documents or reports they might receive. Then they heard an oral presentation of the motion and conducted, when necessary, an examination of relevant experts before engaging in the debate itself. Parliamentary speaking involves talking to a distinct motion in a definite procedural form, whether of the plenary or committee type.

Not all Westminster committees were of the whole House type, but standing and select committees followed the committee style of debating as well. May distinguishes between 'deliberative' and 'investigative' committees, and claims that the whole House type is suited to the former, whereas investigative committees must be select committees (May 1883: 440). An important element in the work of the select committees was hearing officials or other persons relevant for the tasks of the committee. The investigative select committees exhibit some similarities to French and US committees, but, as Campion indicates, Westminster's members do not include experts, but parliamentary generalists who use their political judgment. This distinction is relevant also when the questions before the committee concern the examination of an existing state of affairs, which forms an important part of the parliamentary control of administration.

Weber's defence of the *Arbeitsparlament* includes also the examination committees. In the work of these committees, hearings, examinations of governmental and administrative affairs and assessing various accounts and reports play a central role. In Westminster, Weber admires the range of the different committee types, which could be applied to distinct purposes. The Reichstag was for Weber a mere *Redeparlament*, not only because it lacked the power to elect and dismiss the government (see the criteria for parliamentary government in Weber 1918d: 226–7; for discussion, Palonen 2012a), but also because it did not have a non-specialised committee system similar to the one Westminster had at its disposal. Both aspects were crucial for him, as he discusses in detail in the third chapter of his pamphlet dedicated to the *Beamtenherrschaft* and how far it can be brought under parliamentary control.

Parliamentary control of bureaucratic knowledge

Bagehot assumes that cabinet government would both strengthen parliamentary control of government and cultivate a political culture based on 'government by discussion', an expression that he later developed in more detail in *Physics and Politics* (Bagehot 1872: 114–48). The history of British parliamentary politics, especially the increasing pressure on parliamentary time and the Irish obstruction campaign, led, however, to procedural reform in 1882 that reduced the individual members' occasions to intervene, strengthened the Speaker's power over unparliamentary conduct by members, and tried to establish a fairer distribution of parliamentary speaking time. (On the procedural changes as a response to the campaign, see Redlich 1905: 199–220).

The possibility of dismissing a government in the middle of a parliamentary term, which was of central importance to Bagehot (1867: 124–5), became largely obsolete after the 1867 parliamentary reform. The 'rationalisation' of the cabinet system towards 'party government' illustrated that at Westminster, too, there were some politicians who contemplated reducing the role of parliament to that of a ratifying assembly. Such a system is radically opposed to the Bagehotian vision of a 'government by public meeting', by which he does not mean an actually 'governing parliament', but one serving as a centre of a debating political culture (Bagehot 1905: 99). In the more technical views on 'parliamentary government', this aspect lost much of its significance, albeit never completely in Britain. For example, Ivor Jennings wrote:

> The democratic process is a process of constant argument over different opinions. The House of Commons begins the public debate which is carried on by the weekly journals of opinion and the monthly reviews. From there it percolates into the leading articles and thence into the railway carriage, the factory and the office.
>
> (1941: 53; see also Campion 1953, 1958)

The textbook view of 'parliamentarism' has been limited to a system of government in which majorities depended in the first instance on electoral results, with debate and the control of government and administration no longer perceived as a systematic part of the parliamentary regime.

For Weber, parliamentary control over government was the primary and, at the same time, most demanding requirement for parliamentarism. His critique was, of course, related to the lack of parliamentary government in the German empire, but he stressed also that the Reichstag was lacking those effective means of parliamentary control of government that were available in Britain. His views on the rule of officialdom (*Beamtenherrschaft*) are a corollary of his view of bureaucratisation as an almost irresistible tendency, for which he was searching for counterweights in his 'Parlament' pamphlet, for example (Weber 1918d: 222–3).

Weber's distinction between the necessity for an efficient bureaucracy and for political counterweights to it is also reflected in his acknowledgement of the superior knowledge of officials and the implications of this for parliamentary control. His point, for which he is indebted to Bagehot, is that officials – not only those of Wilhelmine Germany – seldom if ever admit to the limits of their knowledge imposed by the perspective of their offices, or to the need for their offices to put themselves under parliamentary control. For this purpose, Weber calls for professional parliamentarians, whom the state officials view with suspicion as do the party functionaries who remain resistant to parliamentary selection of political leaders. The competent professional parliamentarian is instinctively opposed by the chief administrators in states and parties, who see them as controllers and as rivals for political leadership. This is the main reason why administrators tend to keep parliamentarians in a state of ignorance (*Unwissenheit*) (Weber 1918d: 245).

What makes Weber's proposals to control the rule of officialdom more radical than Bagehot's is his critique of the officials' knowledge claims and his raising of the issue of the officials' claims to have exclusive possession of knowledge against the possibility of parliamentarians gaining access to their factual, official and secret knowledge (*Fach-, Dienst-* and *Geheimwissen*) (Weber 1918d: 236; *see* also Chapters Nine to Eleven in this volume). Weber emphasises that the Reichstag, as opposed to the House of Commons, lacks the basic tools for controlling the knowledge claims of officials. Weber's view corresponds also with his more general perspectivistic theory of knowledge and 'objectivity' (see Weber 1904b). This view is indebted to the rhetorical tradition of debating pro et contra as a necessary condition for a proper understanding of theories, their strengths and weaknesses, for which the Westminster procedure can be seen to provide the best historical approximation (see Palonen 2010b; *see* Chapters Eleven and Twelve in this volume). In other words, Weber seems more than others to have realised that the parliamentary procedure that any motion can be thoroughly understood and properly judged, when it is considered from the opposite points of view, is a true paradigm for a rhetorical view of knowledge and 'objectivity'.

It is this perspectivistic and rhetorical view that makes the officials' claims of superiority due to their exclusive possession of certain kinds of knowledge groundless, in Weber's view. To counter their factual superiority in knowledge, he asserts that parliaments can successfully cross-examine officials and experts by utilising them and their expertise against each other.[4] Weber's view is premised on the Nietzschean insight that 'facts' are facts only in relation to a certain interpretation, and thus may always be disputed from a different perspective (Weber 1904b: 170, 180–1). The cross-examination of officials from different ministries and offices is based on Weber's practical and theoretical insight that officials, besides giving different emphases to the same facts, according to the interest of their offices, tend also to either accord or deny to different matters the status of 'facts'.

This perspectivism is an inherent part of the old Westminster practice of *in utramque partem disputare*, which is visible already in Sir Thomas Smith's *De republica anglorum*, published in 1583, who speaks of disputing as 'a mervelous good order used in the lower house'. A Reichstag that lacks the right to cross-examine officials is for Weber not a proper parliament in the sense of a deliberative assembly. He understands, in line with Erskine May's insight that the plenum cannot act as an examination committee, that the place for such examinations is a smaller parliamentary committee.

The second stage of the officials' advantage in knowledge over parliamentarians is *Dienstwissen*, or knowledge internal to the office itself. Again, this is something that parliamentarians cannot in principle have at their disposal, which makes control over the officials more necessary. To this end, Weber proposes several instruments, including access to files, on-the-spot inspection and again the cross-examination of officials and experts (*see* the quote and translation on p. 146).

It is plain to see how the Westminster Parliament and its committees for monitoring the administration provide the model for the proposed measures. The knowledge of officials is in most cases relatively reliable, but a parliamentarian, at least a member of a select committee, must have the chances to access the original sources in order to check the official interpretations given. Here we can see a linkage to Campion's aforementioned view on the Committee of the whole House as a parliamentary instrument intended to limit governmental and administrative *arcana* and obfuscation.

Weber's third point regarding parliamentary control of administration concerns the parliamentary examination committees. As mentioned above, one of his reform proposals for the Liberals in the constitutional committee of the Reichstag concerned the introduction of such committees (see also Mommsen 1988: 387–8). Weber counterposed official secrecy (*Amtsgeheimnis*) to publicity of administration in a manner resembling Bentham's defence of public parliamentary proceedings in *Essay on Political Tactics* (published posthumously 1843) which Josef Redlich considers a major articulation of the 'theory' of Westminster procedure (1905:

---

4. 'das systematische (eidliche) Kreuzverhör von Sachverständigen vor einer Parlamentskommission unter Zuziehung der betreffenden Ressortbeamten, welches allein Kontrolle und Allseitigkeit der Befragung garantiert' (Weber 1918d: 236–7).

777–803). As the most legitimate and efficient instrument for this purpose, Weber proposes parliamentary examination commissions, or 'Enqueterecht' as the francophone term goes. The right of inquiry appears as an effective measure to protect parliamentary minorities against unscrupulous uses of majority rule: 'ein wirksames Schutzmittel der im Parlament vertretenen Minderheit gegenüber dem Einfluß der jeweiligen Mehrheit' (Weber 1917a: 120). He also defends the measure as a means of increasing the political interest of 'the people', in accordance with the English model (Weber 1917a: 120).

In other words, Weber understands well how a pure majority-based parliamentary government could endanger parliamentary debate and weaken parliamentary control of government and administration. He has identified procedural instruments used in Westminster parliamentary culture, including the setting up of thematic select committees, which allow parliamentary minorities some means to exercise control over the majority. In Westminster these committees are nothing extraordinary, but Weber maintains that in the Reichstag such a possibility would have to be introduced as an explicitly new right.

In his *Parlament* book, Weber again presents the *Enqueterecht* and justifies its parliamentary use. He insists that leading administrators tend to respond arrogantly to parliamentarians' queries and criticisms of their work. A change in this respect will be possible only if the parliament acquires a right to inquire about such factual and technical administrative matters, thus allowing the administrative branches to be scrutinised and supervised by parliament (*see* the quote and translation on p. 66).

For Weber, however, strong means of monitoring the administration should be reserved for extraordinary occasions. The experience from Westminster illustrates that simply the recognition of such a right for the parliamentarians can frequently suffice to make its actual use unnecessary (Weber 1917a: 120; *see* the quote and translation on p. 66). The main point remains that the superior knowledge of officials is part of the *arcana* of an *Obrigkeitsstaat* (authoritarian state), and the parliamentarisation of government must ensure access to such knowledge and thereby exercise control over the bureaucracy.

Taken together, Weber's analysis and proposed measures are based on a well-founded knowledge of Westminster politics, particularly of its non-specialised type of parliamentary committee. Unlike Steffani's claims for the US Congress, there is no need for parliamentarians to be better experts on detailed administrative issues than government officials. Weber's proposals rely on the principle that parliamentarians as political generalists are better than specialists in controlling the knowledge-based powers. They have learnt to debate items pro et contra, remain suspicious towards any claims of authority or superiority, and are able, when having the appropriate parliamentary instruments at their disposal, to evaluate the disputes between specialists. They are thereby able to limit the role of administrative jargon and debate the pros and cons of governmental policies in Westminster committee style.

Types of parliamentarism

A detailed examination of Weber's understanding of the three aspects discussed in this chapter – the parliamentary committees, the parliamentary control of administration and the *Redeparlament* vs *Arbeitsparlament* distinction – allows us to specify the latter distinction. Regarding the character of parliamentary Westminster, the later parliamentary scholars, Steffani in particular, appear simply anachronistic.

However, subsequent discussions also suggest a more complex and nuanced nomenclature for parliaments than Weber provided. From the proposals in the parliamentary literature mentioned above, we can construct a scheme naming six different types of parliaments:

- working parliament
- talking parliament
- committee parliament
- discussion parliament
- debating parliament
- controlling parliament.

Let us take this scheme as the basis for a re-assessment of Weber's distinction. For Weber, the working parliament is obviously better than the talking parliament, as he regards the latter as having only minimal powers. Steffani's work can be understood as a form of paradiastolic redescription (see Skinner 1996: ch. 4) of Weber's view in several senses. He inverts the normative tone of the concepts, if we understand his description of the US type of working parliament as a special form of bureaucracy as a pejorative one. Moreover, he also radically modifies the range of reference (for the term, see Skinner 1979) of Weber's conceptual pair by setting the two types of parliaments into polar opposites that exclude each other, instead of referring to Weber's distinction, where the two were interrelated and separated only by degrees of difference in parliamentary powers. Of course, for Steffani's purposes such redescription might be fully legitimate, but if the aim is to understand why Weber introduced the distinction, then Steffani has completely missed the point.

At the same time, it is easy to admit that the Weberian titles *Redeparlament* and *Arbeitsparlament* are perhaps not very fortunate, because it requires a careful reading in order to detect that he does not speak of them as exclusive of each other. Weber's rhetorical point is that, in a mere *Redeparlament*, talking tends to support declaratory speaking without contributing to a proper parliamentary debate. This is understandable if the declaration of different opinions is the only power a parliament has.

Nicolas Roussellier has proposed another suggestive term, *le parlement de l'éloquence*, for the *Assemblée nationale* of the French Third Republic (Roussellier 1997). This naming is again a paradiastolic move intended to redeem the assembly's reputation. The term refers to an extreme version of a talking parliament, which was, however, not as powerless as the Reichstag. On the contrary, it was extremely powerful insofar as contributions to debate could not only alter parliamentary majorities but also overthrow governments, which they in fact frequently did during the Third Republic. From a Weberian perspective, the fault is the powerlessness of both the Assembly and the governments before the central administration of France (see his critical remarks in 1918d: 1918: 259).

Following the Weberian practice of one-sided exaggeration in order to construct ideal types (1904b: esp. 191) we can speak of two contrasting types of *Redeparlament*. The Reichstag was a 'discussion parliament', that is, it approached a gentlemen's discussion club without politically significant powers and responsibilities. The French Assembly was, in contrast, a 'debating parliament', in which questions about the fate of the government were at the core of debate. Despite this, the French version of *Redeparlament* does not match Steffani's interpretation of the concept, which is based on the presentation and public opinion discussions between the government and opposition. On the contrary, this very divide was unstable in the Third Republic, and the debate itself had the real power to change the votes in rather unexpected directions. Roussellier's point is that France's frequent government crises were not fatal to the regime because it had its own modes of stability and continuity, independently of governmental changes (Roussellier 1997: 9–22). A common feature of both types of *Redeparlament* is, and here Steffani is right, the definite priority of the plenum over the various committees.

The case of Westminster is more complex. For Weber – unlike Bagehot when speaking of the period between the 1832 and 1867 parliamentary reforms – Westminster was no longer a vote-changing parliament, as the French Assembly of the Third and Fourth Republics was. More importantly, in Westminster there was no clear priority between the plenum and the committees, because the difference between them referred to the two states of Parliament with their respective types of debate and ways of regulating debate. The working parliament as understood by Max Weber is a parliament of intensified debate that systematically subjects motions and resolutions to two different types of debating. The Westminster Parliament is for Weber both a debating and a controlling parliament in the sense suggested by Dann, whereas the Reichstag was neither.

As we have seen, in addition to debating, the Weberian *Arbeitsparlament* includes controlling and voting functions, which it conducts through the drafting of motions and documents, reading them, listening to hearings and to the speeches of others, and so on. In a rhetorical sense, we could include activities such as debating and controlling within a deliberative concept of parliament, referring to the very idea of debating *in utramque partem disputare* (for a discussion of this idea, see Skinner 1996 and Hamilton's collection of maxims from the eighteenth century, published in 1927). In a formal sense, we could perhaps best speak of Westminster as a multi-operational parliament, referring to the range of both the powers and activities that it has available. Perhaps the notion of *Arbeitsparlament* is, after all, not so misleading, if we consider that it also takes a lot of 'work' to coordinate the multiple activities that a parliamentarian needs to perform and master in order to be a competent politician.

The discussion of types of parliament also indicates a more general point of view. Today parliamentary studies have been practically relegated to a subfield of political institutions, systems and comparative politics. In Weber's time, discussing parliamentary politics was still an inherent part of political thought and theory. My discussion suggests not only how neglect of this aspect is liable to lead to anachronisms in the way older debates on parliaments are understood, but also how Weber's views on parliamentarism may be used as a marker for how much research has changed. His work illustrates the urgent need to reconnect political theorising with the procedures, rhetorical practices, institutional arrangement and actions of politicians.

List of Abbreviations for the Weber Editions

EW   *The Essential Weber*, ed. S. Whimster, London: Routledge 2004.

GASS   *Gesammelte Aufsätze zur Soziologie und Sozialpolitik*, ed. Marianne Weber Tübingen: Mohr, [1924], 1988.

GASW   *Gesammelte Aufsätze zur Sozial- und Wirtschaftsgeschichte*, ed. Marianne Weber, Tübingen: Mohr [1924], 1988.

GAW   *Gesammelte Aufsätze zur Wissenschaftslehre*, ed. J. Winckelmann, Tübingen: Mohr [1922], 1973.

GPS   *Gesammelte politische Schriften*, ed. J. Winckelmann, Tübingen: Mohr, [1921], 1971.

MWG I/4   *Max-Weber-Gesamtausgabe*, Landarbeiterfrage, Nationalstaat und Volkswirtschaftspolitik: Schriften und Reden 1892–1899, eds W.J. Mommsen and R. Aldenhoff, Tübingen: Mohr 1993.

MWG I/10 *Max-Weber-Gesamtausgabe*, Zur Russischen Revolution, Schriften und Reden *1905–1912*, eds W.J. Mommsen and D. Dahlmann, Tübingen: Mohr 1989.

MWG II/5 *Max-Weber-Gesamtausgabe*, Briefe 1906–1908, eds W.J. Mommsen and M. R. Lepsius, Tübingen: Mohr 1990.

MWG II/6 *Max-Weber-Gesamtausgabe*, Briefe 1909–1910, eds W.J. Mommsen and M. R. Lepsius, Tübingen: Mohr 1994.

MWG II/9 *Max-Weber-Gesamtausgabe* II/9, Briefe 1915–1917, eds G. Krumreich and M. R. Lepsius, Tübingen, Mohr, 2008.

MWG III/7 *Max-Weber-Gesamtausgabe*, Allgemeine Staatslehre und Politik. Mit- und *Nachschriften 1920*, ed. G. Hübinger, Tübingen: Mohr 2009.

MWS I/2   *Max-Weber-Studienausgabe*, Die römische Agrargeschichte in ihrer Bedeutung *für das Staats- und Privatrecht*, ed. J. Deininger, Tübingen: Mohr 1988.

MWS I/8   *Max-Weber-Studienausgabe*, Wirtschaft, Staat und Sozialpolitik, Schriften und *Reden 1900–1912*, eds W. Schluchter and W. Schwendtker, Tübingen: Mohr 1999.

MWS I/10 *Max-Weber- Studienausgabe*, Zur Russischen Revolution, Schriften und Reden *1905–1912*, eds W.J. Mommsen and D. Dahlmann, Tübingen: Mohr 1996.

MWS I/15 *Max-Weber-Studienausgabe*, Zur Politik im Weltkrieg, Schriften und Reden *1914–1918*, eds W.J. Mommsen and G. Hübinger, Tübingen: Mohr 1988.

MWS I/16 *Max-Weber-Studienausgabe* 1/16, Zur Neuordnung in Deutschland, Schriften *zund Reden 1918–1920*, eds W.J. Mommsen and W. Schwendtker, Tübingen: Mohr 1991.

MWS I/17 *Max-Weber-Studienausgabe*, Wissenschaft als Beruf, Politik als Beruf, eds W.J. Mommsen, W. Schluchter, and B. Morgenbrod, Tübingen: Mohr 1994.

PE II   *Protestantische Ethik* II, Kritiken und Antikritiken, ed. J. Winckelmann, Gütersloh: Siebenstern 1978.

Bibliography

Abschlussbericht des SFB 584 (2013) *Das Politische als Kommunikationsraum der Geschichte*, Universität Bielefeld.

Adamson, S., Alexander G. and Ettenhuber K. (eds) (2007) *Renaissance Figures of Speech*, Cambridge: Cambridge University Press.

Angenot, M. (2003) *La démocratie, c'est le mal*, Laval: Les Presses de l'Université de Laval.

Ankersmit, F. R. (1997) *Aesthetic Politics*, Stanford: Stanford University Press.

—— (2002) *Political Representation*, Stanford: University Press.

Anter, A. (1995) *Max Webers Theorie des modenen Staates*, Berlin: Duncker & Humblot.

Arendt, H. (1954 [1991]) *Elemente und Ursprünge totaler Herrschaft*, München: Piper.

—— (1958) 'Totalitarian imperialism: reflections on the Hungarian revolution', *Review of Politics*, 20(1): 5–43.

—— (1960 [1981]) *Vita activa*, München: Piper.

—— (1963 [1990]) *On Revolution*, London: Penguin.

—— (1964a [2003]) 'Personal responsibility under dictatorship', in J. Kohn (ed.) *Responsibility and Judgment*, New York: Schocken pp. 19–48.

—— (1964b [1974]) *Über die Revolution*, München: Piper.

—— (1968 [1977]) *Between Past and Future*, London: Penguin.

—— (1973) *The Crisis of the Republic*, London: Penguin.

—— (1985 [1993]) *Karl Jaspers Briefwechsel 1926–1969*, München: Piper.

—— (1993) *Was ist Politik?*, U. Ludz (ed.), München: Piper.

—— (2002) *Denktagebuch 1950–1973 I–II*, München: Piper.

—— (2003) *Responsibility and Judgment*, J. Kohn (ed.), New York: Schocken.

Armitage, D., Condren C. and Fitzmaurice A. (eds) (2009) *Shakespeare and Early Modern Political Thought*, Cambridge: Cambridge University Press.

Aron, R. (1938a [1981]) *Introduction à la philosophie de l'histoire*, Paris: Gallimard.

—— (1938b [1970]) *La philosophie critique de l'histoire*, Paris: Vrin.

—— (1964) 'Max Weber und die Machtpolitik', *Zeitschrift für Politik*, N.S. 11: 100–13.

Aubrey, W. H. S. (1905) 'The modern trade of politics', *Macmillan's Magazine*, 90: 288–300.

Badiou, A. (1985) *Peut-on penser la politique?* Paris: Seuil.

Baehr, P. (2005) 'Personal dilemma or intellectual influence: the relationship between Hannah Arendt and Max Weber', *Max Weber Studies*, 5(1): 125–30.

Bagehot, W. (1867 [2001]) *The English Constitution*, P. Smith (ed.), Cambridge: Cambridge University Press.

—— (1872 [1956]) *Physics and Politics*, Boston: Beacon Press.

Barker, E. (1942) *Reflections on Government*, Oxford: Clarendon Press.

Barthou, L. (1923) *Le Politique*, Paris: Hachette.

Baumgarten, H. (1866 [1974]) *Der deutsche Liberalismus. Eine Selbstkritik*, Frankfurt/M: Ullstein.

Beck, U. (1993) *Die Erfindung des Politischen*, Frankfurt/M: Suhrkamp.

Bedorf, T. and Röttgers, K. (eds) (2010) *Das Politische und die Politik*, Frankfurt/M: Suhrkamp.

Beetham, D. (1974 [1985]) *Max Weber and the Theory of Modern Politics*, Cambridge: Polity.

—— (1994) 'Max Weber and the liberal political tradition', in A. Horowitz and T. Maley (eds) *The Barbarism of Reason*, Toronto: University of Toronto Press pp. 99–112.

—— (2006) 'Max Weber and Anglo-American democracy', in K.-L. Ay (ed.) *Das Faszinosum Max Weber*, Konstanz: UVK pp. 343–51.

Belloc, H. (1911) 'The change in politics', *Fortnightly Review*, 89: 33–45.

Benjamin, W. (1929 [1988]) *Einbahnstrasse*, Frankfurt/M: Suhrkamp.

—— (1980) *Illuminationen*, Frankfurt/M: Suhrkamp.

Bentham, J. (1791/1999) *Political Tactics*, M. James, C. Blamires and C. Pearse-Watson (eds), Oxford: Clarendon Press.

—— (1843) 'An essay on political tactics', in *Collected Works of Jeremy Bentham*, vol. 1, Edinburgh. http://oll.libertyfund.org/title/1921/113915 (accessed 10 July 2016).

Beranger, D. (1999) *Le parlementarisme des origins*, Paris: Presses Universitaires de France.

Berlin, I. (1958 [1969]) 'Two concepts of liberty', in *Four Essays on Liberty*, Oxford: Oxford University Press pp.118–72.

Beyme, K. von (1970/1999) *Die parlamentarische Demokratie*, Wiesbaden: Westdeutscher Verlag.

Berolzheimer, F. (1907/08) 'Politik als Wissenschaft. Ihr Wesen und ihre Grenzen', *Archiv für Rechts und Wirtschaftsphilosophie*, 1: 210–18.

Björk, A. (2015) 'On time. Very briefly', in C. Wiesner, E. Roshchin and M.-C. Boilard (eds) *In Debate with Kari Palonen. Concepts, Politics, Histories*, Baden-Baden: Nomos pp. 37–40.

Borchert, J. (2003) *Die Professionalisierung der Politik*, Frankfurt/M: Campus.

—— (2007) ' "From Politik als Beruf" to "Politics as a Vocation": The translation, transformation and reception of Max Weber's lecture', *Contributions to the History of Concepts*, 3(1): 40–70.

Botzenhart, M. (1977) *Deutscher Parlamentarismus in der Revolutionszeit 1848–1850*, Düsseldorf: Droste.

Breiner, P. (1996) *Max Weber and Democratic Politics*, Ithaca, NY: Cornell University Press.

Bright, J. (1866) *Speeches on Parliamentary Reform*, Manchester: Heywood.

Browne, T. (1808–10) *The British Cicero* or a Selection of the Most Admired Speeches in the English Language Arranged under Three Distinct Heads of Popular, Parliamentary, and Judicial Oratory with historical illustration to which is prefixed an introduction to the study and practice of eloquence, Philadelphia. /https://archive.org/details/britishciceroor00browgoog (accessed 10 July 2016).

Brunner, O. (1942) *Land und Herrschaft*, Brünn: Rohrer.

Bruun, H.-H. (1972/2007) *Science, Values and Politics in Max Weber's Methodology*, Aldershot: Ashgate.

Bryce, J. (1888/1914 [1995]) *The American Commonwealth I–II*, Indianapolis, IN: Liberty Press.

Buchstein, H. (1992) *Politikwissenschaft und Demokratie*, Baden-Baden: Nomos.

Burke, E. (1774 [1999]) *Speech to the Electors of Bristol*, in Select Works of Edmund Burke vol. 4, Indianapolis: Liberty Fund, pp. 5–14. http:// oll.libertyfund.org/titles/burke-select-works-of-edmund-burke-vol-4 (accessed 10 July 2016).

Burke, K. (1945 [1969]) *A Grammar of Motives*, Berkeley: University of California Press.

Butzer, H. (1998) *Diäten und Freifahrt im deutschen Reichstag*, Düsseldorf: Droste.

Campion, G. (1953) 'Parliamentary procedure: old and new', in G. Campion, L. S. Amery and D. W. Brogan (eds) *Parliament, A survey*, London: Allen & Unwin pp. 141–67.

—— (1958) *An Introduction to the Procedure of the House of Commons*, 3. ed., London: Macmillan.

Catlin, G. E. G. (1929) *A Study of the Principles of Politics*, London: Allen and Unwin.

Chalcraft, D. (1994) 'Bringing the text back in: on ways of reading the iron cage metaphor in the two editions of *The Protestant Ethic*', in L. J. Ray and M. Reed (eds) *Organizing Modernity*, London: Routledge pp. 16–45.

Chapman, N. (1807–8) *Select Speeches Forensick and Parliamentary with Preparatory Remarks 1_IV*, Philadelphia. /https://archive.org/details/ selectspeechesf00chapgoog (acccessed 10 June 2016).

Collingwood, R. G. (1939 [1978]) *An Autobiography*, Oxford: Clarendon Press.

—— (1946 [1994]) *The Idea of History: Revised edition with lectures 1926–1928*, J. van der Dussen (ed.), Oxford: Oxford University Press.

Colliot-Thélène, C. (1990) 'Max Weber, la leçon inaugurale de 1895, ou: Du nationalisme a la sociologie comparative', *Les cahiers de Fontenay* 58/59, June 1990 pp. 103–21.

—— (1992) *Le désenchantement de l'État*, Paris: Minuit.

Constant, B. (1814 [1980]) 'De l'esprit de conquete et de l'usurpation', in *De la liberté chez les Modernes, presenté par M. Gauchet*, Paris: Hachette pp. 117–261.

—— (1819 [1980]) 'De la liberté chez les Anciens comparée à celle des Modernes', in *De la liberté chez les Modernes, presenté par M. Gauchet*, Paris: Hachette pp. 491–515.

Crewe, E. (2015) *The House of Commons: An anthropology of MPs at work*, London: Bloomsbury.

Curzon, G. (1913) *Modern Parliamentary Eloquence*, London: Macmillan.

Dann, P. (2003) 'European parliament and executive federalism', *European Law Journal*, 9(5): 549–74.

Debray, R. (1981) *Critique de la raison politique*, Paris: Gallimard.

Delafosse, J. (1904) *La psychologie du depute*, Paris: Plon.

De Mille, J. (1878) *Elements of Rhetoric*, New York: Harper. http://tinyurl. com/72p4s2u (accessed 10 July 2016).

Draus, F. (1995) 'Max Weber et la liberté', *Revue européenne des sciences sociales*, 33(101): 123–43.

Drysdale, J. (2007) 'Weber on objectivity: advocate or critic?', in L. McFalls (ed.), *Max Weber's 'Objectivity' Reconsidered*, Toronto: University of Toronto Press pp. 31–57.

Easton, D. (1953) *The Political System*, New York: Knopf.

Eliæson, S. (2002) *Max Weber's Methodologies*, Cambridge: Polity.

Flynn, P. (2012) *How to be an MP?* London: Biteback.

Fontana, B. (1991) *Benjamin Constant and the Post-revolutionary Mind*, New Haven, CT: Yale University Press.

Fraenkel, E. (1960) *Das amerikanische Regierungssystem*, Köln: Kiepenhauer & Witsch.

Freeden, M. (1996) *Ideologies and Political Theory: A conceptual approach*, Oxford: Clarendon Press.

—— (2013a) 'Navigating around politics: British progressive thought and the "political" as an expanding transnational perspective', in W. Steinmetz, I. Glicher-Holtey and H.-G. Haupt (eds) *Writing Political History Today*, Frankfurt/M: Campus pp. 127–45.

—— (2013b) *The Political Theory of Political Thinking*, Oxford: Oxford University Press.

—— (2016) 'Review: Kari Palonen, politics and conceptual history', *European Journal of Political Theory*, 15(1): 124–30.

Freund, J. (1965[1981]) *L'essence du politique*, Paris: Sirey.

—— (1990) *Études sur Max Weber*, Genève: Droz.

Gagarin, M. and Woodruff, P. (eds) (1995) *Early Greek Political Thought from Homer to the Sophists*, Cambridge: Cambridge University Press.

Garrigues, J. (ed.) (2005) *Histoire du Parlement de 1789 à nos jours*, Paris: Colin.

Gauchet, M. (1980) 'Preface: Benjamin Constant: l'illusion lucide du liberalisme', in B. Constant (ed.) *De la liberté chez les Modernes*, Paris: Hachette pp. 5–91.

Ghosh, P. (2001) 'Translation as a conceptual act', *Max Weber Studies*, 2(1): 59–63.

—— (2008) *A Historian Reads Max Weber*, Wiesbaden: Harrasowitz.

—— (2014) *Max Weber and the Protestant Ethic: Twin histories*, Oxford: Oxford University Press.

Goldberg, H.-P. (1998) *Bismarck und seine Gegner*, Düsseldorf: Droste.

Greven, M. (2010) 'Verschwindet das Politische in der politische Gesellschaft? Über die Strategien der Kontingenzverleugnung', in T. Bedorf and K. Röttgers (eds) *Das Politische und die Politik*, Frankfurt/M: Suhrkamp pp. 68–88.

Grey, H. G. (1864) *Parliamentary Government Considered with Reference to Reform*, London. http://www.archive.org/stream/parliamentarygo00greygoog#page/n8/mode/2up (accessed 10 July 2016).

Grünthal, G. (1982) *Parlamentarismus in Preußen 1848/9–1857/8*, Düsseldorf: Droste.

Guizot, F.-P. (1851[1880]) *Histoire des origines du gouvernement représentatif*, vol. 2, Paris: Didier.

Habermas, J. (1962) *Strukturwandel der Öffentlichkeit*, Neuwied: Luchterhand.

Hamilton, W. G. (1808) *Parliamentary Logick*, E. Malone (ed.), London. /https://archive.org/details/parliamentarylo00johngoog (accessed 10 July 2016).

—— (1927) *Parliamentary Logic*, Cambridge: Heffer.

Hatsell, J. (1818) *Precedents of Proceedings in the House of Commons; with Observations* London: L. Hansard and Sons. http://tinyurl.com/7p7br4h (accessed 20 July 2016).

Hazlitt, W. (1809–10) *The Eloquence of the British Senate* being a Selection of the Best Speeches of the Most Distinguished English, Irish and Scotch Parliamentary Speakers from the Beginning of the Reign of Charles I to the Present Time I–II, London. /https://archive.org/details/eloquenceofbriti02hazliala (accessed 10 July 2016).

Hennis, W. (1987) *Max Webers Fragestellung*, Tübingen: Mohr.

—— (1994) ' "Die volle Nüchternheit des Urteils". Max Weber zwischen Carl Menger und Gustav Schmoller. Zum hochschulpolitischen Hintergrund des Wertfreiheitspostulats', in G. Wagner and H. Zipprian (eds) *Max Webers Wissenschaftslehre*, Frankfurt/M: Suhrkamp pp. 105–45.

—— (1996) *Max Webers Wissenschaft vom Menschen*, Tübingen: Mohr.

Hexter, J. H. (ed.) (1992) *Parliament and Liberty*, Princeton, NJ: Princeton University Press.

Hiller, K. (1981) *Pazifismus der Tat—Revolutionärer Pazifismus*, Berlin: Ahde.

Holmes, S. (1984) *Benjamin Constant and the Making of Modern Liberalism*, New Haven, CT: Yale University Press.

Holyoake, G. J. (1897) *Public Speaking and Debate: A manual for advocates and agitators*, Boston. http://www.archive.org/stream/publicspeakingde00holy#page/n0/mode/1up (accessd 10 July 2016).

Hübinger, G. (2009a) 'Editorischer Bericht', in MWG III/7, Tübingen: Mohr pp. 43–62.

—— (2009b) 'Einleitung', in MWG III/7, Tübingen: Mohr pp. 1–41.

Hufnagel, G. (1971) *Kritik als Beruf. Der kritische Gehalt im Werk Max Webers*, Frankfurt/M: Propyläen.

Jellinek, G. (1900) *Allgemeine Staatslehre*, Berlin: Häring.

Jennings, W. I. (1941) 'Parliament in wartime IV', *Political Quarterly*, 12(1): 53–65.

Jouvenel, B. de (1963) *The Pure Theory of Politics*, Cambridge: Cambridge University Press.

Jouvenel, R. de (1914 [1979]) *La république des camarades*, Genève: Slatkine.

Kalmo, H. and Skinner, Q. (2010) 'Introduction: a concept in fragments', in H. Kalmo and Q. Skinner (eds) *Sovereignty in Fragments*, Cambridge: Cambridge University Press pp. 1–25.

Kant, I. (1798 [2001]) 'Der Streit der Fakultäten', in R. Toman (ed.) *Der Streit der Fakultäten und kleinere Abhandlungen*, Köln: Köhnemann pp. 5–140.

Käsler, D. (2014) *Max Weber: Eine Biographie*, München: Beck.

Kaube, J. (2014) *Max Weber, Ein Leben zwischen Epochen*, Berlin: Rowohlt.

Kelly, D. (2003) *The State of the Political*, Oxford: Oxford University Press.

Kelsen, H. (1911[1960]) *Hauptprobleme der Staatsrechtslehre*, Aalen: Scientia.

Kluxen, K. (1983) *Geschichte und Problematik des Parlamentarismus*, Frankfrurt/M: Suhrkamp.

Kocka, J. (1981) 'Otto Hintze, Max Weber und das Problem der Bürokratie', *Historische Zeitschrift*, 233(3): 65–105.

—— (ed.) (1987) *Max Weber, der Historiker*, Göttingen: Vandenhoek & Ruprecht.

Koselleck, R. (1967) 'Richtlinien für das Lexikon politisch-sozialer Begriffe der Neuzeit', *Archiv für Begriffsgeschichte*, 11: 81–99.

—— (1979) *Vergangene Zukunft*, Frankfurt/M: Suhrkamp.

—— (1983) 'Begriffsgeschichtliche Probleme der Verfassungsgeschichtsschreibung', *Der Staat*, Beiheft 6: 7–21.

—— (1991) 'Wie sozial ist der Geist der Wissenschaften?', in *Geisteswissenschaften heute*, Frankfurt/M: Suhrkamp pp. 112–41.

—— (1996) 'A response to comments on the Geschichtliche Grundbegriffe', in H. Lehmann and M. Richter (eds) *The Meaning of Historical Terms and Concepts*, Washington: German Historical Institute pp. 59–70.

—— (2000) *Zeitschichten: Studien zur Historik*, Frankfurt/M: Suhrkamp.

—— (2006) *Begriffsgeschichten*, C. Dutt (ed.), Frankfurt/M: Suhrkamp.

Koselleck, R., Moraw, B., Günther, H., Ilting, H.-K. and Hilger, D. (1982) 'Herrschaft' in *Geschichtliche Grundbegriffe*, vol. 3, Stuttgart: Klett-Cotta pp. 1–102.

Koselleck, R., Conze, W., Haverkate, G., Klippel, D. and Boldt, H. (1990) 'Staat und Souveränität', in *Geschichtliche Grundbegriffe*, vol. 6, Stuttgart: Klett-Cotta pp. 1–154.

Lacouë-Labarthe, P. (1983) *Le retrait du politique*, Paris: Galilée.

Lacouë-Labarthe, P. and Nancy, J.-L. (eds) (1981) *Rejouer le politique*, Paris: Galilée.

Lambert, S. (1980) 'Procedure of the House of Commons in the early Stuart period', *English Historical Review*, 95(377): 753–81.

Lassman, P. (ed.) (2006) *Max Weber*, Aldershot: Ashgate.

Leibholz, G. (1957 [1974]) *Strukturprobleme der modernen Demokratie*, Frankfurt/M: Fischer.

Lenman, B. P. (1992) *The Eclipse of the Parliament*, London: Arnold.

Leyret, H. (1909) *La république et les politiciens*, Paris: Fasquelle.

—— (1910) La tyrannie des politiciens, Paris: Comély.

Llanque, M. (2000) *Demokratisches Denken im Kriege*, Berlin: Akademie-Verlag.

Lowe, R. (1867) *Speeches and Letters on Reform*, London: Bush.

Lowell, A. L. (1908 [1921]) *The Government of England I–II*, New York: Macmillan.

Luhmann, N. (2000) *Die Politik der Gesellschaft*, Frankfurt/M: Suhrkamp.

Macaulay, T. B. (1859) 'William Pitt', in *The Miscellaneous Writings and Speeches of Lord Macaulay*, vol. 3. http://www.gutenberg.org/files/2169/2169-h/2169-h.htm (accessed 10 July 2016).

Mack, P. (2002) *Elizabethan Rhetoric: Theory and practice*, Cambridge: Cambridge University Press.

Mann, T. (1918 [1983]) *Betrachtungen eines Unpolitischen*, Frankfurt/M: Fischer.

Marchart, O. (2007) *Post-foundational Political Thought*, Edinburgh: University of Edinburgh Press.

—— (2010) *Die politische Differenz*, Frankfurt/M: Suhrkamp.

Marschall, S. (2005) *Parlamentarismus: Eine Einführung*, Baden-Baden: Nomos.

Mathews, W. (1879) *Oratory and Orators*, Chicago. /https://archive.org/details/oratoryandorato00unkngoog (accessed 10 July 2016).

May, T. E. (1844) *A Treatise upon the Law, Privileges, Proceedings and Usage of Parliament*, London. http://www.archive.org/stream/atreatiseuponla00maygoog (accessed 10 June 2016).

—— (1883) *A Treatise upon the Law, Privileges, Proceedings and Usage of Parliament*, London. http://www.archive.org/stream/treatiseonlawpri00maytrich (accessed 16 July 2016).

Meier, C. (1980) *Die Entstehung des Politischen bei den Griechen*, Frankfurt/M: Suhrkamp.

Meier, U., Papenheim, M. and Steinmetz, W. (2012) *Semantiken des Politischen*, Göttingen: Wallstein.

Meisel, J. S. (2001) *Public Speech and the Culture of Public in the Age of Gladstone*, New York: Columbia University Press.

Mergel, T. (2002) *Parlamentarische Kultur in der Weimarer Republik: Politische Kommunikation, symbolische Politik und Öffentlichkeit im Reichstag*, Düsseldorf: Droste.

Michels, R. (1910 [1970]) *Zur Soziologie des Parteiwesens in der modernen Demokratie*, Stuttgart: Kröner.

Mill, J.S. (1838 [1985]) 'Bentham', in *The Collected Works of John Stuart Mill*, vol. 10 Toronto: University of Toronto Press, 75–116. http://oll.libertyfund.org/titles/mill-collected-works-of-john-stuart-mill-in-33-vols. (accessed 10 July 2016).

—— (1861[1991]) *Considerations on Representative Government*, Buffalo, NY: Prometheus Books.

Miller, J. D. B. (1958) *Politicians: An inaugural lecture*, Leicester: University of Leicester.

—— (1962) *The Nature of Politics*, London: Duckworth.

Mommsen, W. J. (1959 [1974]) *Max Weber und die deutsche Politik (1890–1920)*, Tübingen: Mohr.

—— (1988) 'Zur Entstehung und Überlieferung der Texte', in MWS I/15, Tübingen: Mohr pp. 372–407.

—— (1991) 'Nachwort des Herausgebers', in MWS I/16, Tübingen: Mohr pp. 147–75.

Morgenthau, H. (1929) *Die internationale Rechtspflege*, Leipzig: Noske.

—— (1933) *La notion du 'politique' et les différends internationaux*, Paris: Sirey.

Mouffe, C. (1993) *The Return of the Political*, London: Verso.

—— (2005) *On the Political*, London: Verso.

Narr, W.-D. (2014) *Niemands-Herrschaft: Eine Einführung in die Schwierigkeiten, Herrschaft zu begreifen*, Hamburg: VSA.

Nelson, J. S. (1998) *Tropes of Politics*, Madison, WI: University of Wisconsin Press.

Nelson, J. S., McCloskey, D. and Megill, A. (eds) (1987) *Rhetoric in the Human Sciences*, Chicago: University of Chicago Press.

Nicolet, C. (1982) *L'idée républicaine en France*, Paris: Gallimard.

Nietzsche, F. (1887 [1981]) 'Zur Genealogie der Moral', in K. von Schlechta (ed.) *Werke*, Frankfurt/M: Ullstein II, pp. 761–900.

—— (1995) *Werke: Kritische Gesamtausgabe* 2/4, Berlin: W. de Gruyter.

Oakeshott, M. (1962[1991]) *Rationalism in Politics*, Indianapolis, IN: Liberty Press.

—— (1975[1991]) *On Human Conduct*, Oxford: Clarendon Press.

Oliver, F. S. (1930) *The Endless Adventure*, London: Macmillan.

Ostrogorski, M. (1903 [1993]) *La démocratie et les partis politiques*, Paris: Fayard.

Oxford English Dictionary (1989), vol. 16, Oxford: Clarendon Press.

The Oxford Shakespeare (1914), W. J. Graig (ed.), Oxford. http://bartleby.com/70/ (accessed 10 July 2016).

Page, A. (1913) 'Character or politics', *Blackwood's Edinburgh Magazine*, 193: 573–83 /https://archive.org/details/blackwoodsmagazi193edinuoft (accessed 10 July 2016).

Palonen, K. (1981) 'Allgemeine Staatslehre als Wissenschaft. Rehabilitierende Bemerkungen aus finnischer Sicht', *Der Staat*, 20(2): 229–48.

—— (1985) *Politik als Handlungsbegriff: Horizontwandel des Politikbegriffs in Deutschland 1890–1933*, Helsinki: Societas Scientiarum Fennica.

—— (1989) 'Korrekturen zur Geschichte von "Politisierung"', *Archiv für Begriffsgeschichte*, 30: 224–34.

—— (1990) *Thematisierung der Politik als Phänomen: Eine Interpretation der Geschichte des Begriffs Politik im Frankreich des 20. Jahrhunderts*, Helsinki: Societas Scientiarum Fennica.

—— (1992) *Politik als Vereitelung: Die Politikkonzeption in Jean-Paul Sartres 'Critique de la raison dialectique'*, Münster: Westfälisches Dampfboot.

—— (1993) 'Introduction: from policy and polity to politicking and politicization' in K. Palonen and T. Parvikko (eds) *Reading the Political*, Helsinki: The Finnish Political Science Association pp. 6–16.

—— (1998) *Das 'Webersche Moment': Zur Kontingenz des Politischen*, Wiesbaden: Westdeutscher Verlag.

—— (1999a) 'Max Weber's reconceptualization of freedom', *Political Theory*, 27(4): 523–44. (Chapter Six in this volume).

—— (1999b) 'Rhetorical and temporal perspectives on conceptual change', *Finnish Yearbook of Political Thought*, 3: 41–59.

—— (2000) 'Die Umstrittenheit der Begriffe bei Max Weber', in G. Scholz (ed.) *Archiv für Begriffsgeschichte*, Sonderheft 1, Die Interdisziplinarität der Begriffesgeschichte 145–59.

—— (2001) 'Transforming a common European concept into Finnish: conceptual changes in the understanding of *politiikka*', *Finnish Yearbook of Political Thought*, 5:113–43.

—— (2002) *Eine Lobrede für Politiker. Kommentar zu Max Webers 'Politik als Beruf'*, Opladen: Leske+Budrich.

—— (2003a) *Quentin Skinner: History, Politics, Rhetoric*, Cambridge: Polity.

—— (2003b) 'Die Verzeitlichung der Begriffe bei Max Weber', in J. Kurunmäki and K. Palonen (eds) *Zeit, Geschichte und Politik/Time, History and Politics. Zum achtzigsten Geburtstag von Reinhart Koselleck*, Jyväskylä: Jyväskylä Studies on Education, Psychology and Social Research pp. 85–104.

—— (2004a) *Die Entzauberung der Begriffe: Das Umschreiben der politischen Begriffe bei Quentin Skinner und Reinhart Koselleck*, Münster: LIT.

—— (2004b) 'Max Weber, parliamentarism and the rhetorical culture of politics', *Max Weber Studies*, 4(2): 271–90. (Chapter Ten in this volume).

—— (2004c) 'Parliamentarism: a politics of temporal and rhetorical distances', *Österreichische Zeitschrift für Geschichtswissenschaft*, 15(3): 111–26.

—— (2005a) 'Max Weber als Begriffspolitiker', *Etica & Politica/Ethics & Politics*. http://www.openstarts.units.it/dspace/bitstream/10077/5342/1/ Palonen_E%26P_VII_2005_2.pdf (accessed 18 July 2016).

—— (2005b) 'Political theorizing as a dimension of political life,' *European Journal of Political Theory*, 4(4): 351–67.

—— (2006) *The Struggle with Time: A conceptual history of 'politics' as an activity*, Münster: LIT.

—— (2007) *Re-thinking Politics: Essays from a quarter-century*, K. Lindroos (ed.), Helsinki: The Finnish Political Science Association.

—— (2008a) 'Imagining Max Weber's reply to Hannah Arendt: remarks on the Arendtian critique of representative democracy', *Constellations*, 15(1): 56–71. (Chapter Eight in this volume).

—— (2008b) ' "Objectivity" as fair play. Max Weber's parliamentary redescription of normative concept', *Redescriptions*, 12: 72–95. (Chapter Eleven in this volume).

—— (2008c) *The Politics of Limited Times: The rhetoric of temporal judgment in parliamentary democracies*, Baden-Baden: Nomos.

—— (2008d) 'Speaking *pro et contra*. The rhetorical intelligibility of parliamentary politics and the political intelligibility of parliamentary rhetoric', in S. Soininen and T. Turkka (eds), *The Parliamentary Style of Politics*, Helsinki: The Finnish Political Science Association pp. 82–105.

—— (2009a) 'John Pocock and Quentin Skinner: the Machiavellian and the Weberian moment', *Ideas in History*, 33: 61–79.

—— (2009b) 'The two faces of contingency. *La politique* and *le politique* in the work of Pierre Rosanvallon', *Contributions to the History of Concepts*, 5(2), 2009: 123–39.

—— (2010a) 'Max Weber's rhetoric of "objectivity": The parliament as a paradigm for scholarly disputes', *Max Weber Studies*, 10(1): 71–93. (Chapter Twelve in this volume).

—— (2010b) '*Objektivität' als faires Spiel: Wissenschaft als Politik bei Max Weber*, Baden-Baden: Nomos.

—— (2012a) 'Der Begriff des Parlamentarismus bei Max Weber', in O. Asbach, R. Rchäfer, V. Selk and A. Weiß (eds) *Zur kritischen Theorie der politischen Gesellschaft: Festschrift Michael Th. Greven*, Berlin-Wiesbaden: Springer-VS Verlag pp. 195–206.

—— (2012b) *Rhetorik des Unbeliebten: Lobreden auf Politiker im Zeitalter der Demokratie*, Baden-Baden: Nomos.

—— (2012c) 'The Search for a new beginning: Hannah Arendt and Karl Jaspers as critics of West German parliamentarism', in M. Goldoni and C. McCorkingdale (eds) *Hannah Arendt and the Law*, Oxford: Hart pp. 151–69.

—— (2014a) *Politics and Conceptual Histories*, Baden-Baden: Nomos.

—— (2014b) *The Politics of Parliamentary Procedure: The formation of the Westminster procedure as a parliamentary ideal type*, Leverkusen: Budrich.

—— (2016) *From Oratory to Debate: Parliamentarisation of deliberative rhetoric in Westminster*, Baden-Baden: Nomos.

Parlament. http://de.wikipedia.org/wiki/Parlament/ (accessed 10 July 2016).

Parvikko, T. (2004) 'A note on Max Weber's impact on Hannah Arendt's thought', *Max Weber Studies*, 4(2): 235–52.

Péguy, C. (1910 [1969]) *Notre jeunesse*, Paris: Gallimard.

Peukert, D. (1989) *Max Webers Diagnose der Moderne*, Göttingen: Vandenhoek & Ruprecht.

Perelman, C. (1989) *Rhétoriques*, Bruxelles: Presses de Université libre de Bruxelles.

Pierre, E. (1887) *De la procédure parlementaire*, Paris: Maison Quintin.

Pitkin, H. (1967 [1972]) *The Concept of Representation*, Berkeley, CA: University of California Press.

Plessner, H. (1924[1981]) 'Grenzen der Gemeinschaft', in *Gesammelte Schriften*, vol. 5, Frankfurt/M: Suhrkamp pp. 11–133.

—— (1931[1981]) 'Macht und menschliche Natur', in *Gesammelte Schriften*, vol. 5, Frankfurt/M: Suhrkamp pp. 135–234.

Plunkitt of Tammany Hall (1905 [1948]) *A Series of Very Plain Talks on Very Practical Politics:* delivered by Ex-Senator George Washington Plunkitt, the Tammany philosopher, from his rostrum – the New York County Court-House bootblack stand – and recorded by William L. Riordon, New York: Knopf.

Pocock, J. G. A. (1973) 'Verbalizing a political act', *Political Theory*, 1(1): 27–45.
—— (1975) *The Machiavellian Moment*, Princeton, NJ: Princeton University Press.
—— (1985) *Virtue, Commerce and History*, Cambridge: Cambridge University Press.
Radkau, J. (2005) *Max Weber: Die Leidenschaft des Denkens*, München: Hanser.
'Recent political theory and practice' (1900), *Quarterly Review*, 192: 359–80.
Redlich, J. (1905) *Recht und Technik des Englischen Parlamentarismus*, Leipzig: Duncker & Humblot.
—— 1908 *The Procedure of the House of Commons: A study of its history and present form*, trans. E. Steinthal, London: Constable.
Reinach, J. (1894) *L'éloquence française depuis la Révolution jusqu'à nos jours*, Paris: Delagrave.
Revolution, Rätegremien und Räterepublik in Bayern 1918/19. http://www. bayerische-landesbibliothek-online.de/bayern1918 (accessed 10 June 2016).
Ricoeur, P. (1957) 'Le paradoxe politique', *Esprit*, 26(1): 721–45.
Riddell, P. (2010) *In Defence of Politicians (In Spite of Themselves)*, London: Biteback.
Riescher, G. (1994) *Zeit und Politik*, Baden-Baden: Nomos.
Rochau, L. A. von (1853/69 [1972]) *Grundsätze der Realpolitik I–II*, Frankfurt/M: Ullstein.
Rorty, R. (1979) *Philosophy and the Mirror of Nature*, Cambridge: Cambridge University Press.
—— (1989) *Contingency, Irony and Solidarity*, Cambridge: Cambridge University Press.
Rosanvallon, P. (1992) *Le sacre du citoyen: Histoire du suffrage universel en France*, Paris: Gallimard.
—— (1998) *Le peuple introuvable*, Paris: Gallimard.
—— (2000) *La démocratie inachevée*, Paris: Gallimard.
—— (2003) *Pour une histoire conceptuelle du politique*, Paris: Seuil.
Roth, G. (1995) 'Max Weber: the would-be-Englishman', in H. Lehmann and G. Roth (eds) *Weber's Protestant Ethic*, Cambridge: Cambridge University Press pp. 83–121.
Roussellier, N. (1997) *Le parlement de l'éloquence*, Paris: Presses de sciences Po.
—— (2000) 'Deux formes de représentation politique: le citoyen et l'individu', in M. Sadoun (ed.) *La démocratie en France. 1. Idéologies*, Paris: Gallimard pp. 243–331.
Rühle, O. (1924 [1970]) *Von der bürgerlichen zur proletarischen Revolution*, Berlin: Blankertz.
Sartre, J.-P. [1943 [1977]) *L'être et le neant*, Paris: Gallimard.
—— (1960 [1985]) *Critique de la raison dialectique*, vol. 1, Paris: Gallimard.
—— (1964[1972]) 'L'alibi', in *Situations*, vol. 8, Paris: Gallimard pp. 127–45.
—— (1972) *L'idiot de la famille*, vol. 3, Paris: Gallimard.

Scaff, L. (1989) *Fleeing the Iron Cage*, Berkeley, CA: University of California Press.

—— (2014) *Weber and the Weberians*, Basingstoke: PalgraveMacmillan.

Schelting, A. (1934) *Max Webers Wissenschaftslehre*, Tübingen: Mohr.

Schmitt, C. (1912 [1969]) *Gesetz und Urteil*, München: Beck.

—— (1921[1978]) *Die Diktatur*, Berlin: Duncker & Humblot.

—— (1922 [1979]) *Politische Theologie*, Berlin: Duncker & Humblot.

—— (1923/1926 [1979]) *Die geistesgeschichtliche Lage des heutigen Parlamentarismus*, Berlin: Duncker & Humblot.

—— (1927) 'Der Begriff des Politischen', *Archiv für Sozialwissenschaft und Sozialpolitik*, 58: 1–33.

—— (1928 [1970]) *Verfassungslehre*, Berlin: Duncker & Humblot.

—— (1932a [1979]) *Der Begriff des Politischen*, Berlin: Duncker & Humblot.

—— (1932b [1980]) *Legalität und Legitimität*, Berlin: Duncker & Humblot.

—— (1963[1975]) *Theorie des Partisanen*, Berlin: Dunker and Humblot.

—— (2004) *Legality and Legitimacy*, trans J. Seitzer. Durham, NC: Duke University Press.

Senigaglia, C. (1995) 'Analysen zur Entstehung der Massenparteien und zu ihrem Einfluß auf das Parlament: Ostrogorski, Michels, Weber', *Parliaments, Estates, Representation*, 15(1): 159–84.

Skinner, Q. (1974) 'Some problems in the analysis of political thought and action', *Political Theory*, 2(3): 277–303.

—— (1978) *The Foundations of Modern Political Thought I–II*, Cambridge: Cambridge University Press.

—— (1979) 'The idea of a cultural lexicon', *Essays in Criticism*, 29: 205–24.

—— (1982) 'Habermas's reformation', *New York Review of Books*, 7 October: 35–8.

—— (1984) 'The idea of negative liberty' in R. R. Rorty, J. B. Schneewind and Q. Skinner (eds), *Philosophy in History*, Cambridge: Cambridge University Press pp. 193–221.

—— (1988) 'A reply to my critics', in J. Tully (ed.) *Quentin Skinner and His Critics*, London: Polity pp. 232–88.

—— (1996) *Reason and Rhetoric in the Philosophy of Hobbes*, Cambridge: Cambridge University Press.

—— (1999a) 'Hobbes and the purely artificial person of the state', *Journal of Political Philosophy*, 7(1): 1–29.

—— (1999b) 'Rhetoric and conceptual change', *Finnish Yearbook of Political Thought*, 3: 60–73.

—— (2002a) 'Hobbes and the classical theory of laughter', in *Visions of Politics 3*, Cambridge: Cambridge University Press pp. 142–76.

—— (2002b) 'A third concept of liberty', *Proceedings of the British Academy*, 117: 237–68.

—— (2002c) *Visions of Politics*, vol. 1: *Regarding method*, Cambridge: Cambridge University Press.

——(2007) 'Paradiastole', in S. Adamson, G. Alexander and K. Ettenhuber (eds), *Renaissance Figures of Speech*, Cambridge: Cambridge University Press, pp. 147–63.

——(2008a) 'Political rhetoric and the role of ridicule', in K. Palonen, T. Pulkkinen and J. M. Rosales (eds) *Ashgate Research Companion to the Politics of Democratisation in Europe: Concepts and Histories*, Farnheim: Ashgate pp. 137–49.

—— (2008b) *Quentin Skinner interviewed by Alan Macfarlane, 10 January 2008*. /https://www.repository.cam.ac.uk/bitstream/handle/1810/197060/skinner.%20txt.?sequence=1 (accessed 10 June 2016).

—— (2009) 'A genealogy of the modern state', *Proceedings of the British Academy* 162: 325–70.

Smith, G. (1888/9) 'The American commonwealth', *Macmillan's Magazine* 59: 240–53.

Smith, T. (1583) *De republica anglorum*, London. http://www.constitution.org/eng/repang.htm (accessed 10 July 2016).

Sombart, W. (1907a) 'Unser Interesse an der Politik', *Morgen* 1: 40–5.

—— (1907b) 'Politik und Bildung', *Morgen* 1: 67–72.

—— (1907c) 'Die Politik als Beruf', *Morgen* 1: 195–9.

—— (1907d) 'Vom Stil des politischen Lebens in Deutschland', *Morgen* 1: 223–7.

—— (1907e) 'Die Elemente des politischen Lebens in Deutschland', *Morgen* 1: 255–59.

—— (1907f) 'An Friedrich Naumann', *Morgen* 1: 421–5.

—— (1907g) 'Die Abkehr der Gebildeten von der Politik', *Morgen* 1: 479–83.

—— (1907h) 'Wir müden Seelen', *Morgen* 1: 513–17.

—— (1915) *Händler und Helden*, Leipzig: Duncker & Humblot.

Sorel, G. (1908 [1971]) *Réflexions sur la violence*, Genève: Slatkine.

Spinner, H. F. (1989) 'Weber gegen Weber', in J. Weiß (ed.) *Max Weber heute*, Frankfurt/M: Suhrkamp pp. 250–95.

Steffani, W. (1960 [1967]) 'Über die parlamentarischen Untersuchungsausschüsse', in K. Kluxen (ed.) *Parlamentarismus*, Köln: Kiepenhauer & Witsch pp. 249–71.

—— ([1965] 1967) 'Amerikanischer Kongress und deutscher Bundestag im Vergleich', in K. Kluxen (ed.), *Parlamentarismus*, Köln: Kiepenhauer & Witsch pp. 230–48.

—— (1967a) 'Arbeitsparlament', in H.-H. Röhring and K. Sontheimer (eds) *Handbuch des deutschen Parlamentarismus*, München: Piper p. 33.

—— (1967b) 'Redeparlament', in H.-H. Röhring and K. Sontheimer (eds) *Handbuch des deutschen Parlamentarismus*, München: Piper pp. 418–20.

Steinmetz, W. (ed.) (2005) *'Politik': Situationen eines Wortgebrauchs in Europa der Neuzeit*, Frankfurt/M: Campus.

—— (2013) 'The political as communicative space in history: The Bielefeld approach', in W. Steinmetz, I. Gilcher-Holtey and H.-G. Haupt (eds) *Writing Political History Today*, Frankfurt/M: Campus pp. 11–43.

Steinmetz, W., Gilcher-Holtey, I. and Haupt, H.-G. (eds) (2013) *Writing Political History Today*, Frankfurt/M: Campus.

Stenogaphische Berichte der Verhandlungen des Reichstags 1881, 1884. http://www.digitale-sammlungen.de (accessed 21 July 2016).

Sternberger, D. (1978) *Drei Wurzeln der Politik*, Frankfurt/M: Insel.

Tenbruck, F. H. (1959) 'Die Genesis der Methodologie Max Webers', *Kölner Zeitschrift für Soziologie und Sozialpsychologie*, 11: 573–630.

Tomkins, A. (2005) *Our Republican Constitution*, Oxford: Hart.

Tribe, K. (2012) 'Translating Weber', in M. J. Burke and M. Richter (eds) *Why Concepts Matter*, Leiden: Brill pp. 207–33.

Triepel, H. (1927) *Staatsrecht und Politik*, Berlin: de Gruyter.

Tyrell, H. (1994) 'Max Webers Soziologie – eine Soziologie ohne Gesellschaft', in G. Wagner and H. Zipprian (eds) *Max Webers Wissenschaftslehre*, Frankfurt/M: Suhrkamp pp. 390–414.

Vahland, J. (2001) *Max Webers entzauberte Welt*, Würzburg: Königshausen +Neumann.

Valéry, P. (1974) *Cahiers II*, Paris: Gallimard.

Veröffentlichugen der Vereinigung der Deutschen Staatsrechtslehrer (1929) vol. 5, Berlin: de Gruyter.

—— (1929) vol. 7, Berlin: de Gruyter.

Visscher, C. de (1953[1960]) *Théories et réalités en droit international public*, Paris: Pedone.

Weber, M. (1889 [1988]) 'Zur Geschichte der Handelsgesellschaften im Mittelalter', in GASW, Tübingen: Mohr pp. 312–443.

—— (1891 [1988]) 'Die römische Agrargeschichte in ihrer Bedeutung für das Staats- und Privatrecht', in MWS I/2, Tübingen: Mohr.

—— (1893a [1988]) 'Die ländliche Arbeitsverfassung', in GASW, Tübingen: Mohr pp. 444–72.

—— (1893b [1993]) 'Die ländliche Arbeitsverfassung', in MWG I/ 4, Tübingen: Mohr pp. 165–98.

—— (1894 [1988]) 'Entwicklungstendenzen in der Lage der ostelbischen Landarbeiter', in GASW, Tübingen: Mohr pp. 470–507

—— (1895a [1971]) 'Der Nationalstaat und die Volkswirtschaftspolitik', GPS, Tübingen: Mohr pp. 1–25.

—— (1895b [1993]) 'Der Nationalstaat und die Volkswirtschaftspolitik', in MWG I/4, Tübingen: Mohr pp. 543–74.

—— (1897 [1993]) 'Diskussionsbetrage zum Vortrag Karl Oldenbergs, *Deutschland als Industriestaat*', in MWG I/4, Tübingen: Mohr pp. 626–40.

—— (1898 [1990]) *Grundriß zu den Vorlesungen über Allgemeine ('theoretische') Nationalokonomie*, Tübingen: Mohr.

—— (1903/06 [1973]) 'Roscher und Knies und die logischen Probleme der historischen Nationalökonomie', in GAW, Tübingen: Mohr pp. 1–145.

—— (1904a [1999]) 'Die "Bedrohung" der Reichsverfassung', in MWS I/8, Tübingen: Mohr pp. 16–17.

—— (1904b [1973]) 'Die "Objektivität" sozialwissenschaftlicher und sozialpolitischer Erkenntnis', in GAW, Tübingen: Mohr pp. 146–214.

—— (1904–05/1920[1993]) *Die protestantische Ethik und der 'Geist' des Kapitalismus,*. K. Lichtblau and J. Weß (eds), Bodenheim: Athenäum.

—— (1905a [1999]) 'Bemerkungen im Anschluß an den vorstehenden Aufsatz' [from R. Blank, *Die soziale Zusammensetzung der sozialdemokratischen Wählerschaft Deutschlands*], in MWS 1/8, Tübingen: Mohr pp. 69–72.

—— (1905b [1999]) 'Das Verhältnis der Kartelle zum Staate. Diskussionsbeitrag im Verein für Sozialpolitik', in MWS 1/8, Tübingen: Mohr pp. 95–101.

—— (1906a [1973]) 'Kritische Studien auf dem Gebiet der kulturwissenschftlichen Logik', in GAW, Tübingen: Mohr pp. 215–90.

—— (1906b [1989]) 'Zur Lage der bürgerlichen Demokratie in Rußland', in MWG I/10, Tübingen: Mohr pp. 86–279.

—— (1906c [1989]) 'Zur Lage der bürgerlichen Demokratie in Rußland', in MWS I/10, Tübingen: Mohr pp. 1–104.

—— (1906d) 'Rußlands Übergang zum Scheinkonstitutionalismus', in MWG I/10, Tübingen: Mohr pp. 293–679.

—— (1906e) 'Rußlands Übergang zum Scheinkonstitutionalismus', in MWS I/10, Tübingen: Mohr pp. 105–395.

—— (1907a [1988]) 'Methodologische Einleitung für die Erhebungen des Vereins für Sozialpolitik über Auslese und Anpassung (Berufswahl und Berufsschicksal) der Arbeiterschaft der geschlossenen Großindustrie', in GASS, Tübingen: Mohr pp. 1–60.

—— (1907b [1999]) ' "Verfassung und Verwaltungsorganisation der Städte" Diskussionsbeitrag auf der Generalversammlung des Vereins für Sozialpolitik am 2. Oktober 1907', in MWS 1/8, Tübingen: Mohr pp. 109–14.

—— (1908 [1999]) 'Kaiser und Reichsverfassung' [Bericht des Heidelberger Tageblatts], in MWS 1/8, Tübingen: Mohr pp. 134–5.

—— (1909a [1988]) 'Agrarverhältnisse im Altertum', in GASW, Tübingen: Mohr pp. 1–288.

—— (1909b [1999]) 'Diskussionsbeitrag zum Thema "Die wirtschaftlichen Unternehmungen der Gemeinden" ' in MWS 1/8, Tübingen: Mohr pp. 127–30.

—— (1910a [1978]) 'Antikritisches zum "Geist" des Kapitalismus', in PE II, Gütersloh: Siebenstern pp. 149–87.

—— (1910b [1988]) 'Diskussionsreden auf den Tagungen des Vereins für Sozialpolitik', in GASS, Tübingen: Mohr pp. 394–430.

—— (1912 [1988]) 'Diskussionsrede auf dem zweiten Deutschen Soziologentag in Berlin', in GASS, Tübingen: Mohr pp. 484–6.

—— (1913 [1973]) 'Über einige Kategorien der verstehenden Soziologie', in GAW, Tübingen: Mohr pp. 427–74.

—— (1916a) 'Deutschland unter europäischen Weltmächten', in MWS I/15, Tübingen: Mohr pp. 61–78.

—— (1916b) 'Zwischen zwei Gesetzen', in MWS 1/15, Tübingen: Mohr pp. 39–41.

—— (1917a [1988]) 'Die Abänderung des Artikels 9 der Reichsverfassung', in MWS I/15, Tübingen: Mohr pp. 137–9.

—— (1917b [1988]) 'Das preußische Wahlrecht', in MWS I/15, Tübingen: Mohr pp. 94–101.

—— (1917c [1973]) 'Der Sinn der "Wertfreiheit" der soziologischen und ökonomischen Wissenschaften', in GAW, Tübingen: Mohr pp. 489–540.

—— (1917d [1988]) 'Vorschläge zur Reform der Verfassung des Deutschen Reichs', in MWS 1/15, Tübingen: Mohr pp. 116–28.

—— (1917e) 'Vorträge während der Lauensteiner Kulturtagung' [Aufzeichnung Wolfgang Schumann], in MWS I/15, Tübingen: Mohr pp. 343–44.

—— (1917f [1988]) 'Wahlrecht und Demokratie in Deutschland', in MWS 1/15, Tübingen: Mohr pp. 155–89.

—— (1917g 1988) 'Was erwartet das deutsche Volk vom Verfassungsauschuss des deutschen Reichstages' [Bericht der Münchener Neuesten Nachrichten], in MWS I/15, Tübingen: Mohr pp. 345–47.

—— (1918a [1991]) 'Deutschlands Lage', MWS I/16, Tübingen: Mohr, pp. 125–6.

—— (1918b [1991]) 'Deutschlands politische Neuorientierung', in MWS I/16, Tübingen: Mohr pp. 113–15.

—— (1918c [1991]) 'Das neue Deutschland', in MWS I/16, Tübingen: Mohr pp. 121–3.

—— (1918d |1988]) Parlament und Regierung im neugeordneten Deutschland, in MWS I/15, Tübingen: Mohr pp. 202–302.

—— (1919a [1991]) 'Deutschlands künftige Staatsform', in MWS I/16, Tübingen: Mohr pp. 25–59.

—— (1919b [1991]) 'Erklärung zum Scheitern der Kandidatur für die Wahlen der Nationalversammlung im Wahlkreis 19 (Hessen-Nassau)', in MWS I/16, Tübingen: Mohr p. 52.

—— (1919c [1994]) 'Politik als Beruf' in MWS I/17, Tübingen: Mohr pp. 35–88.

—— (1919d [1991]) 'Der Reichspräsident', in MWS 1/16, Tübingen: Mohr pp. 75–7.

—— (1919e [1994]) 'Wissenschaft als Beruf, in MWS 1/17, Tübingen: Mohr pp. 1–23.

—— (1919f [1991]) 'Zum Thema Kriegsschuld', in MWS I/16, Tübingen: Mohr pp. 60–6.

—— (1921 [1973]) 'Die drei reinen Typen der legitimen Herrschaft', in GAW, Tübingen: Mohr pp. 475–88.

—— (1922 [1980]) Wirtschaft und Gesellschaft, Tübingen: Mohr.

—— (1936) Jugendbriefe, Marianne Weber (ed.), Tübingen: Mohr.

—— (1978) Economy and Society, G. Roth and C. Wittich (eds), Berkeley, CA: University of California Press.

—— (1990) Briefe 1906–8, in MWG II/5, Tübingen: Mohr.

—— (1994a) Briefe 1909–10, in MWG II/6, Tübingen: Mohr.

—— (1994b) *Political Writings*, Cambridge: Cambridge University Press.

—— (2003) *Le savant et le politique*, Préface, traduction et notes de C. Colliot-Thélène, Paris: Decouverte.

—— (2004a) 'Basic sociological concepts', trans. K. Tribe, in EW, London: Routledge pp. 311–58.

—— (2004b) 'The "objectivity" of knowledge in social science and social policy', trans. K. Tribe, in EW, London: Routledge pp. 359–404.

—— (2004c) *The Essential Weber*, S. Whimster (ed.), London: Routledge.

—— (2008) *Briefe (1915–1917)*, in MWG II/9, Tübingen: Mohr.

—— (2009) *Max-Weber-Gesamtausgabe, Allgemeine Staatslehre und Politik. Mit- und Nachschriften 1920*, G. Hübinger (ed.), Tübingen: Mohr.

—— (2012) *Collected Methodological Writings*, H.-H. Bruun and S. Whimster (eds), trans. H.-H. Bruun, London: Routledge.

Weidner, T. (2012a) *Die Geschichte des Politischen in der Diskussion*, Göttingen: Wallstein.

—— (2012b) *Die unpolitische Profession: Deutsche Mediziner im langen 19. Jahrhundert*, Frankfurt/M: Campus.

Weischenberger, S. (2012) *Max Weber und die Entzauberung der Medienwelt*, Wiesbaden: Springer VS.

Weiß, J. (1992) *Max Webers Grundlegung der Soziologie*, München: Saur.

Whimster, S. (ed.) (1999) *Max Weber and the Culture of Anarchy*, Basingstoke: Macmillan.

—— (ed.) (2004) *The Essential Weber*, London: Routledge.

Young-Bruehl, E. (1984) *Hannah Arendt: For the love of the world*, New Haven, CT: Yale University Press.

Index

www.ingramcontent.com/pod-product-compliance
Lightning Source LLC
Chambersburg PA
CBHW072119020426
42334CB00018B/1646